B/

We know that econo...   ...e. But
what if they're not ju...   ...basic flaw
in the way classical ec... ...understands human behaviour?

In his lucid, radical and entertaining book, Pete Lunn ... makes
a compelling argument that the most basic, and therefore least
examined, assumptions of economists are utterly at odds with
the evidence of how we actually make choices.

With both rigorous logic and demotic charm Lunn builds ...
a persuasive and highly thought-provoking case ...

Fintan O'Toole, *Irish Times*

Pete Lunn is an oddity: an economist originally trained as a
neuroscientist ... Lunn has assembled wonderful evidence of
irrational economic behaviour for his contention that economics,
as currently understood, simply does not explain the economy.

[*Basic Instincts*] is a hugely enjoyable string of pearls ... Read this
book for the gems and the pleasing prose style.

Dan Atkinson, Economics Editor, *Mail on Sunday*

This is a most interesting and readable complement to the
standard elementary economics textbook – throwing light on
broader questions which arise when economic theory is applied
to the real world.

**Lord Peston of Mile End, Emeritus Professor, Department of
Economics, Queen Mary University of London and former
Chairman of the House of Lords Select Committee on
Economic Affairs**

BASIC INSTINCTS

Human nature and the
new economics

Pete Lunn

Marshall Cavendish
Business

Copyright © 2010 Pete Lunn

First published in hardback in 2008

This paperback edition published in 2010 by Marshall Cavendish Business
An imprint of Marshall Cavendish International

5F / 32–38 Saffron Hill
London EC1N 8FH
United Kingdom

and

1 New Industrial Road
Singapore 536196
genrefsales@sg.marshallcavendish.com
www.marshallcavendish.com/genref

Marshall Cavendish is a trademark of Times Publishing Limited

Other Marshall Cavendish offices:
Marshall Cavendish International (Asia) Private Limited, 1 New Industrial Road,
Singapore 536196 • Marshall Cavendish Corporation. 99 White Plains Road,
Tarrytown NY 10591–9001, USA • Marshall Cavendish International (Thailand) Co
Ltd. 253 Asoke, 12th Floor, Sukhumvit 21 Road, Klongtoey Nua, Wattana, Bangkok
10110, Thailand • Marshall Cavendish (Malaysia) Sdn Bhd, Times Subang, Lot 46,
Subang Hi-Tech Industrial Park, Batu Tiga, 40000 Shah Alam, Selangor Darul
Ehsan, Malaysia

A CIP record for this book is available from the British Library

ISBN 978-0-462-09963-7

Printed and bound in Great Britain by
CPI Bookmarque, Croydon CR0 4TD

Contents

Acknowledgements

THIS PROJECT BEGAN more than a decade ago with the death of the man I knew as "Grandpa", Walter Crabtree. When he passed away, at the age of 97, Walter left me sufficient money to pay my own way through a postgraduate degree in economics. Walter was one of the most generous and selfless people I have ever known, so it is somewhat ironic that I used his bequest to learn economic theories that deny the importance of these traits. The theories were taught to me by the staff of the Department of Economics at Birkbeck College, London, who I thank for teaching them well and for being open minded enough to admit a neuroscientist-turned-journalist straight on to a postgraduate course. Were it possible to explain to Walter what I learned after he died, I suspect he would dispute the world-view of orthodox economics.

Since then, such a large number of arguments, suggestions and opinions have contributed to the development of this book that it is not possible to acknowledge all of those involved. I am grateful to the many friends who have taken an interest, to former colleagues at BBC *Newsnight* and to current ones at the Economic and Social Research Institute (ESRI) in Dublin, where I would especially like to thank Frances Ruane, Philip O'Connell, David Duffy and Mary Dowling for their constant support. Thanks are particularly due to a disparate group of people who volunteered their time and effort to read and offer detailed comments on earlier drafts. Ciarán Dyar, Tony Fahey, Anne Luke, Becky Lunn, David Murphy, Eddy Taylor and Julian Watts all made constructive and very useful contributions, for which I am very grateful, while any mistakes or misconceptions remain entirely mine.

I would like to extend special thanks to Carl Emmerson at the Institute for Fiscal Studies (IFS) in London, who has the capacity to analyse issues with the precision and rigour of an excellent economist, and yet is able and interested to see things from alternative perspectives. Our many conversations over the past decade have been an important influence on this book, as has Carl's rapid and thorough dissection of each draft chapter.

Much of the research for this book was done in the Harold Washington Library Center, during a year in Chicago, Illinois. The staff of this excellent public library were of great assistance.

Wholehearted thanks also to my agents Elizabeth Cochrane and Lavinia Trevor for giving first-rate guidance to a new author, to Martin Liu and Pom Somkabcharti at Marshall Cavendish for so enthusiastically taking one on, and to Paul Forty for his expert production.

Lastly, I suspect the families of first-time authors suffer a fairly unique experience. Gratitude too warm to describe faithfully is due to my partner Úna and her daughter Sorcha, who have encouraged, helped and endured me during the ups and downs of the past few years, and to little Méabh and Cillian, who might wonder why their dad stares so much at the boring little screen by the wall. In addition to her brilliant and much-needed support, Úna's understanding of the use of language has been invaluable and is something to which I can only aspire. Her scribbles in the margin were educational, greatly improved the text and were frequently a pleasure to read – though perhaps, in this last matter, I am more than a little biased.

Preface

NOBODY TRULY PREDICTED IT. At least, I am yet to see convincing evidence that anyone did. There are plenty of people who claim to have done so; who claim to have foreseen what began as the "credit crunch" and became the global economic crisis. Many commentators did warn that double-digit house price rises were not sustainable, while others also worried about the gung-ho nature of modern financial markets. Yet I can find no one who understood that the bursting of the housing and credit bubbles in America would cause the international money market to freeze, would destroy multinational financial companies of serious pedigree, would spread with devastating effect to Europe, Asia and beyond, and would cause the deepest recession in over 70 years, with a collapse in world trade and soaring unemployment across the globe.

You might think that in order to grasp what caused this mayhem and misery, you need to be a financial expert, to know your "credit default swaps" from your "futures contracts", or what it means to be "highly leveraged" or to "sell short". Sure, knowing about such things is useful if you want to absorb the minutiae, but it is far from necessary to understand what has occurred. In essence, the crisis is quite simple.

Millions of (mostly poorer) Americans took on debts they could not repay, primarily in the form of mortgages. Because borrowers often use biased or faulty financial reasoning, many of these decisions were bad ones. Salespeople in companies that offered the loans were subject to biases and faulty reasoning too, but many were additionally influenced by being paid for making sales yet in no way punished if the loans went sour. Instead, the companies took their cut and then simply sold the loans on to banks and other big financial players, who hoped to make profits from the repayments in return for taking on a manageable level of risk. These institutions thought the risks they were buying were manageable because some of the top financial brains had developed new and clever mathematical techniques to balance different risks against each other. Unfortunately, neither newness nor cleverness is a guarantee against being hopelessly wrong. Sophisticated traders on international financial markets spent billions of dollars buying and selling bundles of mortgages and other loans that were, in reality, going to generate far less revenue than they expected.

When the housing market inevitably ran out of willing buyers in 2007, prices turned and those unable to meet repayments could no longer sell to get out of trouble. In just a few weeks, what had been financial hot cakes became "toxic assets" – a wonderfully oxymoronic expression. Revelation spread quickly and it was rapidly apparent that losses would be massive. Some banks were clearly going to go under, but no one knew which ones were holding the most toxic assets, so the banks stopped lending even to each other and the whirligig of world finance came to a crunching stop. Companies found it hard to borrow. Consumers, many of whom had big debts, became nervous and stopped spending. Wealth, especially house values and shares, tumbled. With less demand for their goods and services, many firms tried to cut staff and wages; others just folded. We entered a huge world recession, with rising unemployment and declining incomes across the globe. We don't know how long it will last.

It bears repeating: nobody truly predicted this. The Turkish economist Nouriel Roubini perhaps came closest. In 2006 he told a seminar in Washington that he believed America was about to experience a "nasty recession", with a "housing slump that could lead then to a systemic problem for the financial system". Thus, Roubini clearly understood what was happening better than the rest of us. And yet, in the same speech, he said "I do not expect a global recession," arguing instead that it would be only a "slowdown". What's more, since it was already autumn 2006, Roubini was really just the first to yell and point in horror at the stable door flapping in the breeze. The horse was already loose, even if the havoc it would ultimately wreak had yet to materialize.

Why does it matter who understood what when? Because the fact that the global economic crisis came as such a surprise reveals how little we really understand about how the economy works. This, I have discovered, is not always a popular view among some of my fellow economists, whose opinions and commentaries have never been in such demand. It is one of the oddities of the crisis that economists are being simultaneously pilloried and courted. In truth, however, orthodox economics has been humiliated by what has occurred.

You don't need to take my word for this. You can instead read the testimony of the man who used to be variously described as the "architect", "guru" or even "maestro" of modern capitalism. Watching the crisis unfold in October 2008, Alan Greenspan, Chairman of the US Federal Reserve for 18 years until his retirement in 2006, told a US Congressional committee that he was in a state of "shocked disbelief". Apparently he was quite upset by the whole thing, confessing that he had thought the world worked a particular way, but that the crisis had proved him wrong. "I made a mistake," Greenspan told the committee. There was, he said in typically mechanistic language, a "flaw in the model that I perceived [to be the] critical functioning structure that defines how the world works... I found a flaw. I don't know how significant or permanent it is, but I have been very distressed by that fact." He sounded rather like the crestfallen inventor of a killer robot. But Greenspan's honesty is to be commended – not all economists have expressed such humility in the face of what has occurred.

For my part, I make no claim to having seen the present crisis coming either, although on returning from America to Ireland in 2005, my partner and I were too suspicious of rocketing prices to buy a house – a decision that is, so far, the source of much relief to us both. But suspicions are not predictions, so it is reasonable to conclude that, like the rest of my profession, I do not understand how the economy works well enough to be able to anticipate such events. Unlike Alan Greenspan, however, my mental state is far from "shocked disbelief". Some time ago now, I reached the point where I had encountered enough evidence about people's real economic behaviour to form the conclusion that markets do not work as the textbook asserts. So when events make that apparent, even catastrophically so, I am neither shocked nor disbelieving.

The evidence to which I refer is supplied by "behavioural economics", a rapidly expanding school of thought which provides the material for this book. Thankfully, to understand the impact of this relatively new school does not require mathematical skill, the ability to decipher charts and tables, nor tiresome visits to an alphabetically ordered glossary. Perhaps the most helpful attribute for absorbing what follows is instead the ability to put yourself in other people's shoes. Behavioural economics is about uncovering our most basic economic instincts – understanding how we instinctively approach doing business with each other, as consumers, workers, managers, traders and so on.

Now, open an economics textbook and you are unlikely to encounter any discussion of our economic instincts. The conventional starting point of my chosen science is instead simply to assume that individuals and firms act independently and rationally in whatever way most benefits their own self-interest. This set of assumptions defines orthodoxy. Yet compare them with recent events. Families bought houses they could not pay for, often with drastic consequences. Consumers, egged on by unprecedented access to credit, made purchases they would later regret. The brightest and best financial minds completely miscalculated the value of assets and so incurred enormous losses. Top investment banks took ruinous commercial decisions. These mistakes were replicated and repeated on a massive scale. As I said, orthodox economics has been humiliated.

Shocks have the capacity to change minds and we should hope this one does exactly that. Long before the present crisis developed, the standard assumptions of economics were being undermined by scientific findings. Quietly, undetected by policymakers and pundits, unseen even by most economists, a disparate group of scientists was busy finding ways to test the core assumptions of orthodox economics. Using economic experiments and field studies, behavioural economists were finding ways to study big questions about what people are like, in economic terms. Are people ultimately selfish? Are they ever unselfish? If so, when and why? Do we know what things are worth to us? How do we decide? What principles determine when we will buy or sell? Why do we choose the jobs we do? What motivates us at work? How do companies take decisions?

The economic experiments, scenarios and field studies employed by behavioural economics suggest profound things about human nature. They reveal that people's instincts are not as economists have traditionally assumed, suggesting that economies will not behave as previously thought either. The findings represent an ongoing process of genuine scientific discovery, the implications of which are also likely to be profound. The primary aim of this book is to bring the discoveries to a wider audience. For they prove that, in reality, we do not behave like the selfish, independent calculating machines economists have traditionally assumed us to be; in many cases, we do not even come close to behaving this way. This amounts to a classic scientific refutation: the theory says the world should look a certain way, but once we've found a way to check, it turns out not to. The observations prove the theory wrong. The big question is: how wrong? If traditional theory is only slightly wide of the mark, then the new findings can be accommodated by changing it only slightly – a tweak and a retune. To me, however, the evidence suggests that standard economics is sufficiently far off the mark that the discipline must undergo nothing short of a scientific revolution. New fundamental principles will emerge and the old ones will be largely replaced.

Meanwhile, the crisis has created an environment in which people are, I am glad to say, engaging with economics again. Back when capitalism and communism were locked in mortal combat, economics was more interesting. Opposing economic ideas were linked to alternative views of human nature. The political left and right were partly defined by contrasting assessments of the willingness of individuals to commit their efforts to the common good, or, as the British Labour Party's constitution rather beautifully put it: "to secure for the workers by hand or by brain the full fruits of their industry and the most equitable distribution thereof that may be possible upon the basis of common ownership ..." As the eventual abandonment, in 1995, of this idealistic, evocative yet ultimately embarrassing constitutional clause indicated, the left had superior prose and inferior economics. Arguably, economics got boring because the left lost. The demise of socialist economics ushered in a period of greater consensus about how the economy works than at any time in the preceding century or more. Yet, logically speaking, just because socialist economics relied on an unrealistically starry-eyed view of human nature does not imply that the theories that triumphed over it are based on an accurate view of human nature.

Those theories are now disgraced and people of all political persuasions are looking for alternative ways of thinking. Barack Obama is taking an interest in behavioural economics and, indeed, designing policies based upon its findings. In the UK, David Cameron is advising his ministers-in-waiting to read about it too. Suddenly, those of us who were desperately trying to get the wider world to take notice of what behavioural economics had to offer, find our mobile phones ringing and invitations to speak landing on the doormat. The global economic crisis is truly awful, but at least it is shaking us out of our intellectual complacency.

The primary purpose of the chapters that follow is to reveal new evidence about our economic behaviour, discoveries that are likely to change our view of how the economy works. The final sections aim to suggest just some of the potential political ramifications. In general terms, the findings of behavioural economics are likely to change beliefs about what markets can and cannot do for us. More specifically, I highlight how they suggest new perspectives on what determines people's economic opportunities; why some people are paid more than others; the debate about sweatshops; the role of marketing; how to motivate workers; how to tackle discrimination; reform of public services; the supposed benefits of competition; what makes a successful business; the power of multinationals; the mantra of "flexible labour markets"; and the obsession with low inflation.

There are doubtless implications for many more issues – these are just the main ones that have occurred to me. Learning about people's basic economic instincts can change your perspective on almost every big economic debate you can think of, because what we are like, at heart, is central to any theory of what happens when people come together to work, share and trade with each other. It also helps if you are trying to understand how we managed to get into such a dreadful mess.

1

Believe it when you see it

IRISH PEOPLE will use the location of a pub to navigate long after the pub has ceased to exist. A pub that was once a landmark becomes a kind of "mindmark". Local people, some too young ever to have seen the pub in question, let alone swallowed a drink in it, will nevertheless refer to it when giving directions. When Dubliners tell someone to turn right at one of these imaginary, long-gone hostelries, they talk as if it is an ongoing and thriving concern. For locals, the navigational system works perfectly, with many major junctions identified by single names all of us know. But for visitors or tourists asking for directions, the system is doubtless enough to make them give up and head for the first pub they can actually see.

Naming junctions after families who lived at the corner is common in many societies – there's nothing uniquely Irish about it. The odds that the family in question ran a pub, however, are probably somewhat higher in Dublin than in most cities. My local mindmark is Leonard's Corner – once the site of Leonard's pub. Ask for "Leonard's Corner" and every taxi driver in the city knows where to drop you. But recently the city council tried to impose a more efficient system, labelling key Dublin junctions with a letter and a number in accordance with location, then commissioning new signs to match. This has probably made matters worse. No Dubliners use the labels, visitors are therefore even more confused, and any tourist who asks a taxi driver to drop them at J14 may well experience a rich stream of Dublin slang that is, thankfully, also beyond their comprehension. The council was doing its best. But the way mutual understanding spreads through a community, be it common understanding of directions or anything else, does not necessarily follow what is most efficient or rational.

Most European cities have locations that look a bit like Leonard's Corner. It is an old area undergoing rapid change. When James Joyce sat down to write *Ulysses* in 1914, he made Leonard's Corner the birthplace of his hero, Leopold Bloom. Then it was the heart of Dublin's tiny Jewish quarter. Now the junction has a cluster of perhaps thirty or forty small shops and businesses serving a truly mixed inner-city area. In the most secluded nearby streets, middle-class urbanites predominate, attracted by the old red-brick terraced houses with their original fireplaces and high ceilings. The houses on the larger streets, more exposed to the constant rumble and throb of city traffic, have mainly been sliced up to make student digs, bedsits and first homes for young couples. Between these older streets are pockets of more modern council flats, with lower ceilings allowing more storeys to be stacked. There is an ethnic mix too. Across the street from a post office that still closes for lunch is an internet café, where the window seats are usually occupied by Muslim teenagers who attend the local college, their headphones clamped around their headscarves. Young migrant workers from eastern Europe also go in and out, taking advantage of cheap rates to call home.

All of this makes Leonard's Corner a fascinating place at which to observe economic life, which is the subject of this book. I use the expression "economic life" as an alternative to "economics" for a reason. Sure, I am an economist and the ideas and arguments that follow contain plenty of economics, translated from the subject's often impenetrable language into language we use every day. But if you are interested in how the world works, demonstrations are compelling. An idea that you see work in practice is an idea you are more likely to believe in. For most sciences, a demonstration requires equipment and a laboratory. But when the science is economics, the laboratory is our economic life. We are the rats in the maze – or perhaps the race. So when an economist explains a theory, we really should be able to identify with what is said. This is not to say that a good economic theory cannot surprise us, only that we should recognize something in it; we should find that it resonates. The insight the economist offers should echo in our minds when we do business with a company, when we decide to take a job, when we choose one product over another or when we walk down to the end of our street to take part in and watch economic life.

Back at Leonard's Corner, at the end of my street, economics and economic life frequently do not match. It is, for instance, an accepted part of economic theory that people are selfish and rational, and that they therefore pay the lowest price possible for whatever they buy. This, as with much economic theory, has been translated into a more reasonable-sounding generalization that forms part of current economic wisdom: competition forces firms to lower prices. Yet competing shops at Leonard's Corner consistently sell the same products at vastly different prices. More intriguingly, some of the junction's small businesses thrive even though their prices are generally much higher than those of larger, more efficient competitors. This is not to say that consumers don't care about prices. It takes no more than a trip to a cut-price outlet to see that they do. The point is that accepted wisdom about free-market competition, the idea that it favours the most efficient company with the lowest prices, does not seem to apply at the end of my street. When I compare economics and economic life on my doorstep, they do not match.

One of the reasons why economic life at Leonard's Corner consistently ignores competitive forces, thwarting the market, is the same as the reason why the council failed in its attempt to change the names of junctions. Economists are like the planners at the council. They calculate what they think is the most rational way of buying and selling, and assume that people gravitate towards it. Often, as we will see, people don't. Simple economic activity, such as buying goods and services from local businesses, has something in common with giving directions. It involves mutual understanding, communication and trust – properties of relationships between people. At Leonard's Corner, the relationships between locals and individual businesses seem strong, owing in part, perhaps, to its history, social mix and ethnic diversity. Often, these relationships prove more powerful than market forces, and so it is they, not competitive prices, which determine economic behaviour.

The difference between economics and economic life, between our theories of how the economy works and our experience of it, matters. A new breed of economist has started to observe economic life more closely. The results, as you will see, are revelatory. We turn out to have strong and reliable economic instincts, which have been ignored by traditional economics, but which may be crucial factors in major economic decisions, and hence important for our futures. This book is about those instincts and how the study of them has begun to revolutionize the science of economics.

People's economic instincts are surprisingly sophisticated and subtle, having adapted over generations of trading with each other. Understanding how these instincts work can not only change the way you think about your own affairs, it can alter how you think about a whole range of economic issues, from what constitutes a fair salary to the impact of globalization. But this is to skip too far ahead. For now, the point is straightforward. There is a gap between our standard explanations of how the economy works and how it feels to live and work in the economy. My aim, in this book, is to help to fill that gap. But first, how wide is it?

All consuming

Recently I started a new job. A few days before I was due to begin, I realized that my wardrobe was simply not up to it. Shirts were faded and frayed, trousers decidedly out of fashion and disappointingly tight. There was only one solution: shopping. This, I decided, was a good opportunity to compare economics with a slice of economic life.

As I walked into town, I contemplated how much I wanted to spend and how I would pay. My new salary is fine, but a good bit less than I have become used to earning. According to standard economic theory, people choose the job that makes them the most money for the least work – theories of wages and unemployment are based on this idea. I realized that I had done the opposite. I chose my new job because I thought the work would be interesting and challenging, though it pays less than I earned before. Still, it's a comfortable middle-class salary. I tried to decide how much of it I could afford to spend on new work clothes, at which point I realized that I hadn't calculated what my take-home pay after tax would be. This was something I needed to know if I was to allocate my budget rationally, as orthodox economics says people do. I also decided to use my credit card, even though I had sufficient money in my current account not to need to. I like to leave some margin for error on my account, because in the past I have miscalculated or forgotten about money due to come out, incurring annoying bank charges as a result. In theory, consumers of financial services products, such as credit cards and bank accounts, are supposed to take rational, informed decisions to finance personal spending as cheaply as possible – otherwise free markets in financial services won't work properly. Personally, I have no idea how the interest on the credit card compares to the bank charges. At this stage, before I'd even made it to town, I had violated orthodox economics on three counts: taking a challenging job for less money, not knowing my own budget, and being irrational and ill informed about financial services products. And I'm an economist.

In essence, the standard economic theory of the consumer is straightforward. For now, here's a simple sketchbook version. We are supposed, as consumers, to make informed, rational choices about what we buy. We choose the combination of goods that makes us most happy, within our budgets. A modern market economy lays out before us an unprecedented and fabulous feast of goods and services from which we choose what we want. The theories of modern economics are thus the ultimate expression of so-called "consumer sovereignty". It is the consumer who chooses – the consumer is king. Companies, like courtiers of old, display and advise on their products, in the hope of getting the regal nod. They understand that the royal money chest is not bottomless, and so they compete to offer the best value for money. Companies make profits because they serve, taking pleasure in our patronage. In theory, then, market forces mean that the consumer is all-powerful. But are consumers really all-powerful?

I arrived in the town centre, crossed the threshold of the first shop and surveyed the corner of my kingdom that is menswear. I was struck, as I am each time I visit this part of my realm, by how segregated it was. There were two distinct regions separated by a clearly marked border. The uniformity on one side of the border was remarkable. On the walls hung row upon row of grey and blue suits, while in the middle were large tables completely hidden by pressed shirts in cellophane packets. The clothing on offer seemed more regimental than regal. Crossing the border into the other region revealed the full extent of my choice, as a supposedly all-powerful consumer. I could choose to look like either a banker or a bachelor. There was nothing in between.

Closer inspection was called for. Returning to the more formal part of my domain, there seemed to be two methods of competing for the sovereign's attention. Most of the suits were priced in big letters, written in black marker-pen, on white tickets, with a bold red border. The intention was to impress me with how cheaply I could kit myself out. But the second opportunity laid before me, adorning the remainder of the display, seemed more in tune with royal status. Should I wish to spend more, much more, I could be assured of a beneficial treaty with one of a number of long-established and successful Italian dynasties.

My problem was that the new job required me to be smart, but not besuited. I again crossed the border into the more lively and colourful part of my realm. The courtiers who had jurisdiction over this less formal area preferred a different method of attracting the royal consumer's gaze. The clothing on offer promised to make me, not a dignified king, but the hottest prince in all the land. Each display appealed to my famously rational decision-making powers with photo backdrops depicting the divine sort of men who wore such clothes; men of passion, with perfect cheekbones and powerful stares. Some of these images featured female beauties who would apparently fawn over me and feel my cloth, if only I would purchase the alluring outfit below. The perfect prince is, of course, a noted warrior. Each garment proudly displayed its 21st-century medal – the logo. For the would-be urban warrior, these inscriptions were post-industrial; clothing named after metal, machinery or fuel. And how much would it cost to buy such magnetic finery? It was almost impossible to tell. Gone were the bold white tickets loudly proclaiming discounts. Instead, a systematic search was required to rescue a tiny tag from inside a pocket, under a collar or behind the washing instructions. If it could be found, the biro scribble informed me of the princely sum required to secure sexual irresistibility.

After this brief inspection of the land supposedly laid out for my pleasure, I felt anything but powerful. In fact, I was pretty depressed. I just wanted a varied selection of smart clothes for work, yet this now appeared a difficult task. I didn't feel like a consumer sovereign spoilt for choice – more like a puppet king struggling for survival.

When you find yourself in such circumstances you need a survival strategy that is in keeping with your psychological make-up. I decided the biggest danger was that the whole thing would get me down and I would end up with nothing to wear on Monday morning. So I decided to ignore the price tags and buy at least two shirts and one pair of trousers that I would feel comfortable wearing as I stood for the first time before my new boss. An hour later, having spent much more than I originally intended, I had my two shirts and a pair of trousers. But I felt better.

Once I had splashed out a bit, things became easier. By the second hour, shirts that previously looked expensive no longer appeared quite so prohibitive – after all, they weren't nearly so pricey as the blue, stripy Italian one I was going to wear on Monday. Also, I began to learn more about which current fashions I liked best. This was generally good for morale, although there were moments when I came across items that were probably better value than things I had already bought. Still, with aching feet and the job nearly done, I stopped for tea. As I looked into my bags, I thought back over the experience. Whatever else I had done, I had not chosen my purchases rationally to maximize my happiness within my available budget – as standard economics would have it. It seemed, rather, that I had benefited from accepting my inability to do this. To be sure of getting the job done, I had virtually ignored prices for a while and certainly not worried overly about my budget, whatever it was anyway.

As I looked over the range of purchases, it was pretty obvious that I had brand preferences. I wondered whether this was the result of genuine differences between clothes made by different brands, or whether I had gullibly paid extra, lured by the lifestyle my chosen brands implied. I wasn't sure. After all, though it's been around for a good while now, I still think there is something pleasing about the irreverence of FCUK.

I sipped some tea. Perhaps other shoppers are consumer sovereigns in command of all they survey, using their money wisely, never regretting their purchases. Maybe the dark, confident guy who casually discussed the merits of different labels with the obliging shop assistant, while I feebly tried to formulate a question about whether a pair of trousers was dry-clean only, never pays an extra twenty quid because some clever marketing type understands his desires. But I don't think so. There are bound to be people who enjoy shopping much more than I do, as my tale doubtless reveals. But to be sovereign is to be the decision-maker. And it doesn't appear to me that consumers dictate what's on offer and how much it costs, no matter how much they enjoy buying it.

I looked around me. Marks & Spencer is an old brand attempting renewal, and part of the process apparently involves the introduction of Fair Trade cafés, one of which I had chanced upon after buying a multi-pack of socks. My decision to stop there for tea was doubtless influenced by the highly visible Fair Trade banners. According to standard economics I shouldn't care about such things. Instead, I should care only about what I can purchase and how much it costs. Nevertheless, despite the higher prices of the Fair Trade café, finding a table at which to drink my tea was not easy. Plenty of consumers clearly care about who produces what they buy – as the marketing people at M&S appear to know.

Pouring more tea, I remembered that there was a time when I and many people I knew habitually looked at labels to check where clothes were made before buying them. Many economists think this behaviour is naive – an issue to which we will return. It is over a decade since the debate about sweatshops truly got started, yet all the while the garment industry has continued its unstoppable globalization. Indeed, for any consumer, naive or not, who worries about who made an item of clothing and under what conditions, the country where it was made has become an almost useless indicator. Although I might still think twice about buying something stitched under the military regime of Myanmar, almost everything is now sewn in a faraway land, in circumstances we cannot know. It is possible to buy Fair Trade shirts, but if I limited myself to clothes whose origins I could be confident of, I would be turning up for my first day at work in my birthday suit. Looking again at my shopping bags, I decided that had the label attached to each shirt told me not only the price but also how much of this went to the person who stitched the shirt, it would undoubtedly have influenced my decisions. I pondered the impracticality of this top-of-the-head product labelling scheme, then considered a lesser version whereby the label told me that the sewing-machinist was guaranteed at least a certain percentage. If I were a true consumer sovereign, I would demand to be advised of this. But, as is the way with puppet kings, courtiers influence decisions by providing selective information.

I needed to get a few things at Leonard's Corner on my way home. In our house we like to cook curries and take a degree of pride in our comprehensive spice cupboard. The previous weekend had seen the last of the turmeric shaken out of its jar. I also needed milk and bread. The small supermarket had a 50g refill of turmeric for €2.99. Two hundred yards further on is a food store that describes itself as "middle-Eastern". If competition truly dictated prices, there would be no point in my making the extra effort by walking further, as in a competitive marketplace it would not be possible for the same product to be sold at radically different prices in the same location – at least, not for very long. Informed consumers would notice the price difference and always buy at the cheaper price until the disparity disappeared. In economics-speak, this is the "law of one price". In fact, I walked for the extra minute or so and managed to buy 100g of turmeric for €2.40. These shops, with total disregard for the law of one price, continue to stock turmeric with a price difference of almost 150%.

My final stop was the local chemist, where I wanted shower gel and razor blades. It's a pleasant shop, with neat shelves and friendly staff. It also operates as a late-night pharmacy, which is very handy for working people. I could have bought the toiletries before I left town, in the identikit store of a well-known chain, where they would have cost a total of more than a euro less. But if everyone did that, market forces might drive the local shop out and leave the community without its independent late-night pharmacy; an outcome that doesn't seem very efficient. I know there are other loyal customers who think like me and pay a bit extra, though there are doubtless some local people who don't.

As a sufferer from mild eczema, I am a frustrated reader of toiletry packaging. Makers of soaps, shampoos and similar products know that there are people like me and adapt their products accordingly. In the chemist I found a shower gel for "sensitive skin", which I compared with another brand that claimed to be "dermatologically tested", then another that insisted it was "hypoallergenic". I have no idea what these descriptions actually signify about what is in the product, nor how rigorously the ingredients must be tested to justify each description. Despite the product information revolution provided by the internet, I cannot find out. Part of me thinks this stuff is pseudo-scientific nonsense, but I always read it and pay extra for its supposed benefits. Occasionally one of these products agrees with me better than others. I buy it until the line is discontinued, which invariably it is. Each purchase of a previously untried product is a gamble with no upside and an itchy downside.

Clutching clothing, spices and toiletries, including a "new dermo-active" shower gel, I finally arrived home. Admittedly, it is not normal behaviour to go shopping for an afternoon and compare your experience with conventional economic theory. Yet my afternoon sample of economic life challenged standard economic principles repeatedly. The gap between the economics I know and my economic life seemed very wide indeed.

To generalize, there are two big differences between how economic life as a consumer is supposed to be, and how it actually seems to be. First, it doesn't only matter what we buy and how much it costs, as traditional economics dictates, because who we do business with matters too. There are many potential reasons why we might prefer to buy from a more expensive supplier, be it supporting a local firm, a liking for how they go about their business, or trust built up over time. In short, as well as prices, our relationship with the seller matters too. Second, we consumers are an uncertain bunch and the companies that sell to us know it. Our economic theories assume that we have much more knowledge and control over our decisions than we actually do. We don't know whether a shirt provides value for money until we discover how long it lasts and get the reactions of others to our wearing it. What seemed a fair price can rapidly feel like a rip-off when a recently bought shirt falls apart, or a person we secretly fancy says it's a strange colour. Nor can we be sure there won't be a better, cheaper shirt in the shop around the corner. We might discover we spent too much only when the next set of bills comes through. Or we may even read the following day that the company that supplied it is responsible for something we don't like. Consumption is not straightforward; it's a guessing game.

Should we care if consumers are not the rational, well-informed people that our economic theories say they are? It is hardly a major worry if a comfortably off middle-class person's trip to buy clothes doesn't work as traditional economics says it should. But what if the rest of economic life doesn't work the way it's thought to either? The theories about consumers, competition and how markets work, which failed to tally with my experience of buying shirts, are also applied to markets that matter much more, such as the housing market, the market for financial services and the jobs market.* They are the very same theories that failed to predict, or even to explain, the catastrophic turns of events in each of these markets following summer 2007. The wide gap between economics and the economic life of consumers could turn out to matter a great deal. Better economic theories may add up to a different overall picture.

The best the man could get

The last item I bought on my shopping trip was a packet of razor blades. I've been buying the same ones, or nearly the same ones, for so long that I can't remember why I chose them in the first place. They are made by Gillette – one of the most successful companies of the twentieth century. If the theory of the consumer is a cornerstone of orthodox economics, then occupying another corner is the theory of the firm. So I decided to see whether the gap between economics and economic life applies to companies as well as consumers, by looking into the history of Gillette.

Here is a simple sketch of the theory of the firm – how

---

* Economists use the term "market" in a way non-economists can find confusing. It is an abstract collective term for a set of possible exchanges between buyers and sellers. It can be defined by exchanges at a physical location (your local market), exchanges of a specific product (the housing market, the market for oranges), or exchanges between types of buyers or sellers (the retail market, the labour market). The "X market" or "market for X" covers all possible ways in which exchanges of X occur.

economists are trained to think of the likes of Gillette. Conventional economics says firms care only about profit. But competition in free markets forces them to charge competitive prices. To make maximum profit, therefore, they have to supply what consumers want as efficiently as possible, ensuring value for money for consumers. Everyday manufactured goods such as shaving products should, in theory, epitomize the benefits of cut-throat competition. Is this how a successful firm like Gillette works?

Anyone who has ever seen a Gillette advert, and few have not, might be interested to learn that for all the images of fine steel gliding through dark stubble on the square jaws of rippling shirtless men, the company's founder had perhaps the least macho name in business history: King Camp Gillette. He was a remarkable character – a millionaire capitalist, yet a committed socialist, named after royalty. The story of his company, beginning in the late nineteenth century, is more remarkable still. It is a case study of how major corporations form and thrive, full of insight into what makes them work. Comparing the richness of the Gillette story to the standard theory of the firm suggests that the gap between economics and economic life is as wide for companies as it is for consumers.

The story begins in 1871, when King Camp was a child, and when the Gillettes were among thousands of Chicago families thankful to be living lakeside. Many more would have perished in the Great Fire of that year had they not been able to escape by wading into Lake Michigan's cool waters. The family had come to the city from nearby Wisconsin to run a small family firm, a hardware business. Their livelihood was destroyed by the fire. Yet King's parents had talent and spirit. They moved to New York City to start again. His mother wrote *The White House Cookbook*, which contained her own experimental recipes and remained in print for a century, while his father worked as a patent agent. Aged seventeen, King Gillette began at the sharp end of business life, as a travelling salesman. He learned firsthand about customers, how they went about making purchases, and how they thought about prices. He began tinkering with products and managed to establish four patents, though none sold well. The company he then worked for belonged to William Painter, an entrepreneur who had made a sizeable fortune as the inventor of the crown cork bottle top. Painter told Gillette that the secret of success was to create something people found useful but threw away – indispensable advice, as it turned out.

Legend has it that, in 1895, King Camp Gillette had his "eureka" moment, appropriately enough in the bathroom, while using an irritatingly blunt razor. A razor is one of those objects that is less dangerous when sharp, so shaving in that era was a hazardous activity. Men used leather strops to condition the blade, but still the consequences of poor concentration were potentially gory. What Gillette saw was the possibility of separating the blade from the razor, to make the blade disposable. This was the moment of conception in the life of a multi-billion-dollar multinational. Yet it took over five years for the company to be born. At first, the metallurgists Gillette approached told him it was impossible to manufacture the sharp, inexpensive, steel blade he required. Undeterred, he eventually met William Emery Nickerson, an engineer who, after much trial and error, proved them wrong. The two men spent plenty of their own money developing the disposable blades and plenty of time wooing sceptical investors to back the product, which together they patented. In fact, had Nickerson not possessed an entertainingly inappropriate name for a razor business, Gillette might not have been "Gillette" at all. The company began trading in 1903, when it sold less than a hundred razors. In 1904, it sold 90,000, and many more blades. By 1910, Gillette was the market leader.

The profit motive, undoubtedly, played a part in the founding of Gillette. But King Gillette cannot have known for sure that his idea would generate profit. Where did he get the confidence to gamble so much time, money and effort on it? Would Gillette Co. have come into being had its founder not had the good fortune to benefit from maternal drive and inventiveness, paternal expertise with patents, parental financial security, an understanding of consumers from his years of selling on the road, and good advice from a former boss? Many people possess the desire to make money, but few have the benefit of such productive relationships and the knowledge and security King Gillette derived from them. Gillette's background, his social and family network, his business contacts, his many doorstep encounters with potential customers, is crucial to understanding how and why the company evolved – perhaps as crucial as the profit motive invoked by orthodox economics.

Once the company had started up, what was behind its quick success? Certainly, competitive pricing is not the answer. Relatively speaking, Gillette products have never been cheap, then or now: if efficiency and price had determined success, many of Gillette's rivals would have fared better. What Gillette had was not a cheaper product but, perhaps, a more useful one and, certainly, a more distinctive one. Separating razor from blade turned out to have big marketing benefits – attributes unrelated to the product's function that nevertheless helped it to sell. Flat, individually wrapped blades could carry a friendly picture of King Gillette himself – sufficient exposure to confer celebrity status in those days. More significantly, because razor handles lasted much longer than blades, once a customer had a Gillette, he would be less likely to switch makes. King Gillette discovered he could sell razors cheaply and make the profit on the blades. In later years, razors were even given away free. Thus, a customer's first contact with the company was an eye-catching offer, likely to establish an ongoing relationship of regular purchases.

This was a clever and lucrative marketing trick, but the success it brought was partly down to luck. Gillette had seen, in his entrepreneurial vision, the desirability of throwing away the blade while keeping the razor. Only later, after he had decided to bet the kitchen sink on the idea, did he discover his razor's additional marketing benefits. A feature of economic life is that luck is difficult to quantify. With each trial and error, both of products and how to sell them, the chances of success can alter. With Gillette razors, unforeseen marketing benefits helped to make their originator a fortune – a word derived from the Latin *fortuna*, which means luck.

In those early years, King Gillette had his fair share of boardroom battles with fretting investors. Yet the company's superior way of attracting attention and loyalty from customers began to deliver the lifeblood of successful business: regular, predictable revenue. This allowed Gillette to plan strategically. Once separating handle and blade was seen to work, the company had the capacity quickly to export the idea. Gillette Co. opened a London office within two years of starting production and was truly international within ten. Its biggest threat was imitation. Yet the company had the funds and the time to enforce patents in court. If litigation failed, Gillette simply bought the rival firm. As industry leader, it could invest more than its competitors in product innovation, patents and, especially, mass marketing and promotion. In 1912, King Gillette went so far as to write: "the whole success of this business depends on advertising". By then, famous baseball players were featuring in Gillette's ads. Money spent on marketing could have been used to reduce prices, but the company understood that competitive pricing was not what mattered. One of King Gillette's strokes of promotional genius was to offer razors to the US Army at cost, in a specially designed tin. They were made standard issue during World War I, which ensured that "Gillette" remained a household name for a generation.

Gillette Co. grew from entrepreneurial idea, to small firm, to large firm, to multinational corporation. Indeed, the company ultimately weathered the stormy economic seas better than its charismatic founder. Like many other businesspeople, and indeed the world's top economists, King Gillette failed to see the 1929 Wall Street crash coming. It swept away much of his personal fortune. Throughout his eventful life, Gillette remained a self-proclaimed socialist, believing that a corporation should not exist only to compete for profit, but as a system of cooperation; a way to engineer a better society. Many have suggested that he was simply confused, or hypocritical. Perhaps. But while Gillette's utopian socialism may have been unrealistic, something in his own motivations and his under-standing of customers indisputably worked in the razor business. He died in 1932, just as the Great Depression, the century's fiercest economic storm, was gathering ominous momentum. His legacy, a world-beating company, was a large and safe enough vessel to sail on through.

Over one hundred years after its foundation, no rival has caught up with Gillette, nor even come close. In most developed countries Gillette dominates the market sufficiently to classify, officially, as a monopoly. A century after its founder's inspiration in the bathroom, Gillette Co. was supplying more than half the "systems razors" sold in the developed world, taking 65% of the US market, 60% in the UK, 70% in France and 85% in some smaller European and Latin American countries. When I bought my razor blades in the local pharmacy, five of the seven packets on sale sported the metallic silver flash of Gillette's logo.

Has a century of competition forced the company to prioritize efficiency and competitive prices? Not at all. Gillette's strategy for success is largely unchanged since the days of its founder: spend on product innovation, patent a new razor, launch it with a massive marketing campaign, make the real money on the blades once people have the razor, then spend enough developing the next generation of razor. In 2004 Gillette launched the "M3Power". It glided across TV screens, over the famously fine features of David Beckham, paid for from an annual marketing budget of about $800 million. That budget could have been used to reduce the price of the razors and blades, but instead David Beckham received a massive fee, paid for by the people who bought them – including me.

In other ways, though, Gillette's strategy did change. With its primary market completely conquered, the main threat became the potential demise of wet shaving itself. When electric shavers, first marketed in the 1930s, began to take off in the 1960s, there was a buzz in Gillette's boardroom. Faced with a risk of uncertain propor-tions, what does a major multinational do? Bet on both horses. By

1967, Gillette was a big enough international corporate player to buy a controlling stake in Braun. Similarly, in the 1990s, as a fusion between small electric and wet razors looked promising, Gillette merged with the leading battery supplier, Duracell. In an uncertain and increasingly globalized world, a company's sheer size and financial muscle help it to respond to threats.

Finally, an era ended for Gillette in October 2005. It was swallowed by a bigger corporate giant, Procter & Gamble; or, as the monster multinational's press release put it, "P&G welcomes Gillette to the family". King Camp Gillette's legacy is no longer a globally successful company. Instead, it lives on as one of the world's most valuable brands – about which more later.

I didn't know the tale of King Camp Gillette until I decided to find out more about my razor blades. Learning his story and delving into the history of his company made the gap between the standard economic theories I have been trained in and the economic life I observe look bigger. The company did not succeed by providing razors people wanted, as efficiently as possible, at competitive prices, in search of profit. It continually produced razors and blades less efficiently than it could have, by spending big money on campaigns to persuade people which razor they wanted. Perhaps more consistently and significantly than anything else, Gillette thrived through investment in clever marketing. But success also depended on an inspirational idea, social and family networks, courage and determination in the face of substantial risk, good fortune, the appeal of distinctive products and, once established, the exploitation of corporate might.

As with consumers, the activity of firms in markets involves human behaviour and relationships, with all the strengths and frailties that implies. In the case of Gillette, the strengths won through, but it is not always this way. What most shocked former Fed Chairman Alan Greenspan, as he watched the financial crisis unfold, was how some of the best and brightest people at major financial institutions had taken decisions so ruinous to their companies' interests. Human frailties, to which we will return, matter too.

Revolutionary talk

Rigorous thinking requires more than anecdotes and generalizations. My experience of a shopping trip, together with a brief history of one successful company, hardly provides the basis for a radical rethink about how the economic system works. Perhaps most other consumers have the good fortune to be much better shoppers than I am and most other companies don't follow the same path as Gillette. Yet, as we will see, the ease with which everyday economic life strays from the path of economic theory is not unrelated to the dramatic departures from theory that have landed us in the mess we are in today. So why is prevailing economic theory such a poor guide to what we see around us?

The main reason is deceptively simple: the task of economists is very, very hard. This does not mean that the theories employed by my profession are more technical or complex than those employed in other fields of study. The scientific toolkit used by economists is the same as that used by numerate researchers in other disciplines, give or take a few specialized tools. Rather, what makes the task faced by economists particularly hard is the system we are working on with those same tools.

The goal of economics, indeed its accepted definition, is to understand how society allocates (or could potentially allocate) resources. More simply: who gets what? The central economic concepts are ownership and exchange – who owns the resources and how they are acquired. This is where most introductory textbooks begin, providing us with an optimistic starting point. The initial concepts of ownership and exchange appear simple and clean. They are the emerging green shoots of an intellectual field. This hopeful perspective quickly changes, however, when we begin to consider the "what" of the "who gets what?". Most obviously, it refers to all manner of material goods, both man-made and raw. But this constitutes a small fraction of the "what". For humans regularly generate, share and exchange at least the following "resources": work, time, protection, ideas, shelter, promises, access, risk, skills, knowledge, rights, transport, experiences, potential, space, data and responsibility. Already the clean green shoots of the economic field are beginning to look messy – many different varieties, all intertwined. Then we must consider the "who" of the "who gets what?". Humans. We are billions of people with different personalities, families, religions, languages, values, limitations, beliefs, identities and abilities; organized into a complex and changeable set of groups, cultures, networks, systems of governance and nations; with their own histories, climates, geographies, laws and leaders. Now the full extent of the challenge is visible. When the huge, evolving, interconnected diversity of people is combined with the changing, subtle and vast array of resources at our disposal, the field of study that is economics looks like a tangled, impenetrable thicket, extending as far as the horizon, from which it is a wonder that any general principles can be made out. The sheer size, density and complexity of the economic system mean that mastering it compares with the task of understanding other vast, complex systems that induce severe scientific brainache, such as the universe and, indeed, the brain itself. The appropriate response to the intellectual vista before the economist, not always provided by my profession, it must be admitted, is humility.

Historically, economists have done two things to make the seemingly impossible problem of understanding the economic system vaguely tractable. First, traditional economics assumes that everything has a price, allowing all resources effectively to be thought of in the same way – resources are just any stuff that has value to people. Second, orthodox economics assumes a set of common characteristics for all of us, from a farmer bartering home-grown produce in an African village to the chief executive of a marketing company atop a Manhattan skyscraper. In two simple assumptions, the "what" is boiled down to the single dimension of price, while the "who" is reduced to a single, supposedly representative, human. In fact, the assumption about "what" is really just another assumption about "who", because all resources have a price only if all of us are prepared to put a price on them, as the supposedly representative human obviously is. To make any headway at all, economists have to simplify the problem, and that means simplifying people like you and me.

Economists are often criticized for simplifying people, but to some extent we have no choice. Any theory of what is likely to happen when people do business must include a theory of what people are like when they exchange things with each other. If we want to know the likely effect of environmental taxes, or the economic impact of a wave of immigration, or what constitutes a fair method for funding higher education, generalizations about how people respond to their economic environment are unavoidable. Indeed, they are essential. Thus, if economists are to be criticized, it cannot be for simplifying human nature. We have to. The question is not whether human nature is simplified, but whether the particular simplification used is the best one available. It should aim to capture the essence of economic activity, leaving the narrowest gap between economic theory and economic life. Thus, the economist needs to isolate the most relevant aspects of our natures; to locate the most powerful determinants of our economic behaviour. I refer to this task as discovering people's "economic instincts".

Mainstream economics decided, some time ago, what people's most powerful economic instincts are. Traditional theory begins with the assumption that individuals are independent, rational, selfish materialists. As consumers, our aim is to get what we want as cheaply as possible. As workers, we desire to do as little as possible in return for as much as possible. Meanwhile the companies we work for care only about making as much profit as possible, because they are governed by rational, selfish owners who are ultimately no deeper than the bottom line. The standard theories of economics, derived by the great economists of the past, now taught as basics to students, parroted passionately by expert commentators, sculpted into soundbites by politicians, are ultimately founded upon this view of what we are like. We are, apparently, at our economic hearts, independent, rational, selfish creatures.

Is this the best description of what we are like? The rest of this book offers an answer to this most fundamental economic question: no. The place to start, however, is with a related question: how should we go about finding out? If the job is to identify our true economic instincts, what is the best way to do it?

As mentioned, before turning my hand to economics, I trained as a neuroscientist and psychologist. To me, the best way to find out what we are like is straightforward: study us. Watch what we do in different situations. Record and analyse the results. Then use the findings to try to discern the strongest forces behind our behaviour when we do business with each other. Build up a picture of what we are like, economically speaking – a theory of people's economic instincts. The theory will be approximate, so some people will not conform to it. It may be useful to know in what ways people deviate from it and in what kind of proportions. This observational approach is imperfect, but likely to be the best that can be done. For me, systematically observing people is the scientist's answer.

It is not, however, the way generations of very clever economists have gone about the task. The version of the human mind employed by mainstream economics is not based on scientific observation of people's behaviour. It is not even based on anecdotal evidence, such as my shopping trip or a brief history of Gillette. Indeed, its genesis may surprise you. Standard economics adopted a set of assumptions about our economic instincts for, primarily, mathematical convenience. The truth is that orthodox economics assumes that people are independent, rational, selfish materialists because it makes it easier to do the sums when you try to add all the people and firms together to get a complete picture of the economy.

In recent times, however, some researchers, including psychologists, sociologists and economists, have begun to examine our economic instincts scientifically. Instead of assuming a version of what our minds are like, for mathematical convenience or any other reason, they choose to investigate the question objectively, using experiments, surveys and data collection. They observe people. This work is developing into a new and influential school of thought in economics, most commonly referred to as "behavioural economics". As with all fields of study, some of the work is very good and some is not so good. What distinguishes behavioural economists from traditional economists is not expertise or technical sophistication, but their scientific approach.

As we will see, behavioural economics questions, even refutes, the traditional assumptions. For example, there turn out to be many economic equivalents of the mindmarks that define Irish street corners – behaviours that appear irrational, but which have evolved over time and seem to work. And, as its many critics have long suspected, traditional economics is excessively pessimistic about our motives. The evidence shows that we are not selfish plotters, out to gain every penny we can from whatever system we live under and everyone else in it. Most people are, in the right economic context, surprisingly selfless.

The material in this book is mostly derived from the work of behavioural economists. The findings suggest that standard economics is not based on a reasonable approximation of our economic instincts, but a distortion of them. The simplification of human nature economists have traditionally adopted is not, it seems, centred on the reality of what we are like. Rather than a rough sketch of our economic character, the version of people adopted by our standard economic theories is more like a cartoon characterization, which vastly exaggerates one side of our natures at the expense of all others. That is, it is not a balanced estimate, which is wrong in individual cases but right on average, but is instead consistently off-beam. Few would doubt that we are, to a degree, independent, rational, selfish and materialistic. But what behavioural economics reveals is that there are other aspects of human nature, which balance these instincts and are crucial to understanding what happens when we do business. The work is uncovering other traits that are vital to our economic life and which most of us share.

Still, adherents to schools of thought can be slow to abandon cherished theories. At various points in the argument that follows, I deal with some of the objections traditionalists have raised. But even those economists who prize dearly the orthodox method are beginning to accept some of the more established findings of behavioural economics. The argument has changed, from refusal to accept findings to asking what those findings ultimately mean. For me, they have begun a revolution in economic thought. I believe this revolution will be very significant. Like the most prominent economic ideas of the last century, behavioural economics has begun to penetrate beyond the dusty journals of academia and into the political arena. Until very recently, it was doing so slowly, but the present crisis has accelerated the process dramatically.

Given the difficulty of isolating our economic instincts and the vast complexity of the economic system, it is surprising how much consensus had previously developed. In what people broadly refer to as "the West", the past few decades were dominated by a pro-market view, which no political movement with serious ambitions for government could afford to challenge. Ambitious politicians repeated the prevailing wisdom: markets are efficient, competition is good, taxes should be low, inflation should be low, labour markets must be flexible, regulation should be kept to a minimum. It is interesting to note that the language used to express these previously unchallengeable maxims, the language that our conventional economic theories were translated into, is very far removed from the simplification of human nature that, ultimately, the theories are based on. For instance, assert that competition is good for the economy and still you may encounter little opposition, but assert that people are essentially selfish, rational individualists and you are likely to find yourself in an argument or two. The latter is a much more discomforting proposition. Ideas can become so embedded and accepted that where they came from becomes largely forgotten. And accepted these ideas were.

How quickly the landscape has changed. In the heat of crisis, the old wisdom prevails no longer, but instead incites immediate objections. Some markets can clearly cause great damage. Intense competition between both loan companies and banks was one of the causes of the crisis. Taxes are necessary to pay for government rescues. Meanwhile, should we worry so much about inflation in the face of mass unemployment? How desirable is labour market flexibility when firms are dumping thousands of good workers at frightening speed? And as for reducing regulation, it may be some time before anyone standing for office is brave enough to revive that notion.

With old ideas wilting, the territory is fertile for new ones. Behavioural economics is receiving unprecedented attention and growing in size and stature. Many more people have become aware of how strongly and successfully it has challenged traditional economic theory, undermining the mainstream textbook account of how the economy works. Nevertheless, as a school of thought, behavioural economics remains young. It is yet to generate a set of coherent alternative theories to explain the new evidence or, relatedly, to be galvanized into a series of principles for guiding policy. In the final sections of the remaining chapters, I try to provide a flavour of what economic theories based on more realistic assumptions about our economic instincts might mean in practice.

This revolution in economic thought is only beginning. Many people are warming to the findings of behavioural economics because they help to make sense of the economy. The ideas resonate when you walk down the street to take part in and watch economic life. Believe it when you see it. But what the findings may ultimately persuade you of, how they may change your world-view, is a much more open and intriguing question. Economics relates to many issues – political, commercial and personal. A revolution in the subject is therefore very likely to change how people regard them. It is an exciting prospect.

2

Marketopia v. Muddleton

WHAT HAPPENS WHEN you think of a light bulb, or the universe, or your worst local traffic problem, or DNA, or the economy? Each of these is a system – a whole made up of interrelated parts. In your mind, it is represented by, or associated with, images, words, memories and so on. If I ask you to rank these five systems according to how well you understand them, how might you go about it? It may be tempting to rank them by how much you can say about each. But loquacity is not understanding – the world has plenty of bluffers. You could rank the systems by how much you know about each. But the bigger the system, the more you are likely to know, however incomplete your understanding. The question, probably, has no perfect answer.

The best answer I can give is that you truly understand how a system works if you have a model of it, in your mind, that behaves like the system itself. I use the word "model" only because that is the word scientists use. Nobody, not even the world's foremost neuroscientist, knows exactly what goes on in your head when you understand a system. But whatever combination of images, words and memories is involved, and whatever method the interconnected mass of nerve cells in your brain uses to generate them, the crucial thing is that what you say about how the system will behave matches how it actually behaves. It doesn't matter whether you can name all the parts, nor whether you can recite its history, nor whether you can reproduce pages of equations purporting to "model" the system, nor how impressive it may appear to others that you can do these things. What matters is whether the system behaves as you think it will. If it does, then you understand the system.

Let's apply this logic to economics. The current economic consensus is underpinned by a particular way of thinking about the economy – a dominant model, which I will describe shortly. Thus, our modern understanding of economics can be judged, to a great extent, by whether the economy behaves like this dominant model. "Competitive equilibrium", as it is called, is the favourite model of neoclassical economics, which has been the foremost school of thought for several decades now. Every economist is taught the model of competitive equilibrium, in increasing degrees of sophistication. It is the centrepiece of a formal economic education – as it was in my own. All trained economists carry this model in their heads, whether we believe in it or not. Very many non-economists have some version of competitive equilibrium in their minds too, though they may not know it as such. Competitive equilibrium is more than a scientific theory. The model's way of thinking, including its assumptions about our economic instincts, has penetrated our culture. It has become an intellectual force to be reckoned with – the scripture of free-market economics.

In a formal version of the model of competitive equilibrium, each person or firm is described by an equation, and the outcome when we all interact is shown as a series of diagrams. I think it is helpful to turn competitive equilibrium into a story about people.

Meet the Marketopians

Imagine an undiscovered country. Picture it as a large island nation where nobody you know lives, or has ever visited. Welcome to "Marketopia". Shortly, you will embark upon a tour of this fictitious land.

Before we get going, please note the following intellectual safety announcement. Because Marketopia is extraordinary, it is important to suspend disbelief and begin with a blank slate. Human history as we know it has not touched the island, which has not shared our experience. The empires, religions, nations and conflicts that dominate our past have no influence here. Indeed, the process of evolution that created Marketopia is unclear. The island is just there – truly a world apart. When you meet the people of Marketopia, note that they resemble us, in that each individual has been assigned different characteristics by the lottery of life. Some are fortunate enough to be healthy, intelligent, strong and beautiful, while others are less so. To this extent it is a typical human society. But "Marketopians" all share the same particular set of values, which makes for a unique culture, aspects of which will appear alien. Still, much is recognizable. Marketopia has citizens who consume, firms that produce and an incredible marketplace. Enjoy your trip.

First, meet Adam, a typical Marketopian. Like his fellow citizens, he is a fairly straightforward individual. He earns money and then uses it to pay for products that make him happier. Adam dislikes going to work, but knows that to keep a roof over his head and to buy the things that make life more enjoyable, he must sacrifice his leisure time to provide things other people want. In his case, the goods in question are hire cars. Adam's job is to check the fuel level, clean the vehicle, squirt in a puff of air-freshener, hook a friendly cardboard welcome pack over the rear-view mirror, and park the car in the pick-up bay for the next customer. Adam could work longer hours, make more money and so buy more of the products that make his life pleasurable. But with an already aching back and bumps on his head, an extra hour's pay just isn't worth another hour of digging sticky crumbs out of car seats. He has carefully balanced the hours he works against the goods and services his earnings will purchase, keeping himself as happy as possible, given his limited opportunities.

Adam lives in a smallish, rather grubby flat in Marketopia's capital city, Port Friedman. Many of his possessions are old and he always wants more than he can afford – a meal out, the latest cool sneakers, a better dentist. In particular, he dreams of owning a fancy sports car. But he makes good use of what he does earn, because Adam is a superb shopper. He likes to go to fruit stalls at one of Port Friedman's many markets, where he compares apples with oranges. Adam can place the whole range of produce in order of preference. He has always liked pears more than apples, but oranges more than pears. So he prefers oranges to apples too. After examining the fruit carefully, Adam usually buys mostly oranges, some pears and a few apples. It would get boring if he ate only his favourite – the third or fourth orange never tastes quite as good as the first. Adam is such a good judge of ripeness that when he gets home he always finds the fruit to be just as tasty as he anticipated. In knowing exactly what he likes and what's on offer, Adam is typical of shoppers in Marketopia. The citizens are famous for spending money wisely. They never splash out on a holiday they can't really afford, or use a credit card to pay for a slap-up meal in an expensive restaurant, only to regret it later.

Next, meet Eve, another Marketopian, who shares many characteristics with Adam. After all, she was born and raised in Marketopia too, learning to be sensible with cash and to assess products accurately from the moment she was old enough for pocket money. She too can place fruit in order of preference, and be sure of its ripeness. But although she has these similar characteristics, Eve's tastes are different. She, unusually, has always preferred apples to more expensive oranges and so she gets her favourite fruit more cheaply. Luckily for Eve it seems there is, after all, a kind of accounting for taste.

Eve also balances time working, which like all Marketopians she dislikes, against the income it brings, to maximize her happiness. Here again, Eve is luckier than Adam, since she is more intelligent than him and is a more productive worker as a consequence. Being a manager for a company running a string of cafés throughout Port Friedman, she commands a considerably higher salary. She has a bigger house, with nice furniture, goes for a weekly massage and drives a fancy convertible sports car of the type Adam craves. Though relatively rich, Eve still wants more and better things. Like Adam, she is ruthlessly logical about her spending. For example, Eve gets much pleasure from chocolate ice cream; even more so than from apples, would you believe. But she knows that eating too many tubs containing "choccy chewy-chunks" will make her overweight and more likely to get diseases when she's older, and that the latest research proves that eating apples protects against cancer. So Eve has an apple every day and only occasionally buys a tub of chocolate ice cream, perfectly balancing pleasure today against the chance of a better quality of life in years to come. Like her fellow citizens, she wants to live a long life, consuming the combination of goods and services that will make her as happy as possible.

Adam and Eve have known each other for a long time, but their relationship is not important. They are independent people, to the degree that although Adam would love to have a convertible like Eve's, he's not jealous. He is as happy as he can be, for a man of his abilities. Eve knows Adam likes the car, but she neither teases him about it nor hopes that he admires it gleaming in the drive. Although she knows that little would please him more than the testosterone surge of getting behind the wheel, the invitation is not forthcoming. It just doesn't occur to her. He has his things and she has hers, with no place for envy or pity. That's the way life in Marketopia is. The happiness of the people is determined by what each can afford of the goods and services they prefer, and how much they have to work to pay for them. They are concerned with their own self-interest and what happens in the lives of those around them is immaterial. What is material is, well, material.

The third and final inhabitant of Marketopia we meet on this short tour made his name in business. Maurice Mule was burdened with a terrible surname. After a childhood of painful playground jibes, he realized that this distinctive and unusual bequest was a commercial advantage. Maurice cares about profit. Only profit. It's not that all the teasing he endured at school caused him to become stubborn in the pursuit of success – all his fellow businesspeople in

Marketopia care only about profit too. Maurice simply figured that even in Marketopia's very competitive catering industry, "Mule's Muffins" would become a winner. And so they did. The muffins are as delicious as any others in the land.

Maurice will tell you the firm turned out exactly as he had planned. Just as Adam and Eve are perfect judges of fruit, so the bankers of Marketopia can accurately assess a business plan. After Maurice walked through the twelve-foot-high oak doors of Arrow-Debreu Bank plc, the loans manager quickly gauged his chances of success. ADBank let him borrow enough money to start up a bakery. He wanted one large enough to produce lots of muffins, but not so large he couldn't manage it and carefully monitor quality. Once he had rented enough space for his manageably sized bakery on the outskirts of Port Friedman, Maurice had to decide how many workers to hire. He took a quick tour of the competitive cafés and shops of Marketopia, meeting owners and managers, including Eve, who told him what price she would give him for each muffin; after her cut was accounted for, naturally. Then he added up his costs: repayments to ADBank, ingredients, cleaning and maintaining the bakery, and the going wage for workers with a bit of catering experience. After a few sums, Maurice reckoned his bakery would make the most profit if he hired 23 workers.

Mule's Muffins now bake over ten thousand muffins a week for the café-goers of Port Friedman. The local suburbs are known for the sugary sweet smell of Mule's bakery. As he arrives home at Mule Mansion, turning through automatic gates, each emblazoned with a letter M, Maurice smells only success.

We have now met a businessperson and two reluctant workers, one well off, one not. Adam and Eve are like all Marketopian consumers: rational, knowledgeable, independent and materialistic. What makes them happy is what they own. Each morning they awake, eager to buy products but resigned to the need to sell their labour. They have no time for worrying about job status, goings-on in the world, social relations or keeping up with the neighbours, when there are products to be enjoyed. Maurice Mule, meanwhile, is typically profit hungry. There are businesspeople like him all over Marketopia. Anywhere there is profit to be made there is a Mule equivalent eager to rake it in.

Now, a look at the markets. The local shops and stalls are a fabulous sight: competitive, noisy and hectic. Businesspeople want profit, consumers want lots of things, so huge numbers of goods and services are bought and sold. Products are laid out in such a way that every consumer can establish the quality and price immediately. The local jobcentre is also a visitor favourite. A huge wall lists all vacancies, for everyone to see, and posts appear and get filled at incredible speed. Marketopia has no government regulations to overcome and complete freedom to buy and sell, so anyone can trade anything with anyone else.

Marketopians themselves proudly believe that their nation is more efficient than any other. They tell visitors that efficiency is guaranteed by freedom. They explain the link like this. Every time two parties in free Marketopia agree a transaction, it is voluntary. Independent, rational and informed Marketopians do not make mistakes, so deals benefit both sides. Detailed discussion takes place over wages, products and prices, as everyone checks all available deals to be sure they earn what they can, work the hours they choose and purchase the items that make them happiest. With no restrictions, everyone buys and sells until they can no longer find another deal that makes them still better off. Complete freedom to trade labour and products means they can take advantage of every possible opportunity. They head for home as happy as can be, with work endured but shopping bags bulging, to spend an evening with the products worth striving to get.

I hope you enjoyed your tour and, as your guide, let me add that there really is no need to put your hand in your pocket. You are in Marketopia now, where people don't give tips, obviously, as they wouldn't get anything in return.

The minds behind the model

This caricature of capitalism is what you get if you take the most influential economic model of modern times and turn it into a story. The process was, for me, surprisingly instructive. I found the model of competitive equilibrium, as a picture of society, more plausible beforehand, when it consisted of textbook diagrams and equations, than when I turned it into characters. Once the model's individuals, firms and markets are described in prose, it is harder to believe that this model of our economy is as influential as it is. And it really is. Every government on Earth has probably changed policies because of arguments stemming from the model of competitive equilibrium. Some countries have undertaken wholesale reform designed to make their societies more like the model. So let's dig a bit deeper.

The model assumes several specific theories about people's instincts, economically speaking. Some behaviours are assumed to be common to all, while others are allowed to vary between us. Most fundamentally, every person's happiness depends only on the goods and services each can buy; what other people get is irrelevant. Thus, our motives are assumed to be those of independent, selfish materialists. We are also all assumed to be rational and perfectly informed about available products and jobs. (These two assumptions are not completely unconnected to the motivational ones, because selfishness might drive us to think hard about our decisions and to ensure we are informed.) Where we vary, according to the model, is in tastes and abilities. Each individual is permitted different preferences for products and different workplace skills (though tastes and abilities do not vary to the degree that anybody actually enjoys work). So the version of human nature assumed by the model of competitive equilibrium holds that independence, selfish materialism, rationality and perfect knowledge of economic opportunities are attributes all of us possess, while tastes and abilities vary between us. This is why Adam, Eve and Maurice are as they are.

Of course, no country has citizens just like Adam, Eve and Maurice. Not even the late Milton Friedman, perhaps the most famous free-market economist, believed these assumptions about people to be completely true. But most economists usually argue that the model contains a reasonable approximation of what we are like. Whether they are right is a question of major importance. If our economic instincts are not at least approximated by those of Adam, Eve and Maurice, then many of our standard explanations of how the economy works could turn out to be inaccurate. For example, the model of competitive equilibrium underpins accepted economic explanations for why some countries are rich and others poor, what causes unemployment, the efficiency of markets, and why free trade is beneficial in principle. Understanding the economic instincts of consumers, workers and businesspeople is crucial to understanding economics as a whole.

So where did this model, with its particular assumptions about our economic instincts, come from? The answer is that, initially, standard economics developed this simplification of human nature because it was a navigable route to an enticing destination: a complete model of the whole economy.

Funnily enough, the first person to piece together an influential big picture of the economy was Adam – the eighteenth-century Scottish philosopher Adam Smith, that is. What exactly Smith believed is a matter of some dispute. The economic model in Smith's mind was quite imprecise, and because his text is dense and difficult, modern thinkers have a habit of trying to work it round to their own point of view. Still, what he undoubtedly and famously realized was that if a rational individual approached buying or selling from a completely selfish perspective, this could nevertheless benefit others in the market. Traders might care only about lining their own pocket, but they would still have the incentive to provide goods others wanted and were willing to part with good money for. Smith was a man of his time, and his time was the Enlightenment. The emphasis on the benefit of free voluntary exchange was in keeping with the liberal philosophy being developed by other British philosophers, such as David Hume and Jeremy Bentham.*

Smith's insight was that trade between a selfish seller and a selfish buyer, trading partners who cared not at all for each other, could bring gains to both. In other words, he showed that selfish motives *could* result in mutual gain. Neither Adam Smith, nor anyone since, has shown either that buyers and sellers actually *are* selfish, or that to enjoy mutual gains from trade they need to be. Casual observation had suggested to Smith that voluntary exchanges generally made people better off. This was evidence that trade produced mutual gains, but it was not evidence about people's motives, or their states of mind more generally.

So why did people's selfishness become a central tenet of economics? In short, it made the mathematics easier. As the subject developed, researchers with increasing mathematical skill wanted to create bigger and more elaborate theories. In the nineteenth century, model economies of hypothetical individuals and products were developed. By assuming that individuals were not only selfish but also rational, economists could reduce human decisions to simple mathematical processes. They treated each person as a little calculating machine, describing their available options with an equation. Hypothetical individuals were assigned different abilities to earn income and different amounts of happiness associated with each product they bought.† Economists could then calculate how many hours each hypothetical individual would work and what they would

---

* It is unfortunate that Adam Smith is most identified with this theoretical insight regarding selfishness. Arguably, his greater achievement was to understand how economic gains come from a combination of trade and the division of labour, which he developed through observing the operation of a pin factory. Perhaps, now this achievement features on the new English £20 note, that will change.

† Of course, the economists couldn't actually assign numbers for happiness, or "utility", as the profession rather dryly calls it. This was the main reason the mathematics took decades to develop. A complex set of technical assumptions was needed that allowed relative comparisons to be made without having to put absolute numbers on people's happiness. Even then, relative comparisons are possible only for the same individual in different circumstances, not between different people.

buy, to optimize their happiness. To work out what each would do, economists also had to assume that the hypothetical individuals had perfect information about available jobs and products, otherwise they might randomly miss the best opportunity through ignorance, and random deviation from the optimal choice would be hard to account for in the model. Better mathematical techniques meant that these models could be expanded to include any number of hypothetical individuals, as well as hypothetical firms that employed workers and competed to sell products for as much profit as possible. With mathematical symbols instead of words, economists had invented Marketopia.

It must have been easy, in the mind-numbing detail of mathematical equations, proofs and solutions, to lose sight of the point of it all. What was driving this ongoing programme of research, developing the model of competitive equilibrium, was the desire to work out from first principles what might happen in a hypothetical economy, in terms of prices and wages; or "who gets what?". Early economists thought that maybe, ultimately, the outcome could be compared with data from real economies, but simply completing the hypothetical model was challenge enough. By halfway through the twentieth century, thousands of economics papers had been published that employed increasingly sophisticated mathematical methods to define model economies of imaginary Marketopians and calculate the possible outcomes. All these models consisted of hypothetical individuals who were effectively greedy, all-knowing calculating machines. Almost no papers were published that addressed, scientifically, whether people like you and me actually *are* greedy, all-knowing calculating machines. In fact, comparisons between these models and the real world were a rarity.

The technical approach to economics, characterized by hypothetical economic models, climaxed in the 1950s, when Kenneth Arrow and Gerard Debreu published a celebrated paper. It used the latest mathematical techniques to derive a proof, which showed that in the model of competitive equilibrium (a hypothetical free-market economy of independent, selfish, rational, perfectly informed individuals and firms), prices could adjust such that the economy achieved a stable equilibrium of perfect efficiency.* This meant that Arrow and Debreu's hypothetical economy benefited from every possible gain from trade; it got the most from the abilities of its hypothetical people, meaning no involuntary unemployment; and it suffered no shortages or excesses, as its hypothetical firms maximized their profit by supplying exactly the amount of each product that individuals demanded. The paper is tough stuff – the mathematics is hard. Yet the authors had proved that Marketopia could be perfectly efficient and, over fifty years on, the equations and diagrams that convey this idea still form the centrepiece of an education in economics.

Today's mainstream textbooks refer to Arrow and Debreu's result, that competitive equilibrium can be perfectly efficient, as "remarkable". It is considered by many economists to be proof that free markets deliver efficient outcomes and to provide a formal statement of the logic behind the success of capitalism as an economic system. Marketopia is, for them, an economic ideal to aim for. For example, Steven Landsburg, a senior American economist and commentator, calls the model and its proof "one of the great intellectual achievements of humankind". In his book *The Armchair Economist*, Landsburg argues that students should have to play a computer-game version of competitive equilibrium, with those who achieve the happiness high score being rewarded with coupons for pizza. Apparently, if colleges provided twelve-inch Margheritas as rewards for being good Marketopians, this would teach students how the real world works before they had to head out into it to make a living.

For all the hyperbole, somewhere along the historical line something got lost. There is no doubt that the development of the model

---

* Arrow and Debreu's *Econometrica* paper of 1954 is the classic reference for the proof, although a similar one was independently derived by Lionel McKenzie, also in 1954. In truth, these papers were the result of a cumulative research programme, involving many economists, that had tried for over fifty years to prove what most economists already believed, that the assumptions of the model led to perfect efficiency.

of competitive equilibrium involved decades of impressive and sustained intellectual effort. Some of those who worked on it, including Arrow and Debreu, are winners of the Nobel Prize for economics. The model and its proof are a genuine intellectual achievement. For one thing, the proof established something that many had doubted, for it rigorously demonstrated that, in principle, it is theoretically possible to have an efficient economic system without anyone in charge. But it did not demonstrate, and nor was it intended to, that the real economy actually is such an efficient system, or that it could be turned into one.

You understand the system if the model in your mind behaves like the system itself. So whether you understand sophisticated mathematics or just know a simple story version like Marketopia, the model of competitive equilibrium helps you to understand the real economy only to the degree that the assumptions on which it is based are a fair reflection of the real world. If, instead, people's economic instincts are systematically different from those of Adam, Eve and Maurice Mule, then the economy is likely to work very differently from Marketopia. The energy and skill of the many fine academic minds behind the model were harnessed to construct a hypothetical economy, not to observe the real one in careful detail. The assumptions these pioneering economists made about our economic instincts, their implicit theories about human nature, were not the result of careful scientific testing, but of mathematical convenience. Making these assumptions allowed them to derive precise calculations, employ the latest techniques and publish mathematical proofs. The economists didn't consider the study of real people's instincts to be within their realm, but rather hoped and, in many cases, perhaps believed that their assumptions would turn out to compare favourably with the real world. We shall see.

But I'm a Muddletonian

Imagine a country discovered long ago. Picture it as a developed nation where some people you know might live, and others could visit. Welcome to "Muddleton".

Meet Terry, who is a teacher. Originally from a fairly rough part of a large city, Terry has a decent brain, benefited from maternal common sense, and inhabits a body which, although short in stature, appears to be made of iron. He likes children and earns their respect fairly easily. Terry would be an asset to any school, but particularly one that has problems with some difficult pupils from poorer backgrounds. He is the sort of teacher who has clearly seen a thing or two; the sort you don't mess with; the sort people describe as "hard but fair". But Terry is troubled. Part of him wants to follow a passion and start his own fitness business. It would be exciting, challenging and, if it worked, would earn him much more money. But Terry went into teaching because he believes in it. He knows that his contribution to the schooling of some kids, particularly aggressive young boys, is positive and not easy for schools to provide. In any case, even if he could wrestle his conscience into submission, he's not absolutely sure how to go about funding and developing a new business. It might be a big gamble. He could make crucial mistakes or, perhaps worse, make no mistake other than to start a venture in the leisure industry just before an economic downturn. He tries to talk to as many people in similar businesses as he can. It is a big decision that will affect his well-being for the rest of his life. Terry, like many Muddletonians, is just not sure – he's been considering it for years.

In a nearby town we meet a younger Muddletonian, Sheila. Working-class, outgoing and very much a family girl, Sheila is the oldest child and plays a pivotal role in family affairs, as the one who gets on with everybody else. Her parents have a rocky relationship and her mediation has doubtless helped them through some difficult times. Sheila is starting her last year at school and doesn't know what to do. She has genuine ability in mathematics. In some school years, when she has found the time to work harder, she's managed to beat the middle-class boy who usually comes top of the class. He's going to university; she could too. The problem is, coming from a small town, she would have to move away from home. She worries about the effect on the rest of the family. She worries too about money, especially the debts she would have to take on, and how she would combine academic work with part-time jobs. She is hardly filled with enthusiasm at the thought of serving bar meals to fellow students, hoping they add a decent tip while paying with Daddy's credit card. What if she dropped out, still owing money? How much better would life with a degree be, anyway? She's just not sure.

In the nearest big city, where Terry was brought up and Sheila might go to college, lives Jim. Jim works for himself, doing decorating and other household jobs. He takes pride in a job well done, earns enough to get by, enjoys nights out with friends, and takes a few holidays. But in quieter moments, perhaps the middle of the night, Jim frets. Already approaching fifty, he can't keep going for ever. Back when he started work, the government provided quite well for people in retirement. It doesn't any more. Anyway, like many people in his profession, Jim has not been entirely straight with the government about how much money he earns. That is, he has fiddled his contributions. So he doesn't even know for sure what his entitlements will be when he retires. Jim is in denial. He doesn't like to think about the problem and doesn't really know where to start. He would enjoy life more if the issue wasn't hanging over him. When it visits him in the night, he takes comfort from the one thing he's confident of – there are many other Muddletonians in a similar position.

On the other side of Jim's city is a small district where Pete, the final person we meet on this short tour, bought his first flat and started his first proper job. After a good few years as a rat in the race, Pete needed a getaway. He found a cheap flight on the internet and headed off to the birthday party of an old college friend, in a city famed for its hospitality. There he met a woman in a green dress. She was unlike any other woman he had ever met. That was over two years ago, during which time Pete and the woman have become very expert at finding cheap flights on the internet. But there comes a point when decisions must be taken. Pete would have to sell his flat and give up a job he enjoys to be with her. The housing market is looking a bit wobbly and, in Pete's line of business, his home city is a much more lucrative place to work than hers. No relationship is certain. The leap of faith required comes with a large but unclear financial penalty. He's been thinking about it for months. His friends have patiently tolerated and contributed to his rambling arguments. They all think he should go for it.

Muddletonians talk a lot about the big economic decisions in their lives. Jobs, homes, relationships and unpredictable futures are staples of conversation; the talk over the pub table, the stuff of dinner parties, the questions ageing parents ask returning offspring at Christmas. Muddletonians are interested in the decisions of others, freely trade experience and advice, but are cautious when taking it. If things work out, they thank their luck. If things do not, they try not to regret, but to learn and move on.

Thank you once again for your attention. There is one final point to note on this short tour of Muddleton. It is not a fantasy land of mathematical precision turned into prose, but a real developed country on planet Earth. Terry, Sheila, Jim and Pete are not made-up characters conforming to simple assumptions, but real people known to the author of this book. Indeed, the last of them is known rather well. And, as it turned out, he did start a new life in the other city where, happily, he remains.

Enter the people watchers

Are you more like a Marketopian or a Muddletonian? Introspective insights, like anecdotes, do not constitute strong scientific evidence. But a bit of introspection is all that is required to raise questions about whether Adam, Eve and Maurice capture the essence of modern economic life. My nature and those of my friends might occasionally be a bit Marketopian, perhaps when doing a weekly grocery shop. But when it comes to big economic decisions that affect long-term well-being (what we do for a living, whether we invest in more education, whether we start or expand a business, where we live, who we live with, who we take responsibility for), automata like Adam, Eve and Maurice seem far removed from the people I know. As well as being more calculating and cold than real people, Marketopians are also too sure of themselves. Our situation is characterized by much greater uncertainty, in the face of which we watch, engage with and learn from those around us. Our behaviour is also constrained by its effects on other people. Communication and reliance on others are not occasional aberrations, but a constant feature of economic life.

Introspection is, however, just a starting point. In 2002, Daniel Kahneman, an Israeli academic at Princeton, won the Nobel Prize for economics.* The award was unusual, indeed controversial, because Kahneman is not an economist but a psychologist. In the 1970s he became intrigued by the list of assumptions traditional economics made (and still makes) about people's nature. As Kahneman put it in the 2003 *American Economic Review*, "I found the list quite startling, because I had been professionally trained not to believe a word of it." As a psychologist, instead of *assuming* how people behave, Kahneman decided to look at how we *actually* behave. An extensive research programme was born and Kahneman has become arguably the biggest name in what is now "behavioural economics". Shortly, we will look at some of the classic results, which are changing the science of economics.

Behavioural economics has introduced new tools to the subject, on permanent loan from the psychologist's kitbag. As well as observing and conducting surveys of people's economic behaviour,

---

* Kahneman's long-time collaborator, Amos Tversky, would probably have been named too had he still been alive, but Nobel Prizes are not awarded posthumously. Kahneman shared the prize with the American experimental economist Vernon Smith.

researchers perform controlled economic experiments.* Using these tools to record how people behave in different scenarios, behavioural economists are pulling the rug from under the traditionalists. One by one, the assumptions that underpin the model of competitive equilibrium, previously untested theories about our economic instincts, are being undermined. Observation, surveys and experiments consistently find people's economic instincts to be very different from those of Marketopians.

In the 1980s and 1990s, many of the results were largely ignored, even ridiculed, by more traditional economists, who didn't like to see their pet theories attacked. After all, few professional thinkers do. Mainstream economics and behavioural economics have had frequent skirmishes which, while contained by the polite discourse of academic journals, have occasionally been quite heated. One top American behavioural economist, Matthew Rabin, wrote in the *Journal of Economic Literature* in 1998 that economists had shown "aggressive uncuriosity" towards behavioural research. Some traditionalists attacked the use of experiments and surveys, while behavioural economists defended them, improved the methods and still found that the results ran contrary to orthodoxy. Clever traditionalists added ingenious twists to standard theories, adapting them to explain troublesome results. Behavioural economists then designed new experiments to rule out these ingenious adaptations. Such is the nature of scientific revolutions.

This intellectual entrenchment has had one unfortunate consequence. Too much of the initial effort went into showing what our economic instincts *are not*, rather than what they *are*. While behavioural economics has now observed, recorded and analysed how people take economic decisions, it has tended to concentrate on the particular simplification of our natures employed by standard economics. As with my shopping trip and the history of Gillette,

---

* There was a pre-existing history of economic experiments dating back to the 1930s, but behavioural economics has resulted in a revival of their use.

orthodoxy provides the starting point. Thus, much time has been spent trying to prove that we are not Marketopians rather than trying to build an explicit alternative – a thorough account of life in Muddleton. There is, as of now, no behavioural equivalent of the model of competitive equilibrium – a list of assumptions, equations and diagrams that describe the world according to behavioural economics.

Had behavioural economics begun with a blank slate, it might have progressed differently. Our economic instincts did not form in a vacuum, but developed through our individual and collective experience of economic life – interaction with an economic environment. Learning to exchange money for goods is a skill that some of us are better at than others, as any parent who has watched the frittering of pocket money well knows. Parents teach children the principles of exchange from a young age. We learn pretty quickly who to share and swap our toys and stickers with in the playground, including who to avoid doing business with if at all possible. Our individual economic instincts develop with experience; reinforced by successful deals and adapted following exchanges we come to regret.

The study of our economic instincts is fascinating – we are, after all, interested in what we are like. But what makes it more fascinating still is that, while instincts are honed by the individual, their genesis is deep. Human economic behaviour has evolved over many millennia. Archaeological evidence concerning the movement of objects suggests that trade goes back tens of thousands of years, perhaps hundreds of thousands. This is easily long enough for inherited traits to play a significant role. Possessing traits useful for exchanging resources with others would have been a big advantage to early humans in the struggle for survival. Our economic instincts are very unlikely to be the bequest of some economic Adam and Eve – a first generation born preadapted to a modern market economy. Instead, they are likely to be strongly influenced by generations of exchanging different resources with each other. Of the resources we trade, work, time, protection, ideas, shelter, promises, access, risk, skills, knowledge, rights, transport, experiences, potential, space and responsibility are not inventions of the modern world. From the list of resources we trade quoted previously, perhaps only data qualifies as such. An extensive and varied range of human resources has been bargained over for thousands of generations.

Without the pre-existing standard economic theories to challenge, behavioural economists might have spent less time contesting orthodox assumptions and more time looking at how our instincts have adapted to help us survive in our economic environment. In particular, it is worth asking what traits would be likely to assist people to conduct transactions beneficially. You might think a cold, calculating Marketopian would have the edge in the competition for scarce resources. On the other hand, a ponderous, personable Muddletonian, who seeks and benefits from good advice, who cooperates as well as competes, might be more likely to thrive. Who comes off better depends on the specific economic environment. It is not the individual, nor the environment, but how the two interact which counts.

What this tells us is that the search for our most powerful economic instincts requires that we observe not only people's economic behaviour, but also their economic environment. Behavioural economics is largely concerned with showing that people are not instinctive Marketopians. But the model of competitive equilibrium doesn't only make assumptions about human nature, it also assumes things about the economic environment humans inhabit. Marketopia is not merely an island inhabited by peculiar Marketopians, it is a peculiar place altogether. Have you ever seen a market where it is possible to see, in an instant, the price and quality of every available product? Have you ever selected a job from a list containing a perfect description of all available posts and associated salaries? The model of competitive equilibrium assumes that society informs everyone fully about all possible economic opportunities. If such a world were possible, a cold, rational, self-motivated Marketopian might prosper. But if our economic environment is characterized by individuals lacking information, or some individuals knowing more than others, other instincts may be more crucial to our survival.

This standard assumption, that individuals and firms inhabit an environment where they have perfect information about economic opportunities (including the quality of all products, the terms and conditions of all possible jobs, the size of all the risks they might take – indeed, the value to them of every possible resource they might trade), has also been the focus of a sustained intellectual assault, which began even before behavioural economics was truly born. In a celebrated paper published in 1970, "The market for lemons", the American economist George Akerlof asked a simple question: what if buyers don't have perfect information about the product they are trying to buy? Effectively, Akerlof worked out what would happen if Adam were to leave the Marketopia he knows so well, and embark on a day's shopping in Muddleton, where he would be unsure what he might get in return for his money. In theory, as the next chapter will show, when this key assumption of free-market economics is reconsidered, when buyers or sellers in a free market do not have perfect information about what they are trying to exchange, trade may not be beneficial. In fact, the market may be very inefficient, or fail altogether, such that transactions cease completely.

Akerlof's insight launched "information economics". Its most ardent proponent now is Joseph Stiglitz, an outspoken former Chief Economist at the World Bank. Stiglitz claims that the assumption that people have perfect information is unrealistic in many important markets. The market for loans is one. In Marketopia, ADBank perfectly judges the likely success of Mule's Muffins and so gives Maurice a loan to start his bakery. But in the real world, banks might not be able to tell which start-up businesses are deserving of loans and which are too risky – it may be too hard to judge on the information available. Some good projects could therefore fail to get backers simply because the banks can't tell the good from the bad. The business banking market may therefore fail. Stiglitz believes this kind of insight is crucial to understanding the problems of developing countries, international crises such as the Asian financial crisis of the late 1990s, and the failure of many countries to benefit from free-market reforms, especially in eastern Europe after the collapse of communism.

Akerlof and Stiglitz were rewarded for the development of information economics with the Nobel Prize for 2001,* one year before Daniel Kahneman won it. Yet information economics and behavioural economics proceed mostly in parallel, in largely separate academic communities. (Interestingly, the notable exception to this generalization is George Akerlof, who has tried to connect the two schools, publishing papers that describe how a Muddletonian economy might work.) After an initial intellectual battle, information economics was accepted into the mainstream and now forms an essential part of a modern economic education. Behavioural economics, on the other hand, is still fighting its way in. Schools of thought often fail to benefit from free trade in ideas, even in economics.

Nevertheless, both perspectives focus on the process by which individuals and firms take economic decisions. Information economics primarily looks at the environment in which decisions to buy and sell are taken, asking what information people lack. Behavioural economics records actual behaviour and tries to understand the motives and strategies behind it. In effect, one school describes the challenges of exchanging and sharing resources, while the other records how we go about meeting those challenges. Furthermore, if our economic environment requires, and has required for many generations, people to secure mutual benefits from exchanging and sharing resources, in an environment where those benefits are hard to assess, we would expect our economic instincts to have adapted specifically to cope. Information economics and behavioural economics are two sides of the same coin.

Although behavioural economics provides the strongest evidence, both perspectives guide the search for our most powerful economic

---

* Fellow American Michael Spence was the other winner in 2001.

instincts. These instincts have developed through generations of economic activity, during which a fundamental issue has always been the outcome of decisions to exchange or share resources, made by people who cannot reliably predict the consequences. This may seem a blindingly obvious aspect of economic life – some decisions we look back on with relief, others with regret. But traditional economics has worked with an uncompromising version of people and our environment, which says that driven by selfish instincts we take rational decisions, based on perfect information, to maximize our own gain.

In the life of a scientific school of thought it is still early days. Behavioural economics is no longer in its infancy. It is walking and talking confidently, asking tough questions of its elders who, faced with a crisis, are belatedly realizing that its new ideas are needed. But behavioural economics is far from fully mature, since its ideas are not yet as developed as those of the preceding generation. Thus, the implications of this revolution in progress are unclear. I am confident that the findings reveal much about our real economic instincts. But I am far less sure what will occur when these new economic ideas interact with political ideas, as economic ideas usually do.

The impact is likely to be significant. Take wages, for example, which are the biggest source of people's income. According to the model of competitive equilibrium, the reason some people earn more than others is the reason Eve earns more than Adam; namely that her abilities make her a more productive worker. The distribution of income is therefore believed primarily to reflect the distribution of people's productivity. But this is only true if people are like Adam and Eve; if they make rational, informed choices about how many hours to work and which job to do, balancing income against leisure to maximize happiness, given their ability and willingness to expend effort. In fact, evidence shows that people are neither very rational nor fully informed about jobs, and that maximizing their income is in any case not what motivates them. Studies of bargaining experiments, of the link between income and happiness, of discrimination, and more, suggest that wages are strongly affected by factors other than productivity, including social networks and groups, access to institutions, family background, willingness to forgo income to help others, and a pretty large dose of luck. This different understanding of what governs wages has provocative implications for fair wage structures, fair systems of tax, efforts to fight discrimination, and doubtless related issues that I have not thought of. New ideas and understanding drive new debates.

Nevertheless, before we delve into the evidence, a word of caution is needed. The research I am about to describe finds orthodox economics wanting and, to many people, it may confirm a long-held suspicion about the scientific validity of free-market economics. But the evidence does not suggest there is *no* truth in the model of competitive equilibrium. Most scientific revolutions produce improvements, perhaps dramatic improvements, on what was previously understood. But rarely do scientific revolutions replace what went before completely. The bigger the revolution, the more the models (images, ideas, whatever you wish to call them) of the world in our minds become like the world itself. To continue the example, people's wages *are* related to how productive they are, it's just that the relationship is probably much weaker than standard theory would have it. Behavioural economics suggests other explanations for wage levels; important factors conventional theory has missed. Yet the alternative explanations are not necessarily in direct opposition to each other. More than one factor lies behind what we get paid. The scale of revolution in economics depends on how important the alternative factors ignored by orthodox theory turn out to be.

In my view, behavioural economics is already proving more than a minor refinement of what went before. It is genuinely revolutionary. My guess is that history will judge it to be a very significant change in our economic thinking, one that greatly narrows the gap between economic theory and economic life.

It's now time to see whether the evidence persuades you too.

3

We have been misled

IMAGINE THE FOLLOWING SCENARIO. You sign up to take part in a research study, which I am conducting. When you arrive for a one-hour session of filling in questionnaires, I give you a coffee mug as a gift, to keep. It's one of those large, chunky, branded mugs – a souvenir for the cappuccino generation. Get a good picture of it in your mind. Now, suppose that, as you leave, I ask you what price you would accept from me to buy the mug back from you. Before reading on, come up with a price for your imagined souvenir – how much would you want for it?

Now consider the same scenario with a different twist. Again, you turn up to spend an hour answering questions about which newspapers you buy and whether you prefer spreadable butter. This time, instead of giving you a gift, I offer to sell you the exact same coffee mug. How much would you be willing to pay for it? You should now have two prices. How do they compare?

Daniel Kahneman and two American behavioural economists, Jack Knetsch and Richard Thaler, have done this experiment for real, using a large number of experimental subjects. People in the first scenario require a much higher price to sell back the mug than people in the second scenario are willing to pay to buy one. Usually, the price we will accept is about twice what we will pay – a big difference. This finding defies standard economics. A Marketopian like Adam would simply decide what value the mug had to him. He would happily accept anything more than his valuation to sell the mug in the first scenario, and would readily buy one for anything less than his valuation in the second scenario. Real people don't do this. Across many simple transactions we appear to value something we already own about twice as much as something we stand to gain, even when it is the same object. This basic finding of behavioural economics is called the "endowment effect" – when we own something, our instinct is to value it much more highly.

From the perspective of traditional economics this behaviour looks "irrational". A "rational" person would value the same object at a consistent price. To do otherwise, to value objects inconsistently, could make you miss out on possible gains. For instance, suppose we adapt the experiment a little. The subjects are split into two groups. Half of them are given a mug, the other half chocolate. They are then asked whether they would like to swap their gift for the other one. Some of the people who got a mug would have preferred to get chocolate and vice versa. On average, you would expect half of them to want to swap. But, in fact, fully 90% decide to keep what they have. Many of those who would have preferred to receive the chocolate won't then swap their mug for it. People refuse a gain from a seemingly simple transaction.

Interestingly, when it is explained to subjects in these experiments that their behaviour is "irrational", the subjects tend to disagree, often stridently. They are not making simple errors that, when pointed out, they immediately correct with a slap of the forehead. People will gladly defend their instinct to value what is already theirs more highly. So, are people really being irrational, as traditional economics would have it, or is something more subtle going on?

To answer this question we need to consider the economic equivalent of the atom. The transaction, the exchange of one thing for another, is the essential particle of the economy. Transactions seem simple enough. But they are not as simple as you might think.

Fancy a jar?

Try another scenario. Imagine you are enjoying a pleasant Christmas drink with four friends, when a charming stranger in a Santa hat appears at your pub table. From his pocket he produces a small glass jar and asks you to watch. Intrigued, you observe him go to the bar and hand the jar and a credit card to the barman, who, with a shrug, takes the jar over to the till. When Santa returns, his jar is full of 50-pence pieces. He places it on the table and, with a mischievous grin, says: "Merry Christmas. How much will you good people give me for this?"

A good-natured discussion begins. One friend counts the coins visible through the bottom of the jar, then counts up the side, before stating that with at least eight coins per layer and fifteen layers, there must be over 120 coins, or £60 inside. He suggests offering £55 for the jar. Another friend thinks there is probably more and agrees to the £55 offer. The third member of your group shakes his head, laughs and suggests having nothing to do with this escapade. When the fourth nods in agreement, Santa bemoans their lack of Christmas spirit, before attention turns to you. Two friends want to bid £55, two want to bid Santa good day. The casting vote is yours. What would you do?

There are at least six reasons why this transaction could go wrong. Suppose you decide that your friend's calculation looks sensible and your group buys the jar for £55. One possibility is that when you open it, you discover that a bunch of coins in the middle have fallen at odd angles and are therefore less densely packed, so the jar contains only £53. Nine times out of ten it would have contained more. Your guess was good, but you were unlucky. A second danger is a simple mistake. Perhaps your friend counted the only column up the side of the jar with fifteen coins, while most had twelve or thirteen. There's actually only £51 in total. A third possibility is that there is something surprising about the jar. Perhaps, as you unscrew the lid and Santa disappears through the pub door, you find the jar has a false middle. Or maybe some ten-pence pieces were accidentally mixed in at the till. Either way, it contains only £47 because of something you simply did not foresee. That's now three possible ways to overvalue the jar – bad luck, a mistake in calculation, a surprising twist. But problems can occur even if you initially valued the jar accurately. One possibility you can never rule out is that this genial Santa is nothing but a petty thief. As you produce your £55, he just snatches it and flees. Then, fifth, suppose you discover to your delight that the jar contains £64. But as you divide the loot a row breaks out. The two friends who had not wanted to make any offer insist they were in on the deal and the evening ends early in acrimony. Despite the £9 gain, subsequent events make you wish you had never bought the damn jar. Finally, should Santa ever visit your pub table, there is one killer argument for not buying his jar at any price. Why? It is a decent assumption that Santa knows how much fits in the jar. Unless he intends to lose money, he will sell it to you only if your bid is higher. Otherwise, Santa will take his jar and Christmas fun elsewhere. So there is no point offering anything, because either you get a jar worth less than you pay, or you get no jar – you cannot win. So the sixth pitfall is that Santa always wins, because he has better information about the value of his jar than you do.

So what has this Christmas caper got to do with economics? It is designed to highlight six problems that potentially arise whenever we exchange one thing for another with someone else; issues that could affect any transaction. Three are problems with our initial judgement about the value of what we exchange, which for short let's call luck (L), mistakes (M) and surprises (S). The remaining three are about the environment in which we trade, or how it might change. The other party may be dishonest (D); subsequent events (E) may alter the value of what we obtained; or our trading partner might have better information (I) than we do about the value of what is exchanged. These issues overlap somewhat. Santa's dishonesty could be behind a surprising feature about the jar, such as a false middle. But surprises are possible that do not involve dishonesty, such as the barman accidentally putting ten-pence pieces in. Generally, every transaction could be affected by any combination of these six hitches, to each of which I have assigned a letter. The letters can be rearranged into the acronym MISLED. Thus, by saying we are "MISLED", I mean that we lose out in an exchange for one of these six reasons.

Obviously, the situation with Santa's jar is contrived; a thought experiment that highlights all six ways we can be MISLED. Are people MISLED in the real world? Frequently. When buying financial services, people often make mistakes (M) because they don't read the small print. People pay for medical procedures, car repairs or computer software that they don't actually need, because they follow the recommendation of the more informed (I) people who sell such technical services. In the labour market, when people arrive to take up a new job they are sometimes surprised (S) to discover what the work truly entails. People can look up reliability statistics for electrical goods in magazines, yet still have the bad luck (L) to buy an item that keeps going wrong. People purchase shares in companies the value of which is subject to unpredictable subsequent events (E). People suffer the dishonesty (D) of others, though less often via theft than through hidden charges, dodgy goods, undelivered services, missing payments, wasted time, etc.

We have all been MISLED. We have a whole language for it. We can be "ripped off", "fleeced" or "done". We can "fall for the marketing". We were "had" or met an "operator". They "saw us coming" or "took us for a ride". Sometimes the boot is on the other foot, as we "snap up a bargain", get it "for a song", pay "next to nothing", or declare "it's a steal".

One hallmark of economic development is that the chances of being MISLED are reduced – transactions in developed economies are more reliable. Yet even in a modern, sophisticated market economy, with more consumer protection legislation than ever before, transactions do not always produce mutual gains. Many things we buy are surprisingly like Santa's jar, in that we have some idea of the value to us of the product, but ultimately make a rough judgement on limited information. This analogy to the jar of coins applies least with goods we buy repeatedly. Milk and coffee from the supermarket are likely to be worth the same to us as last week. But with occasional or one-off purchases, we tend to be less sure what we will get for our money. Buying electrical goods, financial services or a house, or engaging someone to do a job for us, is quite like buying Santa's jar. Before the deal is complete we are unsure. We try to judge what's on offer and what the seller is like, to avoid being MISLED. We cautiously ponder our options, like the Muddletonians we truly are.

None of this is to suggest that, overall, transactions are to be avoided. On average, trade is beneficial and has worked wonders for humankind. We take it for granted now – trade is simply what humans do. But it is not simple.

Exchanging things is a skill, at which some of us are better than others. We read the intentions of trading partners, learn to trust repeated transactions, perceive and remember slight differences in the things we buy and sell. When we hesitate, it is because our economic instincts tell us to be careful – we may be MISLED. The possibility of being MISLED is as old as trade itself. From the earliest times, skills for avoiding it would have been important tools in the human survival kit. They still are.

Yet back in the fantasy land of traditional economics, Marketopia, the simple-sounding assumption that consumers have perfect information about economic opportunities rules out the possibility of being MISLED. In Marketopia, people always know exactly what they give up and exactly what they get in return. Marketopians don't have to worry about mistakes, better-informed trading partners, surprises, luck, subsequent events and dishonesty. But once we recognize, instead, that our economic environment is one where we can be MISLED, then behaving like a Marketopian may not be the best strategy. In such an environment, it might be rational to turn down some apparently beneficial transactions.

Now that we have more insight into exchanges, let's return to the endowment effect. Why do people value what they already own more highly? The possibility of being MISLED may be behind it. It makes sense to value an object we possess more highly than one we don't if swapping it for something else means there is a chance of being MISLED. Familiarity with something we own, even for a short period, makes us more sure of its value. That is, we probably have a more accurate idea of the value to us of something we already have than of something we do not. Familiarity improves our perception of value. Moreover, to benefit from something we already own requires no risk of being MISLED in a transaction, because no transaction is needed to get it. We have it already – it is the bird in the hand. So perhaps it is not irrational to value the same object more highly when it already belongs to us. In an economic environment where value is not always instantly obvious and transactions are less than perfectly reliable, it is likely to be a very useful economic instinct. Thus, when traditional economists label the endowment effect "irrational", they may be failing to see that the cautious Muddletonian instincts responsible are designed to overcome problems that don't exist in Marketopia. Conventional theory just assumes them away by taking beneficial exchanges for granted. The less predictable environment in which our economic instincts developed, however, may favour Muddletonians, who prize what they already know and have.

An evolving story

In economic experiments, such as the one with the coffee mug, people turn down what initially look like straightforwardly beneficial exchanges. The endowment effect is just one demonstration of this – we will meet others shortly. Such experiments suggest that our economic instincts are not those assumed by orthodox economic theory. We are more cautious than Marketopians and, like Muddletonians, wary enough of some transactions that we prefer not to trade.

Testing theories against evidence and adapting them accordingly is how science is meant to proceed. Nevertheless, the behavioural approach to economics remains a minority taste and most economists tend to be dismissive of findings such as the endowment effect. They find the evidence unconvincing and persist with the idea that we are, ultimately, like Adam and Eve. Or, at least, that Adam and Eve are the best approximation of what we are like, economically speaking. Before going further, it is worth knowing why.

The University of Chicago's Gary Becker is another Nobel Prize-winning economist and one of the ultimate believers in competitive equilibrium – the model behind Marketopia. During an interview with *The Region* magazine in 2002, Becker was asked about behavioural economics. He said, "There is a heck of a difference between demonstrating something in a laboratory, in experiments, even highly sophisticated experiments, and showing that they are important in the marketplace ... The theory [orthodox economics] is not about how people answer questions. It is a theory about how people behave in market situations." Becker went on to argue that because life in a competitive market economy pushes us to do what we are good at, people who may behave "irrationally" in an unfamiliar experiment will nevertheless be "rational" when doing a job for which the market dictates their suitability. More generally, he compared being in a market to playing dice, where if you wrongly believe some numbers come up more often, say on superstitious grounds, other players will keep taking your money. In such circumstances, as Becker put it, "you will continue to lose until either you change your beliefs, or you lose your shirt".

Becker is really making two arguments here. Indeed, they are the two most common objections that economists raise to behavioural evidence. The first is the straightforward claim that people behave differently when they volunteer to take part in artificial experiments than they do in the real economy. Becker's second argument is less straightforward and, interestingly, employs the logic of evolution. The claim is that people must be "rational", because life in the marketplace forces them to be so, on pain of poverty. Market forces are like evolutionary forces, but instead of survival of the fittest the market ensures the survival of the most "rational". Becker is saying that those who behave like Marketopians do better in markets, making more money, owning better things and being more attractive to employers. He believes that if we deviate from Marketopian behaviour, by for example turning down beneficial deals, or dithering while others grab our opportunity, we will consistently lose out until we change our behaviour. For Becker, the market has its own form of natural selection and the inevitable end-point of economic evolution is Adam and Eve.

The first argument can be dealt with fairly briefly. The notion that economic experiments don't tell us how people behave in the real economy is being undermined by results. Many of the "irrational" behaviours that first emerged in artificial experiments or surveys have since been observed in real markets (and as we encounter more experiments I will provide examples). For instance, an effect just like the endowment effect has been recorded in data from the financial markets, where instead of trading cheap coffee mugs, people trade shares and currencies worth large sums. Traders often do not sell investments they already hold, even though they could trade them for assets they would prefer to invest in if starting from scratch. In fact, so many apparent "irrationalities" have now also been found in the financial markets, usually having first emerged in simple experiments involving games with things like mugs and chocolate, that a parallel scientific school of thought, "behavioural finance", has appeared alongside behavioural economics. Those who insist that experiments don't tell us about the real economy are fighting the tide. Experimental findings are, increasingly, backed up by data from the real economy.

The second argument, however, raises the more contentious issue of evolutionary forces in economics. Generally speaking, people are often sceptical about evolutionary explanations of sophisticated human behaviour. Plenty of pseudo-scientific speculation fancifully invokes evolutionary forces; some of the better-known examples being supposed explanations for gender differences based on our lives as hunter-gatherers. But the existence of fanciful theorizing, often by second-rate researchers courting publicity, does not mean that evolutionary thinking should be dismissed in social sciences like psychology and economics. The long history of trade means that inherited traits almost certainly do affect how people conduct trans-actions and how successful we are in markets. There is interesting and thorough work being done in this area – some of which will be described later.

In any case, Becker's argument is not about genetic selection – organisms with certain inherited traits being more likely to repro-duce. Becker is talking about market selection – certain behavioural traits making some people more likely to get rich. It is part of the genius of evolutionary thinking that non-inherited traits can also be analysed with evolutionary concepts. Traits possessed by individuals and firms in markets are a good example. For instance, we can think of Gillette's development of personalized marketing as the develop-ment of an advantageous trait that made the company more likely to survive in the market for shaving products. In fact, research has thrown up interesting parallels between the failure of businesses and the extinction of species. Similar patterns emerge in data recording the frequency of species extinctions and the frequency of business failures – about which more later. It is probably true, therefore, that analysing whether particular traits are advantageous in economic life, be they inherited or otherwise, can help us to understand our economic instincts and hence more about how the economy works.

The problem with Becker's stance, then, is not that evolutionary arguments do not belong in economics. The problem is that his par-ticular evolutionary argument does not stand up. Evolutionary scien-tists would see a common fallacy in it, which is to believe that evolution consists of progress towards a perfect being. In nature, an organism may gain a survival advantage from a particular trait, like sharp teeth. But millions of years of evolution have not therefore given all organisms the dental weaponry of the tiger. Whether a trait is successful depends on what other traits you possess and what traits you don't possess but that others do. There is no point having predatory teeth if all other organisms are faster than you or can see you coming and climb the trees. Many traits are successful in different combinations: good eyesight, high intelligence, production of venom, camouflage, temperature control, egg production, sonar, water retention, etc. The list is long. Similarly, having the "rationality" of a Marketopian may (or may not) be an advantage in markets. But even if it is, to deduce that therefore everyone in a mature market economy is forced to be "rational" like Adam and Eve is to fall for the fallacy. Other traits will matter in markets too. These include persuasiveness, diligence, creativity, perceptiveness, uniqueness, eloquence, affability, cautiousness, trustworthiness, attractiveness, etc. The list could be long. The way to identify our most powerful economic instincts, those most common to us all, is to observe how we behave in a variety of economic situations. This is exactly what behavioural economists are doing. Becker's argument assumes the answer without bothering with the evidence.

Unfortunately, in the intellectual battle over whether we are instinctive Marketopians, behavioural economists have tended to avoid evolutionary arguments, probably because they are viewed as ammunition for the other side. Many orthodox economists with little or no training in evolutionary theory argue, by analogy to evolutionary theory, that market forces inevitably make us Marketopians. This is testimony to the powerful legacy of the model of competitive equilibrium. Training in economics makes it hard to escape such thinking. Marketopia is the first model that comes to a trained economist's mind and it seems that everything points towards it. But, as we have seen, it is the interaction between the individual and the environment which matters. Behaving like a Marketopian would be an unassailable advantage if the world were just like Marketopia. But it isn't.

In fact, far from being the ultimate economic organism, a "rational" Marketopian may be at a disadvantage in economic life.

Adam and Eve are only perfect economic creatures in the land of Marketopia, where perfect information about all economic opportunities makes beneficial transactions easy. If Adam and Eve were suddenly thrown into an economic environment where they found it hard to assess what things were worth, where they had to judge the motivations of trading partners, and where they were required to make guesses about what could happen in an unpredictable future, they might not fare so well. In a world like Muddleton, Marketopians might get eaten for breakfast.

A little knowledge

We have thus far met just one of the classic results of behavioural economics: the endowment effect. It shows that we value what is ours more highly and, therefore, turn down seemingly beneficial exchanges. Traditional economists have argued that this kind of "irrational" behaviour could not occur in real, "red in tooth and claw" markets. Yet it may be a sensible survival strategy, because exchanges are more unpredictable than conventional economics assumes. In fact, one school of economic thought, "information economics", which is more accepted by the mainstream than the behavioural school, pointed out difficulties with supposedly simple transactions some time ago. Markets are not red in tooth and claw – they require grey matter instead.

As a first-rate theoretical economist, George Akerlof is more inclined to formal mathematics than to storytelling. But when Akerlof gave the hypothetical model of competitive equilibrium a tweak, he produced a highly influential contribution to economics that translates easily into storybook form. He effectively asked: what would happen if a Marketopian suddenly found themselves in the alien situation of being unsure about the value of what they might buy? The history of Akerlof's famous 1970 paper is indicative of how economists have taken everyday transactions for granted. His analysis was initially dismissed as "trivial". It was rejected by three top economics journals before a fourth one finally published it. Three decades later, this trivial analysis won him the Nobel Prize.*

In the 1960s, Akerlof observed that some free markets didn't seem to work very well. For an explanation, he looked back at the model of competitive equilibrium and decided that the assumption that people have perfect information about economic opportunities could be to blame. He worked out, in theory, how imperfect information could damage trade. Akerlof maintained all the other assumptions of the standard model, including that people are "rational", but allowed for just one of the six ways people may be MISLED – the case where one party to a transaction has better information (I) about the product being sold.

Recall that Santa knows best how many coins fit in his jar. Akerlof theorized about a market where the product is quite similar to a jar of coins: used cars. A used car might be very reliable or a heap of junk. The owner, just like Santa, knows its value better than anyone else. Akerlof showed that in this situation, where buyers have imperfect information about the quality of cars but sellers have perfect information, buyers and sellers might not manage to agree a price.

The argument went as follows. Imagine a particular model and age of car and suppose you are a buyer. You decide these cars range in true value from £2,000 for a dodgy one to £6,000 for a good one. You decide to take your chances and pay £4,000 – a price that reflects average quality. Any seller who knows their car is more reliable than average won't want to trade at that price, just as Santa won't sell his jar for less than he knows it contains. So only sellers whose cars are worth between £2,000 and £4,000 will want to sell to you. Thus, you are most likely to end up with a car worth more like £3,000, and almost certain to get one worth less than £4,000. Assuming you work

* The paper was published in 1970 by the *Quarterly Journal of Economics* and is now required reading for all economists. Although Akerlof has published a large volume of research since, this original and thrice-rejected paper, entitled "The market for lemons", was the one cited by the Nobel committee.

this out, you might try to pay less, say £3,000. But if you look for a car at that price, even owners of average cars now won't sell, because they know their car is worth more than that. So the likely outcome is an even worse car, worth between £2,000 and £3,000. You are like a donkey chasing a carrot on a stick – when you suggest a lower price, the quality of cars owners will sell at that price falls further still, always a step ahead. Just as with Santa's jar, you cannot win, because the seller knows more than you do. Unless buyers accept bad deals, or sellers can somehow prove the quality of their car, people simply won't trade – the market will fail completely.*

Akerlof had discovered the problem of "asymmetric information", which arises when one party has better information about the quality of what is being traded than the other. This is the fundamental insight of information economics. The problem is not just for buyers who, unsure of quality, want to avoid being a sucker. Sellers are affected too. When buyers are aware of their own relative ignorance, it is hard to convince them that a high-quality product on offer is actually as good as it is. If both buyers and sellers were equally in the dark there would be no problem – an average price would seem fair to both. It is the asymmetry which makes for distrust, thereby damaging trade.

Of course, back in the real world, people do trade used cars. Does this mean Akerlof was wrong? Not really. The market for used cars does not fail completely, as he showed was possible, but it does work less efficiently than markets for things like furniture, where quality is much easier for buyers to see. Cars plummet in value as soon as they leave the garage forecourt. Think of it from a buyer's perspective: you would be suspicious about a car someone wanted to get rid of so soon after purchasing. Dealers and sellers try to get around asymmetry of information, by offering guarantees, road tests and so

---

* Economists apply the term "market failure" to situations where the market fails to provide mutual gains from trade, either because someone experiences losses rather than gains, or because possible exchanges between people that would be mutually beneficial don't manage to occur. In the present case, it is the latter.

on, to gain buyers' trust. But it remains hard to sell a good used car for a decent price and so people are deterred from trying. Those cars that are on sale therefore tend to be the poorer ones and so the potential mutual benefit from trading quality used cars is lost. Some people end up regretting their purchase, meaning that used car salesmen end up with a reputation you wouldn't want. Although we try to patch it up, the market for used cars is inefficient – it doesn't work very well.

Perhaps Akerlof chose the used car market to make his case because his explanation chimed with its poor reputation. In many other markets, we manage to get around the problem with a bit of patching up, mostly through communication to reduce the information gap between buyer and seller. Companies offer guarantees, free trials or demonstrations. Magazines, newspapers and websites review products. Laws govern how firms must describe them. We try to redress the asymmetry by informing and reassuring buyers about quality, making transparently beneficial trade more likely. Moreover, many firms need regular customers and must establish and maintain a reputation to keep them. Becoming known for products that appear fine but turn out to be trashy is a ticket to bankruptcy. Overall, communication between firms and consumers combined with firms' need to protect their reputation, plus a degree of back-up through legislation, helps to immunize markets for many everyday goods against information asymmetry.

But everyday goods are only one kind of resource that we exchange with each other. In markets for many other kinds of resources, information asymmetry is unavoidable because what is traded depends on people's subsequent behaviour. The commonly quoted example is insurance. Here, the buyer has the information advantage. When we buy insurance, we pay a company to shoulder our risk. But we are more familiar with and control our own behaviour – such as how carefully we drive or how healthy our lifestyle is. So the insurance company has poorer information about the risk being traded. People who know they are the highest risk have the greatest incentive to buy insurance, and once they've bought it they then have less incentive to be careful. So the company's customers will probably be riskier than average, meaning that if the premium is based on average risk of accident or sickness, the insurer is likely to pay out more than it gets in. As the company increases the premium, the first customers not to renew will be those who least need insurance, so as well as losing some customers the remaining ones will be of still higher risk. In some insurance markets, it may be impossible to make a profit, because at any possible premium the people who will buy the insurance will be too likely to make a claim – the company is now the donkey chasing the carrot. Information asymmetry is why insurance works best when it is a legal requirement, as with motor insurance. Compulsion doesn't alter people's incentive to be careful, but it does provide companies with enough low-risk customers to make a profit. Information asymmetry is also why you can't get insurance for the biggest risks in life, such as unemployment or family breakdown.* And it is a leading explanation for why millions of Americans live in one of the world's richest economies without health insurance. In other developed countries the government steps in because the market cannot provide.

There are many important markets where behaviour forms part of the deal and so asymmetric information can cause problems. Most obviously this includes the labour market – we know better than our employers what we can really do and how hard we will work. But it also includes many service industries, where we decide to pay for labour before we see the results, and markets for credit, be it business loans or credit cards.

In each market affected by information asymmetry, the degree to which prices, quality, availability and volume of trade are damaged is simply unknown. Economists argue about how large the impact is,

---

* It is possible to get payment protection insurance on mortgages or other individual loans that might cover the possibility of, say, being made redundant. The point here is that you can't simply buy an insurance policy that covers you for the losses associated with unemployment or family breakdown, as you can for car accidents.

but there is no agreed way to measure it. Those who specialize in information economics say many markets are inefficient. They criticize those economists who promote free markets for refusing to recognize this, and often call for government intervention to help correct the problem. Others play down the significance of information asymmetry and point out that people find ways to overcome it. Wherever one stands on this argument, however, information economics raises a bigger issue. Because even if people do overcome the problem, the instincts and skills required to do so must be important to how markets really work.

Remember, it is the interaction between individuals and their environment which matters. Our most powerful economic instincts have adapted to help us survive the economic challenges we face. So the point of information economics is not only that some markets fail because of information asymmetry, but that to make some markets work at all we need to take decisions when we don't have perfect information. Thus, perceptiveness and guesswork may be important, as might the social skills required to establish mutual trust. In such an economic environment, independent, rational, selfish people like Marketopians may find fewer trading partners. After all, what sensible person would trust a selfish Marketopian? If our economic environment is different from Marketopia, our instincts will not be those of Marketopians. When in Muddleton, do as the Muddletonians do.

Chance encounters

Transactions, exchanges between people, are the essence of economic activity; the economic atom. They are far less predictable than the creators of our current economic theories realized. Information economics raises the issue that transactions may be difficult if one party in an exchange possesses better information – the I of MISLED. There are at least five other ways people may be MISLED in a transaction, and hence may decide not to enter into it in the first place.

Our economic environment is characterized by our having to make judgements about things we do not know for sure: the likely value to us of what we are buying or selling, how that value might change over time, the likelihood that we are making a mistake or could be surprised, and the trustworthiness and knowledge of our partner in trade. In short, we have to assess and take chances. This is the unpredictable economic environment in which our instincts developed; an environment characterized by different degrees of risk and uncertainty surrounding each exchange.

I use these two terms, "risk" and "uncertainty", alongside each other for a reason. There is a subtle and important distinction between risk and uncertainty, which we'll get to soon. But, for now, consider both of them as ways to describe chance – any situation where the outcome is unpredictable.

To some degree, people vary as to how they approach chance. Try for yourself. Suppose I offer you the following bet: we toss a coin; if it comes up heads you give me £10, and if it comes up tails I give you £10. Would you bet with me? If not, what if we make it so that heads means I get £10, but tails means you get £11, £12, £15, £20? At what point would you bet?

Researchers have conducted many gambling experiments for small stakes like this. A few people accept fifty-fifty (coin-toss) bets for small sums like £10. But the overwhelming majority of us don't. To persuade us to gamble we have to be compensated with a significantly higher pay-off. Some people will take a £10 versus £11 bet at fifty-fifty, but most still decline. Some people won't even consider £10 versus £20 on the toss of a coin. Despite this considerable variation in people's attitudes, however, the overall trend is undisputed: almost everyone is "risk averse" to some extent. A gamble must usually be stacked in our favour before we will take it, heavily so for many people.*

---

* Gambling provides obvious exceptions to our risk-averse natures. If there were not some people who gamble for the hell of it, bookmaking would not be the multimillion-

There is one interesting exception. In the example above, people were asked to chance a loss (£10) against a possible gain (£10–£20). The gain must be considerably larger before we bet. But if the comparison is between different degrees of loss, the outcome changes. For example, if people face a choice between losing £500 for definite, or taking a fifty-fifty bet on losing £1,000 versus losing nothing, most people opt to take the bet. When losing, in desperation, we seem to be instinctive gamblers. What underlies this different attitude is a flourishing research area – as of now, we don't know.

Transactions, however, are about exchanging something we have for something we want more. So they are about trying to make gains. What the experiments show us is that where there is risk involved, we build in considerable margin for error – what we might gain must be worth a good bit more to compensate us for the unpredictability.

The main point bears repeating: it is the interaction between our economic instincts and our economic environment which matters. Traditional economics has underestimated the degree of unpredictability in economic activity. The possibility that we might be MISLED in any given transaction means that economic life is full of chances. This aspect of the economic jungle is mirrored in our instincts: we prefer less risky options, and we require compensation to put up with the risk. Years and generations of experience have taught us that, unlike in Marketopia, where every possibility is accurately laid out before us, in our world appearances can be illusory. We seek the more predictable deals. So, of the many deals available to us in economic life, how do we identify which are the less chancy ones?

---

pound business it is. For a very few people, gambling becomes addictive. Most of us will bet at poor odds on occasion – fund-raising events, holidays, a big game for a favourite team, etc. Such betting is not really an attempt to increase income, but a contribution or purchase of entertainment, and our willingness to engage in it is therefore very different.

Familiarity breeds content

Our dislike of unpredictable outcomes is consistent with the endowment effect. One reason to value what we own more highly than what we don't is that something we already own does not require an unpredictable transaction to obtain it. We are also more sure of the value of things we own, because they are more familiar to us. In an unpredictable economic environment, we can be more confident of what we know best. The products, people and companies we are most familiar with are the most predictable for us. Liking what is familiar is a way to reduce unpredictability and to improve our chances.

If this explanation is right, then the strength of the endowment effect should vary with people's degree of familiarity with the product and the environment in which it is traded. If we know the goods well and are in a place where we have traded them many times before, the effect may not occur. Indeed, the American economist John List has shown that experienced traders who go to collectors' fairs seem to overcome the endowment effect. For these people, whose degree of familiarity with pins, sports cards or some other inanimate object borders on obsession, value does not depend on ownership.

Ownership is only one source of familiarity. There are many other findings in behavioural economics that suggest we instinctively prefer what is familiar. Indeed, an instinctive bias towards the familiar can explain many of the decisions traditional economists view as "irrational". In an unpredictable economic environment, it is not irrational to go for what is familiar – it is good strategy.

Perhaps the most basic demonstration of a bias towards what is familiar is the "mere exposure" effect. Studies show we favour something we are already aware of, even if we possess no specific reason to think it good or bad. Just knowing the name of a product makes us more likely to choose it. We have enough doubts about what we buy that simple familiarity with the name seems better than no knowledge at all. And it probably is, because our recognition of a brand may, on average, be more likely to stem from a good reputation than from a bad one.

Of course, there is something conservative about a bias towards what is familiar, because it also implies that we are instinctively biased against change. Results back this up. When opinion surveys ask people to state preferences between alternative spending plans (say for governments, local authorities, companies or individuals), if the accompanying description reveals which option is the current one, many more people choose it. This "status quo bias" is also found in experimental economic games, in which people are given scenarios and must select strategies to win or lose money. People are often slow to abandon their current strategy and switch to a more profitable one. Status quo bias is part of our common understanding, summarized by "better the devil you know".

Those who remain suspicious of the claim that behaviour in experiments translates into behaviour in the real economy should note that the phenomenon of status quo bias has also been observed with company pension schemes. Participation rates alter radically according to whether the default option is to be in or out of the scheme, even though it is the same product. Joining a pension scheme is a major financial decision in a real market that will affect well-being in years to come, yet people seemingly approach it with "irrational" biases. In Marketopia, Eve would embark on a detailed reading of the small print and calculate the trade-off between her present and future spending power so that it maximized her happiness across her lifespan. We don't. Status quo bias has now been so consistently observed that pension policy in the USA and the UK is trying to use it to raise the level of savings for retirement. In an early example of the revolutionary power of behavioural economics, schemes are being designed so that the default is to opt in rather than opt out, meaning that status quo bias increases saving. As we'll see shortly, other findings of behavioural economics may explain why so many people fail to save enough in the first place.

A related effect is referred to by psychologists as

"belief perseverance". Experiments and surveys show that once an individual is persuaded of something it can take a disproportionate amount of evidence to change their mind. The mere exposure effect, status quo bias and belief perseverance show that we tend to be cautious and stick with what we know, unlike Marketopians who immediately spy cheaper or better options and switch to get the benefits. Our instinct is that a move away from what is familiar increases the chance of being MISLED. Only once a perceived gain is sufficiently large and we feel confident about it do we take the chance and change tack.

Our instinct to prefer what is familiar is well known to innovative companies trying to push new ideas. Pioneering firms know that new products don't become popular simply by being better quality, but require considerable marketing effort. Marketing professionals try to exploit consumers' instincts to trust what is familiar, which is partly why they worry so much about creating "brand awareness" and positive "brand attributes". Once they've got a recognized brand with one or more positive attributes widely believed, selling a product is much easier. This is why King Camp Gillette spent so much money marketing his razors when he could instead have reduced their price. Of course, this raises a big issue. We like familiarity because we associate it with reliability. But if marketing experts can exploit our instincts, making things appear familiar and reliable when in fact they are just well marketed, then the marketing may get around our instinctive defences and increase our chances of being MISLED. Ask a businessperson this: would they rather be the producer of a good brand or a high-quality product? Many will admit, albeit after you point out that "the two go together" is an inadequate answer, that the brand matters more. There is much else to say on marketing, which must wait for a later chapter.

Finally, familiarity may well explain another classic finding of behavioural economics. Imagine you head out to the theatre. On arrival you are annoyed to discover, after a fretful search in every pocket, that you have definitely lost your ticket, which cost £20. The box office still has tickets. Do you buy another one? We'll now twist the scenario slightly. Suppose you plan to buy your ticket at the theatre, but when you turn up you discover a £20 note you had ready to pay has disappeared. Do you get a ticket anyway?

A study by Kahneman and Tversky found that almost all subjects said they would still buy a ticket if they had lost the banknote, but less than half would buy another ticket having lost one ticket already. Again, this behaviour appears "irrational". A Marketopian like Eve wouldn't care whether she'd lost the ticket or the note, but would simply decide afresh whether to spend £20 on the play, knowing that she was £20 poorer than before.

The lost-ticket scenario is usually presented as an example of different behaviour occurring in logically identical circumstances – supposed proof of our irrationality. The result is entirely consistent, however, with a sensible bias towards what is familiar. Banknotes are familiar objects with which we have a long history of mostly positive associations. We have all lost money from time to time, so losing the note hardly changes how we feel about money nor, more importantly, how we feel about a theatre ticket we are about to buy. So we are inclined to shrug it off, dig into our pocket for another note and buy a ticket. Losing our ticket is different, however. The surprise loss of the ticket means it turned out to be a waste of money. We have been MISLED. This may well change how we feel about buying another one – a feeling summed up by the phrase "once bitten, twice shy". These tickets are less familiar than banknotes and our bad first experience of them is off-putting. It associates the tickets with unpredictability. Having lost our ticket for this play once already, what is to say we won't lose another? Thus, losing the familiar banknote changes our attitude little, but losing the less familiar theatre ticket means our feelings about buying another may well become more negative. In the predictable world of Marketopia such Muddletonian behaviour is "irrational". In reality, it is just human.

Our preference for the familiar would be irrational if we lived in an economic environment where we could be immediately sure of the value of everything. Our Muddletonian natures would lead us to miss out on beneficial opportunities. But in a world where people can be MISLED, we have learned to reduce unpredictability by preferring what we know. If this behaviour were genuinely irrational, we might expect it to be overcome by education. But highly educated people turn out to be subject to exactly the same biases as everyone else. It is not irrational to like what we know. Our economic environment is, and always has been, unpredictable. Valuing what is familiar is therefore a useful instinct.

A bad deal, frankly

Since humans first began trading with each other, many thousands of years ago, we have doubtless developed skills and instincts that make us better at it. The challenge of our economic environment is to ensure that the transactions we enter into make us better off. Simple exchanges, the very essence of economics, are a bigger challenge than they first appear.

Experiments with mugs and chocolate, betting games and surveys asking about hypothetical theatre trips may all seem academic and unworldly. But the results provide us with insights about people's instinctive approach to doing business with others. We prefer what we already own, what we recognize, what is already the case, and what we have already come to believe. Because we often pay a price to stick with what we know, these instincts can make us appear irrational, especially from the perspective of traditional economics, which has underestimated the unpredictability of economic life. But our liking for the familiar is sensibly cautious in a world where we may be MISLED. We try to avoid taking chances and we instinctively prize what is familiar in order to avoid them.

Given this, consider an issue on the front line of the battle over what markets can and cannot do. Developed countries provide secondary education free at the point of use. But they differ over the extent to which the market or the state provides third-level education. Free or heavily subsidised college and university places can be a middle-class perk. But, where students have to pay for their own education, a major worry is whether able young people from poorer backgrounds are excluded. Economists produce models to inform policy in this area, to determine how much the state should pay to assist poorer students. The economic models compare the benefit students get, primarily in terms of higher wages for graduates, with the fees and maintenance students must fork out. In theory, this is a straightforward mutually beneficial transaction. Politicians who sell these schemes repeat the figures over and over. When, in 2004, Tony Blair defended his introduction of university tuition fees in the UK, he explicitly compared the cost of getting through college with loan repayments and likely earnings after graduation, concluding, "I think that's not a bad deal, frankly." The logic is that if it is "rational" for poorer kids to go to college, meaning the costs incurred are small relative to extra income after graduation, then they will not be put off. Adam and Eve would sign up, whatever their backgrounds.

Now apply the ideas from this chapter to the issue. We will turn down an apparently beneficial transaction if we perceive too much risk. This particular transaction, an exchange of current financial cost for higher graduate income in the future, is very unpredictable. There is a danger of failing the degree (or dropping out for other reasons) having incurred some or all of the costs. Income after graduation is also hard to gauge, as is exactly how well a student is likely to do. Meanwhile, any estimate of income for graduates in four or more years' time depends on the future state of the economy. Even where repayments on official student loans are based on ability to pay, unpredictability is involved. People must assess the chances that the official system will fail to provide adequate funds, requiring them to take on additional debts. They must judge the likelihood that the government will reform the system while they are in it. The risk is more substantial for students from disadvantaged backgrounds, because the income forgone and debts incurred are a larger proportion of family income – sometimes much larger.

People try to reduce risk by favouring what is familiar. But poorer kids also tend to be less familiar with the issues surrounding college funding. They are less likely to have parents, siblings and friends who have been to college and who work in lucrative professions. This means they are less familiar with the benefits of college degrees, the banking services and products they must engage with, the terms and conditions attached to debt, and the labour market in which ultimately they aim to work. Lack of familiarity increases the unpredictability facing those from disadvantaged backgrounds.

We should therefore not be surprised that the evidence, based on surveys of prospective students and data on the decisions they subsequently make, reveals that disadvantaged kids have a greater fear of debt and that this fear puts them off going to college. This is true despite the fact that standard economic analysis shows, quite clearly, that they would be likely to benefit. The evidence is, however, absolutely in keeping with the behavioural evidence. (Note that this explanation does not mean that less advantaged children or their parents have a different attitude to the benefits of education. Rather, they just apply the same economic instincts as everyone else to a decision that, for them, involves higher risk, and with which they are less familiar.)

One of the four real-life Muddletonians you met earlier, Sheila, ultimately chose not to go to college despite her rare ability in mathematics. The market for higher education doesn't work the way orthodox economic theory says it should.

Education is an important market, because it has a dramatic effect on life-chances. There are other markets that have a particularly significant impact on life too, including health, housing, labour, pension, credit and savings markets. These key markets for people's well-being are not characterized by repeated, regular transactions that are predictable and familiar. They often involve large one-off decisions, in which people must weigh up risks and often engage with firms and institutions for the first time. It is in these areas of economic life, which have the biggest influence on our economic fortunes, that the transactions we engage in are most risky and least familiar.

In our economic environment we frequently don't know for sure what the outcome of a decision will be. But even this description does not do justice to the complexity of the decisions we take in our economic lives. For, in many situations, we don't even know what is relevant to the decision. That is, we don't know what we don't know. Fortunately, we at least know this. Confused? Don't worry. This very distinction clearly bamboozled the best and brightest financial traders in recent years and, as we are about to see, your instincts have adapted to cope with it.

4

What you don't know can hurt you

THERE ARE CERTAIN one-off decisions with which it pays not to be familiar. Try this one. You are 40 years old and possess some information that has the potential to save thousands of lives. You cannot be sure whether it will or not, but there appears to be a good chance. The problem is, if you release the information you will commit a crime so serious that it carries a 115-year sentence. What do you do?

This was the dilemma facing Daniel Ellsberg. As an award-winning student at Harvard and Cambridge, a former rifle company commander in the Marine Corps and a high-ranking US government adviser, Ellsberg had an impeccable record. He had worked for the Pentagon and the State Department, and as a consultant to the White House on strategic nuclear planning, nuclear command and control and crisis decision-making. In 1971, he had a decision of his own to take.

A few years earlier, Ellsberg had been commissioned by Defense Secretary Robert McNamara to prepare a top-secret study of US decision-making in Vietnam from 1945 to 1968. After two years of work, he became convinced that the government was deceiving the American public about the likelihood of success in Vietnam. If he were to leak the critical report, the war might come to an end. But there was a very good chance that he would be convicted of the unauthorized release of classified documents under the Espionage Act – a crime that could see him live out the rest of his days in prison. Given the almighty rumpus that would assuredly follow any leak, and all the possibilities that could arise, it perhaps mattered little that Ellsberg was a leading expert on crisis decision-making. For someone in his position, as the saying goes, anything can happen.

Ellsberg made multiple copies of the 7,000-page document, later to become known as the "Pentagon Papers", and gave them to the *New York Times*, the *Washington Post* and seventeen other newspapers. All hell broke loose. After two weeks in hiding, Ellsberg handed himself in and was duly charged with twelve felonies.

The leak was so damaging that the Nixon administration was not content for Ellsberg merely to be convicted – he had to be discredited. The administration was provoked into its infamous "plumbing" operation, a euphemism for fixing leaks. Part of it involved hiring heavies to rough Ellsberg up, tap his phone and burgle his psychoanalyst's office in search of damaging material. Two of the men involved became rather more famous than they intended. Gordon Liddy and Howard Hunt are better known for breaking into the Democratic National Committee Headquarters in the Watergate Building. As Nixon drowned in Watergate, the government's misconduct against Ellsberg also emerged, causing his trial to collapse.

Hindsight makes the twists and turns of historical events appear much more likely than truly they are. As we look back down history's path, the incalculable number and variety of alternative routes are hidden from view. We know only what occurred and little of what did not. No one can ever know what odds Ellsberg faced of spending the rest of his life languishing in jail, or perhaps succumbing to a worse fate. His own guess as to his likely fate probably changed as the extraordinary events unfolded.

Doubtless the irony of Ellsberg's dilemma was not lost on him. Ten years earlier he had completed a PhD in economics entitled *Risk, Ambiguity and Decision*. He would have known better than anyone that, to be precise, the decision he faced was one of great uncertainty, rather than risk. A scenario contained in that PhD thesis helps to explain the difference. As we'll see by the end of this chapter, had governments, regulators and financial institutions had more respect for the distinction, we might not be in today's deeply unpleasant economic fix.

The urn of uncertainty

Imagine this. In front of you is a dark urn from which coloured balls will be drawn at random. You will get two picks and you win £10 each time you guess the colour right. The urn contains 90 balls, of which 30 are red. Each of the remaining 60 is either yellow or black. There is at least one ball of each colour. On the first pick you can either bet on "red" or on "black". Which would you choose? On the second pick, your options are to bet on "red or yellow" or on "black or yellow". Which option would you choose now?

At first sight, the subtlety of this experiment can be hard to see. The split between black and yellow balls could be anything from 30–30 to 59–1. Look carefully and compare options between first and second pick. There is no incentive for the experimenters, who have to pay out any winnings, to stack the numbers of black and yellow balls one way or the other. An urn with fewer black than yellow balls would reduce the odds of people winning with "black" on the first pick, but would increase the odds of people winning with "red or yellow" on the second pick, by exactly the same amount. There is no reason, therefore, to believe the balance between black and yellow is stacked one way or the other. In other words, there is no "right" answer. The crucial difference between the options, on both picks, is whether the odds of success are known for sure. You know there are 30 red balls and hence a one-in-three chance if you go for "red" on the first pick. You know there are 60 balls that are either black or yellow and hence a two-in-three chance if you go for "black or yellow" on the second pick. But with the alternatives ("black" on the first pick, "red or yellow" on the second), you don't know the exact odds. You are actually as likely to succeed whatever option you choose (although, interestingly, some people can be hard to convince of this), but with one option you know the odds and with the other you don't. This is the difference between risk and uncertainty.* Ellsberg's urn is a brilliant invention, because it neatly manages to separate the two.

Economic transactions are unpredictable – we can be MISLED. But the kind of unpredictability involved is usually more accurately termed "uncertainty" than "risk". Suppose you choose between two cars. A consumer magazine might tell you that one make has a 5% chance of breaking down in its first three years, while the other has a 10% chance. The outcome of the purchase is unpredictable (the car could be reliable or break down). But, subject to the accuracy of the magazine report, you know the odds (5% or 10%). In this case you are up against risk. Yet most transactions are not quantifiable like this. When it comes to whether we are about to be MISLED in a transaction, it is generally very hard to quantify the risk. How can you put a figure on the chance that you might make a mistake, be poorly informed, be surprised, get unlucky, change your mind later, or be dealing with someone dishonest? All these things are possible but of unknowable likelihood, so we have to cope with uncertainty. Even in the case of the well-researched purchase of a car, how sure can you be that the magazine has got it right? How accurate was the survey? What are the chances of a printing error?

Most economic decisions involve both risk and uncertainty. Someone investing in a new business may be able to assess their risk by putting a rough figure on the chance that the venture fails, say 50–50 or 70–30. But they will also be aware that this figure is a guess.

---

* To the best of my knowledge, this distinction was first made in economics by the American Frank Knight. The distinction is crucial, but is not always followed, even in the economics literature. When "uncertainty" is defined as circumstances where not only is the outcome unpredictable but the odds of alternative outcomes cannot be quantified, it is often referred to as Knightian uncertainty. Throughout this book, that is what I mean by "uncertainty".

Business-speak reflects our understanding of uncertainty. "Off the top of my head" it is possible to give you a "guesstimate", but it's only a "stab in the dark".

We know from gambling experiments that people don't like risk. But how do we handle uncertainty? Behavioural economists and psychologists have shown that we don't like uncertainty either. Faced with Ellsberg's urn, almost everyone selects "red" on the first pick and "black or yellow" on the second. We go for the option where the odds we face are known. The other options give us neither better nor worse prospects but greater uncertainty, because the odds are unknown, and we are averse to this.* The strength of our aversion can be measured by changing the prizes, such that if you choose "red" on the first pick you get maybe £9, or £8, if your ball comes out, but if you go for "black" you still get £10. People typically sacrifice 10 to 20% of their potential winnings to avoid the uncertainty, sometimes much more. We like to know exactly how many potential winners are in the urn on each pick, even at a cost to ourselves.

Our economic instincts to avoid both risk and uncertainty are not just manifestations of a personality trait that some people might possess, like cowardice. Almost everyone's instinct is to avoid both risk and uncertainty. Yet there is a distinction in our behaviour that matches the conceptual one. Those people who sacrifice the most potential winnings to avoid uncertainty, when facing Ellsberg's urn, are not the same people who are most risk averse in gambles where the odds are known. People who are willing to take risks may not be so brave in the face of uncertainty, and vice versa. The two concepts are different and we appear instinctively to know it.

---

* In the academic literature, this effect is often referred to as "ambiguity aversion". I prefer to use "uncertainty", because "ambiguity" is more usually associated with the unclear formation of language than with economic or physical outcomes.

What are the chances of that?

Here's another unlikely yet informative scenario. You are in a game show and have made it to the final round. The host sidles up to you with a cheesy grin, puts his arm around your shoulders and wishes you luck, before turning you round to face three doors. Behind one is a brand-new car. Behind the other two are goats. Your job is to pick the right door. Say you choose door No. 2. The host, who knows which door hides the car, walks over to door No. 1 and flings it wide open to reveal one of the goats. "Now," he says, "it's your final choice. Do you want to stick with door No. 2, or switch to door No. 3? The choice is yours."

The "game show problem" was sent in by an American reader to the "Ask Marilyn" column of *Parade* magazine in 1990. The column-ist, Marilyn vos Savant, who is listed in the *Guinness Book of Records* as holding the world's highest IQ score, gave the correct answer. But she had little idea that she was about to cause a national controversy. Believe it or not, and in my experience most people don't, you stand a better chance of winning if you switch doors. When the answer was printed, it proved to be a postbag-buster. Thousands wrote in to say that vos Savant was wrong, including large numbers of professional scientists and mathematicians, many of whom had to admit their own error later. The debate and exchanges of letters rumbled on for years. Many people became convinced only by actually playing the game over and over between themselves. There were even articles written in the *American Statistician* about it.*

Generally speaking, we are dreadful at reasoning with numerical probabilities. Psychologists have recorded dozens of experiments that reveal, unequivocally, that our intuitive judgements run counter to the mathematical principles of probability, as they do in the game show problem. Furthermore, where numerical probabilities are called

---

* At the time of writing, a flavour of the debate and an explanation of why switching doors is the right answer can be had at www.marilynvossavant.com/articles/gameshow. html.

for, they are subject to large biases. Here is just one: about twice as many people will opt for a medical procedure described as having a "90% success rate" than when the same procedure is described as having a "10% failure rate". Judgements of numerical probability just don't chime with our intuitions.

Why? Any neuroscientist will tell you to be sceptical if you encounter a claim that there is a basic skill that humans, as a whole, are very bad at. The human brain is the most remarkable object, adapted by millions of years of evolution to achieve tasks that are beyond the most advanced artificial intelligence systems ever developed. Our brains can recognize thousands of faces from the full range of angles, comprehend and learn languages, and work out the intentions of others from the twitch of an eyebrow. No machine we can build can do any of these things. Because the human brain is so wonderfully adapted to the challenges it faces, if we can't do simple numerical probability problems, it can only be because for the greater part of human existence we have inhabited a world where we didn't need to. The problems we have faced for generation after generation are not those of quantifiable risk but those of unquantifiable uncertainty, in which ability to solve numerical probability problems doesn't help very much.

This observation is not limited to economic decisions, but it nevertheless includes them. In every transaction there is a chance that we may be MISLED, but this chance is not easy to quantify. What's the probability of making a mistake, lacking crucial information, being surprised, suffering bad luck, changing our mind, or suffering from the dishonesty of others? We just don't know and, in the case of being surprised, we don't even know what we don't know. We can only guess. Our instinct to stick with what's familiar helps – if something worked out well before it has a better chance of doing so again.*

* A philosopher might object to this statement, as it seems to be a form of naive inductive logic. Philosophers point out that just because something has happened every time previously doesn't mean it will occur the next time. I haven't the space to deal with this argument properly, but I'll bet that those same philosophers are more likely to return to a restaurant that fed them well last time.

But for one-off decisions, or in circumstances that are new to us, we need other instincts to help us cope with uncertainty. One of them is straightforward: we adjust our chances up or down in response to how we perceive and judge the intentions and motivations of those we do business with.

Given this, it can be argued that people's instinct with the game show problem makes perfect sense. We are almost never given highly valuable objects for free, and yet before us is a disarmingly charming individual who appears to be willing to give us a car. He already knows whether our initial choice is a winner or not and is nevertheless now offering us the opportunity to change that initial decision. Every intuition we possess should tell us to stick with our original choice, which is what people tend to do. The idea that someone would encourage us to switch doors if he knew that by doing so he would have to hand over a car rather than a goat is such a ludicrous assumption in terms of our normal experience that even people with mathematics degrees struggle to abide by it. The mathematics gives the right answer only if we assume, *with absolute certainty*, that the controllers of the game show don't care whether they have to give us a car or not.

To a Marketopian like Adam or Eve, there appears to be a right answer, as defined by mathematics. Indeed, when the problem is presented as a mathematical probability problem, there is a right answer, and it is to switch doors. But to describe the problem solely in numeric terms in the first place requires one or more assumptions that people are uncertain about. Because our environment has for generations been characterized by uncertainty rather than risk, we are far more inclined to judge by social signals than by numeric calculation. Unsurprisingly, therefore, we are not very good at probability problems yet quite brilliant at decoding social signals.

Perhaps the same kind of reasoning explains the medical procedure finding. When somebody chooses to describe a procedure by its success rate rather than its failure rate, they send a social signal that potentially offers us vital information. Is it a subtle sign of confidence, perhaps even a recommendation? When, instead, they choose to describe the procedure by its failure rate, the social signal is different. Are we being encouraged to think twice? Does the description imply lack of blame if the procedure goes wrong? Even assuming that the success or failure rate is accurately compiled from past performance, might a patient reasonably believe that a physician who emphasizes the strong chance of success, rather than the distinct possibility of failure, is likely to be more motivated and to have greater feelings of responsibility while carrying out the work? What initially appears to be an irrational response may not be. The scenario has a dubious assumption buried in it; namely that there is, in reality, no difference in the future outcomes of procedures *described* as having a 10% failure rate and those *described* as having a 90% success rate. Perhaps there is a difference. Even when risk is quantified with precise figures, there is reason to question their accuracy and continuing applicability. As in the mug and theatre ticket experiments, once the uncertainty surrounding our decision is taken into account, what at first appears to be irrational behaviour, certainly by Marketopian standards, may turn out to be sensible.

Behavioural economics has now thrown up very many instances where people behave differently facing what appears to be the same decision, numerically speaking, presented in two different contexts. They are referred to as "framing effects". I know of at least eighty of them in published work, and there are probably more. Examples include the fact that people are more likely to ignore a "cash discount" and pay with plastic than to ignore the same differential when labelled a "credit card surcharge", and that we are more inclined to pay a price of "27 pence a day" than "£100 a year". Once you consider the social signals involved, it is often straightforward to construct an argument to justify these kinds of behaviours. Calling something a "surcharge" implies that only a few people pay it and so you may appear foolish if you are one of them. Choosing to ignore a discount does not have the same negative connotations. A price described as "27 pence a day" implies something about how it may be levied, and we might prefer to pay gradually. If you care about appearing foolish or payment methods, you may behave differently for good reasons.

This analysis leads to a very different way of viewing the vigorous debate in economics about rationality. It is absolutely clear that we do not take decisions as Marketopians do. But this does not mean we are irrational. With the mug, theatre ticket and medical procedure examples, and perhaps the two examples just given, we may view the decision as involving sufficient uncertainty that we don't treat it as a simple, well-defined numerical problem. Given this, whether we are or are not "irrational" is very hard to say. Obviously, once people accept that a decision requires a numerical calculation, they usually try to get it right, and some people are clearly better at calculations than others. But the bigger question may be whether it is sensible to reduce an uncertain decision to a straightforward numerical problem in the first place.

Here's a final example that makes the point clearer. Products priced at £4.99 instead of £5.00 attract disproportionate extra buyers. Given the tiny price difference, this behaviour looks like irrationality – people simply placing too much weight on a single penny. But perhaps not. Suppose I'm deciding whether to make a particular purchase and I check the price tag. I face uncertainty about whether the product is available cheaper in other shops: should I buy it here and now, or move on and look elsewhere for a better deal? But suppose I believe, either consciously or otherwise, that a retailer who prices at £4.99 is more likely to be a retailer who aims for low prices generally. Whether this assumption is true or not I have no idea, but the existence of "99p stores" suggests it may be. If I'm right, it makes more sense to buy when I see £4.99 than when I see £5.00, because I am less likely to find a cheaper product elsewhere. Again, what looks like a simple numerical problem depends on a dubious assumption, namely whether a "something-99" pricing policy says anything about prices in a shop generally. What are the chances that this assumption is right? The problem with uncertainty is that, by definition, you can't put a figure on it. Even if you have a perfectly rational brain, it is of little use when faced with such a question. You can only make an intuitive, rough guess.

The problem for standard theory is not whether people are or are not rational. As common sense correctly suggests, some people are more rational than others, in the sense of being able to apply logic or to calculate things accurately; although all of us sometimes make mistakes. The problem for standard theory is that there are very many economic decisions that cannot be reduced to simple numerical problems, because our economic environment is too uncertain. Our economic lives are governed by guesswork. This does not mean that we deviate randomly from standard theory. The instincts that govern our guesswork are systematic and, hence, it should be possible to generate new theories to describe our economic decisions more accurately.

As well as using familiarity as our guide, we instinctively seek and process information contained in social signals, which we use to adjust our guesses up and down. It is very likely that our skills at decoding social signals are much more sophisticated than our skills at numerical probability because, throughout human history, they have proved far more useful. We have inhabited and continue to inhabit Muddleton, not Marketopia.

It's anybody's guess

When we do business with anyone, perhaps the most important initial decision we have to make is whether they are trustworthy. If we have dealt with them before, this is easier. If they have a reputation to protect, we have more reason to trust them also. We are very sensitive to the character, attitudes and attributes of the people we deal with and we use our judgement to avoid being MISLED. But, in any transaction where the value of what is to be traded is at all uncertain, which covers almost every exchange that is not a regular one, we try to pick up any signals we can to reduce our uncertainty.

Suppose you are one of those people who has taken a long time to get round to converting to a digital camera. You have finally decided to take the plunge and you are resigned to trying to get your head around such things as mega-pixels, user capacity and minimum system requirements. The first shop you visit suggests two cameras that might be right for you, one for £100, the other for £130. The second camera has more mega-pixels, which you have worked out means it takes clearer photos. But you are not sure whether to pay the extra. You decide to look in another shop. There, you find the same two cameras at the same price, but the man behind the counter thinks you might prefer a third option. This is supposed to be a better camera still, because it apparently contains a superior lens and possesses what the shop assistant keeps referring to as "improved functionality". It is priced at £180. Which camera do you buy?

Experiments have been conducted in which consumers are given budgets and exposed to different product ranges. One of the findings is that the inclusion of a third option can change our preferences regarding two others. In the case above, the appearance of the more expensive option suddenly makes us more likely to buy the £130 camera – the middle option. Why do we do this? Again, it could be that we are just irrational. Adam and Eve would not change their minds about the relative merits of two products just because a third one appeared. But assume that, especially with products that are new to us, we are very uncertain about which combination of price and quality to go for. In these circumstances, the range of products available is a signal regarding the preferences of everyone else. Thus, picking the middle option is likely to be closer to the average choice, which for most people is probably a good guide. There are people who always seek the cheapest option and others who only ever consider better models. But the expressions "bottom of the range" and "top of the range" carry connotations that many of us tend to avoid – we like to be somewhere in between.

This finding may also explain a puzzle found in industry data. Standard theory predicts that when a new product is launched, the products already available in the market will lose market share. If consumers behaved like Adam and Eve this would be true. Yet often markets do not work out this way. The appearance of a new product sometimes increases the share of one or more existing ones. When people are uncertain, the range of available products can alter decisions to the degree that it changes the balance of a whole market.

It isn't just consumers of newfangled electronic goods who try to reduce uncertainty by looking at what others do; picking up subtle social signals. This instinct was a major cause of the financial crisis, as both consumers and financial traders copied each other's erroneous valuations of houses and so-called "mortgage-backed securities" respectively. The final section of this chapter will explain how our various instincts for coping with uncertainty relate to what occurred. But it really shouldn't have taken a crisis of such magnitude to alert us to the possibility that these instincts have the potential to cause havoc in markets. The evidence has been there for some time, especially in data relating to the stock market.

When a trader buys a stock or share,* they buy a small part of a company. The share price should reflect the company's value – its likelihood of future profit. When the price rises, it is because traders decide the future profits of the company are likely to be higher. Now, if traders form rational independent judgements about the future profitability of companies, then you would expect changes in share prices to be closely related to changes in actual profits. On the other hand, if traders are uncertain about the true value of shares and are therefore influenced by the valuations of other traders, then you might expect larger swings in share prices than in actual company profits. In fact, this is exactly what occurs: share prices vary much more than company profits do.

The likely reason for this is that traders "herd". Where they see

---

* The terms "stock" and "share" are often used confusingly. They are the same thing – ownership of a small part of a company. "Stock" is more common in the USA, "share" more common elsewhere, though "stock market" is standard for places where shares (stocks) are traded.

the price of a share rise, they assume that other traders have information suggesting that the company is doing better, and so they become more likely to buy it themselves. The result is that small events or changes in sentiment can be exaggerated into larger price swings. Indeed, looking at stock market trends, it is almost impossible to conclude that traders form independent rational judgements about company values. Share prices rise disproportionately in January, fall on Mondays and go up on Fridays. They also rise at the end of each month, before holidays and towards the end of the day. No rational assessment of company values explains these fluctuations, which match obvious mood patterns. Prices of individual shares also tend to be cyclical, as if traders simply guess that each price is likely to continue on the same rising or falling path. The leaders of the herd change direction faster than the rest of the pack.

Stock market crashes, which occur pretty regularly, are also hard to reconcile with the idea that traders form independent rational judgements, again suggesting that they herd. On 19 October 1987, so-called "Black Monday", share prices in New York sank by 23%. The ripples rocked markets around the globe. By the end of that October, UK shares were down by a quarter, while the Australian market lost 40%. Why this happened still baffles scholars, as no obvious negative news event suddenly damaged the prospects of all the thousands of companies whose shares were being traded. The 1980s stripy-shirt brigade seemingly reacted to the infectious mood and copied the behaviour of colleagues, causing worldwide panic selling – a yuppie epidemic of contagious downward mobility.

Just like consumers, stock market traders read signals about the opinions of other traders and adjust their own guesses accordingly. Bubbles and crashes make stock market traders appear irrational, just as consumers appear irrational when the launch of a new product increases the market share of a pre-existing one. In both cases, the phenomenon can be explained by uncertain individuals changing their guesses about what things are worth, after reading signals about what others are doing.

There are in fact circumstances in which backing your own judgement and ignoring what everyone else is doing can be a serious mistake. Back in the 1950s, US oil companies began drilling in the Gulf of Mexico. New technology had made offshore drilling look like a highly profitable option and companies competed strongly for drilling rights. A decade or so later, however, the expected bonanza had still not materialized – profits were poor. Three engineers named Capen, Clapp and Campbell, who worked for one of the companies involved, ARCO, sussed out what had happened. In doing so, they unearthed a new economic concept.

The problem, once again, was uncertainty. When new drilling rights were offered, each company bid for them and the rights went to the highest bidder. For any given location, the oil available and the difficulty of extracting it were uncertain. The result was that the oil company that won the rights was always the one that had been most optimistic. Yet, in such a competition, it's a fair assumption that the average bid will reflect the true value of the site. Hence, the bid that won was usually too high and the winning company struggled to make a profit. Capen, Clapp and Campbell also managed to show that engineers invent better jargon than economists, by giving the phenomenon a wonderful name: winner's curse.

For some time after their explanation appeared, there was debate about whether winner's curse really was a problem in competitive bidding situations. Many economists resisted the idea, presumably because it suggested, heretically, that companies might behave irrationally. It didn't take long, however, to show how easy it was to induce winner's curse in experiments. Behavioural economists found that if you auctioned a jar of coins to a group of bidders you normally made a profit – someone would guess too high, win and suffer the curse. They then showed that experienced businesspeople fell for winner's curse in experiments too. Since then, the phenomenon has been recorded in a number of industries. Examples include publishers bidding to offer advances to famous authors, professional sports teams bidding for individual players in the transfer market, and other instances where companies bid for rights to extract oil and gas. In each case, the winner is the firm that guesses most optimistically, usually too optimistically, hence suffering the curse of paying too much and making no profit.

Winner's curse can also occur when firms bid competitively to carry out work. This has strong implications for procurement and outsourcing in the public and private sectors. It is widely believed that competition for a contract should lower the cost of buying in the service, as firms compete to do the job more efficiently than each other. But the phenomenon of winner's curse suggests that this will work only where the differences in efficiency between the competing firms are greater than the uncertainty that surrounds the cost of completing the work to the required standard. Otherwise, the firm that is most likely to win is simply the one most likely to be unable to do the job for the cost they specify, because they were the most optimistic. If you've ever wondered why major projects so often come in over budget, winner's curse may well be part of the answer. The contractor engaged to do the work is the one least able to do what they said they could do, so they come back to the table to renegotiate, complaining of unforeseen technical problems and extra costs.

There is a final twist to the phenomenon of winner's curse. Individuals and firms that go in regularly for competitive tendering processes may become aware of the curse. If so, the sensible thing for them to do is to bid more cautiously – quoting a higher price for their services. If bidders get wise like this, there is an interesting implication. Once a number of the bidders are wise, increasing the amount of competition might actually increase the cost of the service, not decrease it. Indeed, this effect has been found in data. With many bidders going for the same contract, they start to worry about being the lowest-cost bid and so add a premium. You can understand the insecurity – if they are the lowest, they must have missed something. Similarly, research on internet auctions shows that bidders put in more cautious bids once there are many others involved – you wouldn't want to be the only one who thinks it's worth that much.

Adam and Eve are independent and rational. Consumers, stock market traders and companies are not. They all behave in a manner that suggests they are uncertain about the value of what they purchase, or uncertain about what it will cost them to do a job. Quite sensibly, they observe the behaviour of those around them to try to improve their guesses. But when the degree of uncertainty is large enough, everyone may copy each other's mistakes, producing bubbles and crashes. Or someone may get the judgement wrong, and so win an unprofitable contract. Or people may be so put off by the uncertainty that they don't bid competitively in a contest. Thus, uncertainty means that markets can be inefficient.

Gather ye rosebuds

How much is getting something a day earlier worth? Suppose I offer you a choice between the following fairly pleasant options. I will either give you £100 today, or I will give you £110 pounds tomorrow. Which would you prefer? Now compare this choice with the following similar one. I will either give you £100 in 30 days, or I will give you £110 in 31 days. Which of these two would you prefer?

When faced with scenarios like these, people differ in their preferences, but there is a clear pattern. Quite a lot of people will go for £100 today in the first instance, but take £110 after 31 days in the second, while almost no one opts for £110 tomorrow and £100 in 30 days. Thus, we do not place a consistent price on a one-day delay. The closer the day in question is to the present, the more the day seems to matter.

This behaviour may again make sense in an uncertain world. The future is particularly uncertain – anything can happen. You might legitimately reason that there is a chance my generosity will not last until tomorrow, so you are better off taking the smaller sum now while I'm in the mood. Similarly, there may be a greater chance that in 30 days' time I won't cough up. But there is probably little difference between the chance that I will have changed my mind after 30 days and the chance that I will have done so after 31. So it may make sense to wait the extra day and go for the higher sum.

Another interpretation of this experiment is that we are simply impatient, or perhaps impulsive; that we know we'd be better off waiting for the higher sum, but we just can't resist the temptation to cash in now. Impulsiveness is a strong instinct and one that makes sense in an uncertain environment – you may not get the chance again.

This kind of inconsistent approach to time is fairly easy to observe in the real economy. A good example is the purchase of energy-efficient appliances – or rather the non-purchase. Efficient appliances usually cost extra initially, but will ultimately save more on energy bills than the extra paid. Yet studies show that even in circumstances where consumers have access to information on the relative energy consumption of electrical goods, where it is apparently clear that they will recover more than the price difference, they are still biased towards buying the cheaper, less efficient appliance. Again, perhaps this is just impulsive unwillingness to part with the money then and there. Alternatively, people might be sceptical of the promise of reduced energy bills. They can see the price difference in front of them, but the energy calculation is uncertain – a promise of jam tomorrow. You can't see the contribution of an individual appliance on your electricity bill. Is the efficiency saving believable? And if you buy a more efficient washing machine, might it just tempt you to wash your clothes more often? Maybe it's not surprising that people are more influenced by the immediate price difference, of which they are certain.

Standard economics is at odds with how we assess the future. Adam and Eve would price a one-day delay consistently and, because they live in Marketopia, would have perfect information about energy-saving appliances and simply compare the costs and benefits. In Muddleton, life is less certain. Yet while sometimes it may be sensible to avoid uncertainty and stick with what we know, there are circumstances in which our instinct to prefer the definite and the present causes us problems. It would be better for our bank balances and the environment if ways could be found to increase our confidence in energy-efficient solutions across the whole range of products. There are also many issues that seem to produce conflicts between our long-term and short-term preferences. "Rational" Marketopians have stable preferences – they know what they like. Real people don't. We might have the best long-term intentions regarding what we eat, whether we smoke, whether we drink too much, whether we take exercise, whether we save for the future or splurge on a credit card, yet we often fail to live up to them. Orthodox economics assumes that we have stable preferences, but our preferences actually change over time, with opportunities and moods.

We often lack the self-control to resist temptation and we have an expression for such purchases – "impulse buys". This problem, if indeed we consider it to be a problem, probably arises because some of our economic instincts were formed in an environment of much greater uncertainty than the one we occupy now. Our ancestors lived in a world of scarcity and shorter life expectancy, in which no sensible human turned down high-energy food, rest or other opportunities for instantaneous benefit. Now, at least in developed countries, we are sufficiently wealthy that people count calories, suffer from sedentarism and indulge in a large variety of pleasures that do long-term harm.

In an era where priority is given to individual choice, it can be hard to discuss these issues without being criticized for being patronizing or paternalistic – who am I to suggest that people don't know their own minds? On a societal level, people often complain about the "nanny state". Yet economic behaviour suggests that we sometimes actively try to limit our own future choices. Alcohol clinics or fat farms are examples where people hand over money to firms promising to control or deny choice of drink or food. We can instantaneously behave in a way that our long-term selves dislike and, knowing this, we take decisions aimed at controlling our unstable desires. Compare smoking and taking exercise. Smokers could save money by buying in bulk, but buy small packets instead, in the hope it will reduce their smoking. In contrast, people buy access to gym equipment through large monthly or yearly subscriptions. Studies show this entices healthier future decisions, as higher initial payments increase the frequency of use. In both cases, the size of the initial purchase is designed to control our fluctuating preferences. Back in Marketopia, Eve's ability to buy just the right amount of chocolate ice cream to balance desire and health, for maximum happiness, appears inhuman because it is.

This kind of inconsistent behaviour is not confined to addictions and bad habits, but can affect financial planning too. People will place funds in savings accounts that limit access when they could get a better interest rate elsewhere, because they don't trust themselves not to dip in. Christmas clubs are an extreme example of this, where people sometimes forgo interest on their savings to limit their access until the tinsel is on the tree.

Clearly, some of our more impulsive instincts developed to cope with a short, changeable and uncertain life. Thus, they may not always be ideally suited to our longer and somewhat more certain modern lives. Interestingly, as well as valuing the immediate future too highly, experiments also reveal that we overvalue the lessons of the immediate past relative to those of longer ago. If asked to place bets on future outcomes, such as sports results, stock returns or election results, we are inclined to pay too much attention to what has occurred most recently and too little to what happened longer ago. It is as if our instincts are tuned to a more changeable world than the one we now inhabit, leading us to respond excessively to temporary trends.

Our instincts for valuing time help to explain something that standard economics simply cannot: why people fail to save sufficiently for retirement. Adam and Eve would save exactly the right amount during the period they were earning to spread their spending power evenly across their lifespan. We don't. When families are surveyed about the issue, a large number report that they wish they were saving more for the future. Somewhere over a third usually report that they intend to increase their saving levels. When surveyed again at a later date, in most cases they have failed to do so. In countries with large baby booms, the impact of under-saving on the financial well-being of retired people is likely to become a big issue.

Behavioural economics is beginning to offer solutions to the problem. Changing the default option on company pension schemes, such that status quo bias works in favour of joining the scheme rather than against, is just one technique. But in America, behavioural economists Richard Thaler and Shlomo Benartzi have devised and piloted an entire scheme based on evidence about our economic instincts, called Save More Tomorrow (SMT). The SMT plan takes advantage of the fact that people are happy to pre-commit to better long-term behaviours in future. SMT, as its name suggests, does not start immediately, but kicks in only at the time of a worker's next pay increment. Then the contributions to the scheme increase each time pay increases. Thus, the worker never experiences a fall in their familiar disposable income. When it was piloted in a medium-sized manufacturing company, it proved attractive: many more people joined SMT than were prepared to join the firm's standard pension scheme, and they saved at higher rates too. Note that orthodox economics would predict that no one would join the SMT – being "rational", the workers would already be saving at their optimal rate.

Our Muddletonian nature leads us to favour the familiar and to look for all kinds of signals from others regarding the value of what we exchange – sensible instincts in an uncertain world. The ability to avoid being MISLED in transactions has mattered throughout human history and matters now too. But some aspects of the economic environment have become more certain, including our access to essentials, such as high-energy food, and our longevity. By revealing our true economic instincts, behavioural economics can be used to design economic systems that are better suited to human nature. The SMT scheme appears to be one.

Crash, bang, wallop

Behavioural findings relating to uncertainty strongly suggest that we need to reassess what markets can and cannot do. There is no question that economic success consists of widespread gains from mutually beneficial trade, but the view that free markets provide such gains reliably is questioned by a deeper understanding of our economic instincts. More obviously, it is contradicted utterly by what has occurred in the world economy since summer 2007. A free market is efficient only when the transactions within it are predictable – transparently beneficial to buyers and sellers alike. Our real economic environment is just not like that. Instead, economic decisions are frequently taken in circumstances of genuine uncertainty, to which our instincts have adapted. Yet it is apparent that once they operate across millions of people in a complex modern economy, these instincts can cause major economic problems.

The housing bubble that burst catastrophically in 2007 is not an isolated incident. There have actually been over 40 house price bubbles across the OECD countries over the past 50 years. This is not surprising given the behavioural evidence presented in this chapter, which shows how we rely on the valuations of others to guide our own decisions, how we value the immediate future too highly and how we are excessively influenced by the most recent trends. When people watch others pay high prices for houses, see the trend rising steeply, then weigh up the immediate satisfaction of a new home against having to make large repayments well into the future, they are very strongly tempted to buy. Hence, our instincts for coping with the uncertainty, which may well have been sensible in other uncertain environments, cause bubbles in a modern housing market.

Behavioural economists have even learnt to generate mini-bubbles among people playing simple trading games in the laboratory. Subjects in these experiments buy and sell tokens, the future value of which is uncertain, because it is partly governed by chance and partly by what the other people in the game may be prepared to pay. The subjects respond too strongly to short-term trends and follow too readily the first enthusiastic buyers, causing bubbles and crashes in the price. In other words, bubbles are a scientifically replicable piece of human behaviour when trading assets of uncertain value.

The distinction between risk and uncertainty, which lies at the heart of this chapter, also offers insight into how the instincts of traders scuppered some major financial institutions. In the build-up to the crisis, financial traders began using increasingly sophisticated risk management models, which balanced risk across different assets in a mathematically sound manner, but started from the assumption that accurate probabilities could be assigned to returns on each asset. For example, some models were based on an initial probability that Americans in lower socio-economic groups would fail to meet their mortgage payments. In truth, such probabilities were incalculable. Historical patterns permitted an educated guess, but that was all. The mistaken belief that the risk models were accurate representations of an uncertain world was a big factor in the collapse of firms of international pedigree.

Interestingly, once it became apparent that the estimates of default probabilities were bad, perceptions changed. Major losses looked inevitable, but nobody knew which financial institutions were holding the most toxic assets. Banks suddenly stopped lending to other banks, because traders decided it was impossible to calculate the probability of default. The bizarre result was that after granting huge loans to poorer Americans, who despite being previously considered unsuitable for credit were perceived by the market as a manageable risk, financial traders stopped lending to the biggest and most prestigious financial institutions in the world, because they perceived the loans to be subject to too much uncertainty. This behaviour is truly irrational, but understandable if you know how people typically perceive and react to risk and uncertainty.

The financial traders also fell prey to herding. Once some of them enthusiastically led the way in trading "mortgage backed securities", bundles of mortgages bought and sold as a single asset on the financial markets, the herd followed. More and more bright, numerate financial professionals began buying up these pieces of paper for millions of dollars – far more than they were truly worth. The herd was so enticing that it attracted more than one species: credit rating agencies and regulators joined it too. All were seemingly persuaded of the value of these innovative financial products.

We will come to the relationship between behavioural economics and marketing in Chapter 6, but for now note that marketing professionals have known for decades that individuals who are uncertain about what things are worth can be strongly influenced by the opinions of other people. This is why marketers prize "testimonial" adverts, in which real consumers talk about mundane household products as if they've just fallen in love for the first time. To a behavioural economist, the cleverest financial professionals in the world behaving as irrationally as consumers hearing stories about the brilliance of the latest washing powder is not a surprise. Clever people are still instinctively human.

The naive free-market model of predictable transactions between informed traders is unlikely to survive the coming revolution in economics. Our economic instincts suggest that our economic lives are not like that. Facing unpredictable transactions, unsure of the outcomes, we stick with what is more familiar to us, employ educated guesswork and respond strongly to social signals about value. The result is that our behaviour is subject to systematic biases, which when compounded across individuals can produce very large pricing errors. In some markets these effects appear to be endemic. Financial crises and bubbles are a recurrent theme of economic history. If we are to prevent them in the future, we need to start by understanding their causes. Then we need to develop regulations that help people to take better long-term decisions, or at least limit the damage if they don't.

There is one more implication of the powerful role played by uncertainty in transactions that deserves mention. In an uncertain economic environment it is inevitable that some people gain more from trade than others. What you don't know can hurt you. Knowledge is not evenly spread. What is familiar to us depends on who is familiar to us. The social signals that guide us vary with who we have access to. Our economic fortunes will thus be determined not only by ability and effort, but by our relationships with others, including our social, occupational and family circles, to a much greater extent than economists have been inclined to believe.

How we interact with other people may therefore have a big impact on economic well-being. Independent, selfish Marketopians don't worry about such things – they are, after all, independent and selfish. But we Muddletonians do. So the next question is: what does the evidence say about how we interact, economically speaking, with others?

5

Establishing the motive

IN SUMMER 2005, Irish Ferries, a company that runs sailings between Ireland, Britain and France, told 543 of its staff to accept severe cuts in pay and conditions or take a redundancy package. The workers were to be replaced with cheaper labour from eastern Europe. The company's ships were to be "re-flagged" to sail under the flag of Cyprus. Workers could then be outsourced to an agency and paid below Ireland's minimum wage. Following the company's announcement, there was an almighty row.

The dispute was emblematic of our globalized age. Irish Ferries said that without large cost savings it would soon be unable to compete and that this was not its fault – every ferry company was outsourcing cheap labour. The union representing the workers disagreed. It accepted that savings needed to be made, but said the scale was excessive. The company was engaged in a "race to the bottom" over labour standards, it said. A stand had to be made, or workers in other industries would suffer similar ultimatums to cut pay or lose their jobs.

Strike! Docks went silent, pickets formed, seamen locked themselves in engine rooms, security personnel were hired to deal with them. Ireland's union movement organized a national day of protest and thousands of people marched in the streets of the country's largest towns. The union, however, had to decide how far it was prepared to go. Continued industrial action could cost its members their redundancy money. If action went on for long enough, the company could be destroyed along with all the jobs. Irish Ferries had to decide how far the union was prepared to go too. Would union members jeopardize their money in support of principles, or would self-interest force the union to give in?

Bitter words were exchanged in the media. Right-wing commentators bemoaned a return to the bad old days of trade union power. Left-wing commentators invoked the bad old days of nineteenth-century labour standards. But, as months passed, the union's resolve and public support remained for all to see. Irish Ferries was forced to negotiate a deal. Cost savings were scaled down, options facing existing workers were improved, and the minimum wage was secured for incoming foreign workers, who were not members of the union.

Such events do not occur in Marketopia, where it is assumed that only selfish motives operate. Other motives were at work in the Irish Ferries dispute. They included three economic instincts, each of which can be identified with a well-documented laboratory experiment and frequently observed in the real economy also. These instincts, relating to fair shares, to economic cooperation and to group identity, are shared by the majority of people, which may go some way to explaining why public sympathy was with the union.

You can keep it

Suppose I give you £10 on condition you share some of it with a stranger, according to simple rules. You must offer them a proportion of the money. It is entirely your decision how much. If the stranger, who knows the total amount to be divided, accepts your offer, both of you leave with the sums agreed. But if they reject it, the money is returned to me and both of you leave with nothing. There is no negotiation and no second chance. How much would you offer? Now imagine the positions are reversed. Instead, the stranger has £10 to share with you, according to the same rules. What offers would you accept and what would you reject?

This is the "Ultimatum Game", invented in the early 1980s by a German sociologist, Werner Güth. In the past twenty years, researchers have played it with thousands of people, in many countries, for different amounts. How do your answers compare? Standard practice is to call the player who presents the ultimatum the "proposer" and the player who must decide to accept or reject it the "responder". The most common offer from proposers is 50%, or £5 in this case. Most proposers offer at least 30%. Responders, meanwhile, usually reject anything less than 30%. Very few accept offers below 20%, while some responders even reject anything below 50%. The response to a miserly take-it-or-leave-it ultimatum is: "you can keep it". So let's call this the *yucki* instinct.

This is another result that violates standard economics. If the world were like the model of competitive equilibrium, all offers above zero would be accepted. Marketopians get happiness only from their own income – other people are irrelevant. If Adam were the responder, he would accept any amount, preferring the little happiness gained from an ungenerous sum to the alternative of nothing. If Eve were the proposer she would offer just a penny, knowing that because Adam has no *yucki* instinct, he would accept.

The *yucki* instinct seems to be universal and strong. Whether in America, Europe or Asia, in developed or developing countries, in isolated tribal societies, and even when the game is played with complete anonymity via isolated computer terminals, the Ultimatum Game gives a similar result.

The intuitive explanation is that, in this context, instincts associated with fairness are stronger than our selfish desire for money. But an alternative explanation of our behaviour as responders is that we are buying revenge. We might weigh the little bit of pleasure gained from the paltry amount offered against the enjoyment of punishing the proposer. We may prefer the revenge to the money on purely selfish grounds. This revenge theory predicts that if the stake were increased, the effect would disappear, as the amount of money began to outweigh the pleasure of giving a tight-fisted proposer a slap in the face.

But the *yucki* instinct is stronger than that. An Australian economist, Lisa Cameron, played the Ultimatum Game with Indonesian volunteers using very large sums. In one instance the proposer was asked to split 200,000 rupiah, which was roughly three months' income for the players.* The average offer was 42% and all offers below 25% were rejected, as were some over 30%. These Indonesians said "you can keep it" even when the "it" was enough to widen the eyes – far more than would be exchanged in everyday transactions. The *yucki* instinct really does seem to override self-interest.

What about proposers? An offer over 30% is not necessarily selfless. If proposers think responders have a *yucki* instinct, a generous offer may reflect a selfish desire to avoid ending up with nothing. To test intentions of proposers, the Ultimatum Game has been transformed into a "Dictator Game", in which responders have no option to reject offers. Rather than presenting an ultimatum, the proposer dictates. In Dictator Games, the average split tends to be less equal and some people offer nothing, so self-interest does play a part. But most proposers still offer significant amounts and many continue to split the money evenly. Fairness plays a part too.

The Ultimatum Game is, obviously, artificial. But there are everyday situations quite like it. In fact, the *yucki* instinct could, potentially, affect any transaction.

Imagine you are shopping for a child's present when your eye is caught by a big teddy bear. He is well made, but what has captured you is his slightly quizzical expression. Dangling from his fluffy brown ear is a price tag. Will he be yours? According to standard

---

* It is a common practice in behavioural economics to travel to a developing country to do tests involving significant levels of income for the people involved. The cost of playing the game for three months' income with a large sample of Australians would exceed an entire research grant.

economics you simply decide how much the bear is worth to you. Perhaps you decide he's worth £25. If the actual price is below your valuation, you buy him; if not, you move on. You will buy even if the price is £24, because you are still happier owning the bear than the money.

But suppose the *yucki* instinct comes into play. You may care about how much money the retailer makes too. To the retailer, your cuddly character is just another toy that must fetch at least £10, say, to deliver a profit. Now make the analogy to the Ultimatum Game, with the retailer as proposer and you as responder. The difference between £10 and £25 is like the sum to be shared, because at a price of £10 the shop makes no profit and at £25 you gain nothing from buying. Effectively, the price is an offer regarding how £15 should be shared,* which the retailer proposes. If the *yucki* instinct is involved then we have a prediction. At a price of £24, with the retailer making £14 and you making £1, you won't buy the bear even though you would marginally gain, because you will judge your benefit to be unacceptably small compared to the retailer's. You will buy only if the price drops to maybe £20 or less. Does the *yucki* instinct affect ordinary transactions like this?

Richard Thaler developed an experiment that you can again try for yourself. Imagine it is a long, hot day. You are on the beach with a friend. He leaves to make a brief phone call and offers to bring you back a cold bottle of beer from a nearby hotel bar. He says it might be expensive and asks how much you are willing to pay for the beer. How much do you tell him? Once you have decided on an answer, try this twist. The scenario is exactly the same, but instead of a hotel bar, your friend says he will go to a nearby grocery store. Does this make a difference? Thaler found his American subjects would pay, on average, up to $2.65 for a beer from the hotel bar, but only $1.50

---

* Economists refer to this £15 as the "surplus", or total gain from trade. Of course, in this situation you are unlikely to know the exact size of the surplus and would have to guess the size of the retailer's mark-up. A precise figure is used here for illustrative purposes.

from the grocery store. Instead of putting a price on their desire for a beer and stating this price as their maximum, subjects adjusted their maximum price for different sellers. They appeared to account for profit, realizing that hotels have higher costs to cover. If the grocery store tried to charge hotel prices, it would be hit by the *yucki* instinct. People will forgo the bottle of beer to deny excess profit, even though they would rather have the beer than the money. Thaler's finding is related to the common idea of a "fair price". When we say a price is fair, we are not referring to a figure that expresses a buyer's desire for a product. We mean that the price represents a balance between the buyer's gain and what the seller deserves in return.

If this is right, then the *yucki* instinct has the capacity to influence every transaction we conduct; to be a key property of the economic atom. Modern economics is based on the idea of mutual gains from trade, yet it looks as if we disregard gains when we think they are not mutual enough. It is therefore remarkable how little research has followed up Thaler's study, which was conducted in 1984 – when a beer really could be had for $1.50.

Thaler's experiment took place in a laboratory. Is there evidence that the *yucki* instinct affects real markets? Take arguably our most important transaction: wages in exchange for work. Employers make money from our work and offer us a proportion of it. If the *yucki* instinct affects this transaction, it will influence salary offers and acceptances. Wealthy firms that gain more from our work will offer higher salaries, and we will not accept the job unless they do. What does the evidence say? Surveys of job adverts and salary levels, going back to the 1950s, produce what economists call "inter-industry wage differentials". In ordinary language, this means that large, profitable industries pay more for the same work. An administrator, secretary or accountant in, say, a wealthy oil company gets paid considerably more than someone doing exactly the same job for a local hotel. One published estimate found that an administrator in the petroleum business might get 70% more than they would get for doing the same job in education. Standard economic theory says this won't happen, because administrators will be desperate to leave schools and colleges and join oil companies, which, with more people knocking on their doors, could then lower their wages. So market forces ought to make the pay differential disappear. Instead, it persists. The *yucki* instinct provides a simple explanation of why. We won't accept pay deals unless we get a fair share of the profit we help to create, even at a cost to ourselves.

As with the arguments about rationality, much of the research done on the Ultimatum Game has aimed to disprove the mainstream economic view; to show that people are not always selfish. Less work has focused on what might actually lie behind the behaviour of proposers and responders in the game. Furthermore, traditionalists have again argued that competitive markets would not allow such behaviour; that someone who makes sacrifices in the name of fairness, especially when dealing with completely anonymous strangers, just wouldn't survive. To see why this isn't so, we need to play a classic game.

We're in this together

"Prisoner's Dilemma" is a bizarre, imaginary scenario that contains deep insight. At first glance, it may appear complicated, unrealistic and, more to the point, not about economics. But it is cleverly designed and highly relevant. Understanding the dilemma and people's responses to it can change how you think about many issues, be they occupational, economic, environmental or even personal. Prisoner's Dilemma was devised in 1950, by a Canadian mathematician, Alfred Tucker, who translated a numerical problem on a blackboard into a now well-known scenario – one which may, or may not, be difficult to imagine.

You are a hardened criminal. You and your long-time partner in crime, "Hoodie", have just been arrested in relation to a serious offence, and are being held in separate prison cells. Your interrogators are encouraging you to confess. This will apparently shorten your sentence, but the exact term will depend on whether Hoodie confesses too. If you both own up, you each get five years. If one of you talks and the other holds out, the one who confesses gets just one year, the one who holds out gets seven. If neither of you confess, you will be convicted of a lesser crime and serve two years each. You cannot talk to Hoodie. What would you do?

The logic of Prisoner's Dilemma is subtle. Suppose Hoodie refuses to confess. Then, if you talk, you get just one year, while if you are tight lipped you do two. Your sentence is shorter if you confess. Now suppose Hoodie confesses. Then, if you stay quiet, it's seven years, but if you also confess it's five. Again, confessing shortens the sentence. Thus, whatever Hoodie does, you get a shorter sentence if you own up. From a purely selfish point of view you should confess. But the irony is that if both of you follow this self-interested logic and confess, you end up serving five years each, a total of ten between you, which is the worst possible outcome collectively. You might therefore think that it makes sense to keep quiet. Refusing to confess, however, is a selfless act, because it increases your sentence by a year even if Hoodie follows suit. It also requires trust, because if you keep quiet and Hoodie confesses, he gets just one year and leaves you to rot for seven. To resolve the dilemma successfully, both of you must care about your partner in crime enough to sacrifice at least a year's liberty, and trust each other to do the same in return. You would want to have known Hoodie a long time.

Situations with the same logic as Prisoner's Dilemma are surprisingly common. They arise whenever two (or more) people's individual incentives are at odds with their best collective outcome. Consider two colleagues chatting, as people often do, about their work–life balance. They agree that their hours are too long. While their job should not require them to stay later than six o'clock, being seen to go the extra mile may nevertheless help them to get on in the company. These workmates are in a Prisoner's Dilemma. The best solution is for both to leave each day no later than six. But if one leaves on time, the other has an incentive to stay a bit longer and so appear more hard working than their colleague. Each must ignore this temptation and trust the other to do the same, or both will be consistently late home.

What actually happens when people face a Prisoner's Dilemma situation? Obviously, in its original form Prisoner's Dilemma is not an easy experiment to set up. But simple economic games just like it can be designed. Suppose you are placed at a computer screen, while at another terminal somewhere, in another room, is your anonymous fellow player, "Manikin". Both of your screens present a choice between two buttons, A or B. If you click A and so does Manikin, each of you gets £5. If you select A and Manikin clicks B, Manikin gets £7 to your £1 – you are the dummy. The other way around and you get £7 while Manikin gets the dummy's sum. If you both go for B, you get £2 apiece. You are facing Prisoner's Dilemma, to gain money, rather than to avoid years in a prison cell. To go for the best collective outcome both of you must hit A, which requires selflessness and trust. Which button would you click?

In fact, around half the people facing this game click on A. In other words, half the population violates standard economic theory, which predicts that because you are selfish you will click on B, the option that improves your money whatever Manikin does. This is more evidence that our economic instincts are not purely selfish.

That said, the Prisoner's Dilemma result is less emphatic than the Ultimatum Game result, where a very large majority of people behave unselfishly, not just half the population. There are obvious differences between this Prisoner's Dilemma game and the Ultimatum Game. In particular, although responders in the Ultimatum Game have just two options (accept or reject), as in Prisoner's Dilemma, the proposer has many more, because they can offer whatever proportion of the money they wish, across a whole range. Prisoner's Dilemma games can be designed to give people a range of choices too.

Again, suppose it's you and Manikin. This time each of you has been given £10. You can either just keep it, or you can contribute all, some or none of it to "the pot". The total amount in the pot, after both of you have decided how much to contribute, is going to be increased by 50% then divided equally between the pair of you. How much would you put in the pot?

This is a more sophisticated version of Prisoner's Dilemma. However much Manikin contributes to the pot, you make more money by putting nothing in. This is because each pound you contribute will be increased to £1.50, but then split between the pair of you. So for each pound you contribute you get only 75p back. But if both of you submit all your cash to the pot, you both go home with £15 instead of £10. This is the best collective solution, but it again requires selflessness and trust to reach it. If one of you puts in the whole £10 and the other puts in nothing, the selfish one leaves with £17.50 and the generous one with £7.50. Still, in this game you can compromise by putting only a proportion of the money in the pot. You don't have to be entirely selfish or completely selfless and trusting.

With this version of the experiment, the large majority of people contribute to the pot. The average response is to put in about half the money. Thus, once the number of choices in a Prisoner's Dilemma situation is expanded, people go against conventional economics by abandoning selfishness. This result, as with the Ultimatum Game, has been recorded many times in many places. The game can be expanded to include more than two players, with everyone contributing to a collective pot that is going to be increased and split. Versions have been tried with over a hundred people. Interestingly, contributions to the pot tend to be higher, though there is variation. Some people contribute everything, others nothing, while still others make a sacrifice for the common good, albeit not so much as to appear gullible. But the majority of players, despite complete anonymity, appear to reason that "we're in this together" – so let's call it the *witt* instinct.

As with the *yucki* ("you can keep it") instinct, we can ask whether the *witt* instinct motivates behaviour in the real economy. The experiments are known as "Public Good Games" because the pot of money is like a public good in the real economy – something from which everyone can benefit. In the games, the public good is extra money to be evenly split, but in the real economy public goods are what the contributions pay for. Many public goods are provided by government, such as infrastructure, public information, defence and police forces, environmental protection, public space, and so on. But while it is common to relate Public Good Games to taxation, contributions to "the pot" are very different from taxation. Tax revenue is not shared equally. What it is spent on is often contentious. Contributions are not voluntary, but enforced by law. The *witt* instinct probably plays a part in how people feel about tax, but many other factors are involved.

Nevertheless, there are situations in the real economy where the *witt* instinct clearly operates. One is "honesty boxes". Some businesses simply provide a payment box with a slot and trust that people will pay. The high-street retailer WHSmith successfully introduced honesty boxes in Britain for sales of newspapers in 2000. The company hoped the *witt* instinct would kick in and people would pay, realizing that if everyone stumped up then queues for morning newspapers could be avoided. WHSmith discovered that the *witt* instinct was nearly universal – only a few people failed to pay. Some even compensated for not having the right change one day by making up the difference the next. Studies have found that honesty boxes are successful in many contexts, including for car parking, farm produce, coffee, visitor attractions, golf course and swimming pool fees, specialist music downloads, hiking trails and campsites. Not everyone contributes: while honesty boxes often produce compliance levels upwards of 90%, they don't tend to make it to 100%. Unmonitored payment boxes are, after all, usually locked and chained to the table.

The *witt* instinct works well when people are clear about what good or service they are ultimately contributing to. Most people tip waiters they will never see again, make contributions to charity and ignore many opportunities to escape without paying. We are all made better off, through better table service, charitable provision and easier payment methods. If too many people were to be selfish, the system would break down. Only social convention determines whether it works. The *witt* instinct is encouraged in children and reinforced by strong social norms, which when we occasionally break them induce the memory of a parental voice: "… just imagine if everyone did that!" Indeed, sharing within families is perhaps our introduction to the idea, and the dilemmas, of public goods.

In other contexts, especially where people are doubtful about the benefits of a particular public good, the *witt* instinct is not strong enough. Although many people will sacrifice their own economic self-interest (money, time or comfort) to purchase more expensive (or less effective) environmentally friendly products, or to recycle their waste, or to conserve resources like water, many others will not. We'll return to how to get the best from the *witt* instinct. For now, it is important simply to note that it can work very effectively and that it motivates behaviour in at least some areas of the economy.

How do you eat yours?

Jonathan Swift, the author of *Gulliver's Travels*, didn't require cleverly designed experiments to grasp the workings of the mind. Swift's hero, Gulliver, after arriving in Lilliput, is told how the land has become involved in a long and bitter war with a neighbouring country. The dispute apparently escalated from a deep philosophical disagreement; a fundamental issue that left "Big Endians" and "Little Endians" at each other's throats. Big Endians fervently believe people should start at the big end, while Little Endians are just as convinced it should be the little end – when eating a boiled egg, that is. Satire often consists of an accurate social observation exaggerated out of all proportion. *Gulliver's Travels* was published in 1726 and this passage satirized, brilliantly, the similarity between Catholics and Protestants, who were seemingly unable to live together with their differences. By homing in on the arbitrariness of how people group themselves together and the powerful effect of belonging to such groups, Swift had hit upon a strong human instinct.

Just how strong was revealed by the groundbreaking social psychologist Henri Tajfel. A Polish Jew by birth, Tajfel was a chemistry student at the Sorbonne in 1939. Called up into the French army, he was captured by the Nazis, who throughout his long imprisonment never realized that Tajfel was Jewish. By the time the war was over, he had developed an understandable interest in the psychology of group behaviour, which he turned into a highly successful career. Tajfel's most celebrated contribution was the development of the "minimum group paradigm". The idea was to create groups using minimal and arbitrary criteria, then explore the effect on people's behaviour of being identified with a group. One method was to flash dots on a screen, ask subjects to guess the number, then divide them into high-guessers and low-guessers. Another similar method employed the colour that half the population insists is blue, the other half green. Having assigned people to groups, Tajfel discovered that being a member of a group changed behaviour, even though the criterion for membership was utterly arbitrary. In subsequent unrelated activities and games, which included economic tasks such as dividing money between others, subjects would systematically discriminate in favour of members of their own group. This favouritism occurred even with decisions that did not involve teams, competition or face-to-face interaction. The mere knowledge of group membership changed behaviour.

Tajfel did not try assigning people to groups by asking whether they were a Big Endian or a Little Endian. But if grouping people by how we label borderline hues affects our behaviour, it seems sure that he would have got the same result with groups defined by how people eat boiled eggs. Swift, I suspect, would have been unsurprised.

So let's call this instinct to form and favour group ties the *endian* instinct.*

The minimum group paradigm is most often cited by those seeking to explain discrimination. Indeed, on learning of this experimental demonstration of the *endian* instinct, some people react with despair at what it suggests about human susceptibility to prejudice, as if it constitutes proof that people are instinctive bigots – prone to racism and unable to grow out of picking on the kid with ginger hair. Sure, there is an ugly side to the *endian* instinct, as Swift foresaw 250 years before Tajfel studied the issue scientifically. But the *endian* instinct would be unlikely to play such a prevalent role in our natures were it solely destructive. Just as our selfish instinct can inspire cowardly acts of greed or courageous acts of self-preservation, so the *endian* instinct can foster blind prejudice or reinforce social solidarity. Having observed at first hand not only the group mentality of Nazi guards, but also solidarity between prisoners of war, this point was one Tajfel was inclined to remind people of.

Again, the *endian* instinct is not hard to locate in the wider economy. Identifying with a group changes what people will pay. The price of football shirts is testimony to the power of the *endian* instinct. Marketing people exploit it constantly. Adverts imply that by driving a certain car, wearing a particular brand or drinking a specific liqueur, one becomes part of a social elite. Others suggest that eating domestically reared beef is an expression of true patriotism. It's all nonsense; but it's effective nonsense. American colleges and universities provide a nice example too. They obtain over 30% of all donations from former students. Research on these donations shows that the alumni who give the most tend to be the richest, as one might expect. But some studies have found that subjective surveys of college loyalty predict donations better than objective measures. Those who have

---

* Personally, I am a Little Endian who is constantly surprised by the tendency of Big Endians to defend their clearly impractical method of tackling a boiled egg. They even attempt the impossible task of converting me to what they, incomprehensibly, see as a superior approach.

fond memories or were in social fraternities give more. Donations are higher around reunion years and even rise and fall with the performance of college sports teams. Higher education is a public good to which alumni make greater financial contributions when they feel part of a group.

Studies also show that people tend to trade and hire more within their own ethnic or national group. Once again, this can be viewed negatively or positively. Sometimes, it reflects narrow-minded racism. On the other hand, mutual economic support within, say, a disadvantaged immigrant community can be crucial to overcoming the economic barriers it faces. For now, the issue is not whether the *endian* instinct is ultimately good or bad, but whether it operates in real markets, which it appears to do.

Selfishness is not alone

In the Ultimatum Game, people make sacrifices, even large sacrifices, to punish those who deny them a fair share of a gain – the *yucki* instinct. Evidence suggests the *yucki* instinct influences everyday transactions, through people's willingness to pay prices and agree wages. In Prisoner's Dilemma and Public Good Games, people make individual sacrifices to achieve better solutions for all – the *witt* instinct. Contributions to public goods in the real economy show how sometimes we all benefit from the *witt* instinct. In the minimum group paradigm, people alter their economic (and other) behaviour according to their membership of groups – the *endian* instinct. Generosity towards others and choice of trading partners in the wider economy are influenced by the *endian* instinct. The *yucki*, *witt* and *endian* instincts all lead people to defy standard economics, in laboratories and real markets. These instincts therefore prove more powerful, in many situations, than the selfish instinct to maximize our own individual gain. Selfishness is not the only economic motive. This is what the evidence shows.

It is often difficult to make these arguments without being drawn into a long-standing and deep philosophical argument about whether true selflessness, or altruism, really exists. Some argue that any act people voluntarily undertake must be selfish, or else they wouldn't undertake it. This view reduces generosity to the desire for the nice feelings or plaudits that accompany it. The games and situations described above studiously ignore this inviting intellectual cul-de-sac. To truly understand economic behaviour is to be able to explain and foresee people's decisions. Orthodox economic theory, based on a simplification of our minds that says people are selfish and independent, predicts particular outcomes in the examples above. Its predictions are wrong. Arguing that people are similarly selfish, whichever option they choose, contributes nothing to our understanding; although it may salve the consciences of those few who always prioritize their own pocket. Isolating other instincts permits more accurate predictions of people's behaviour, adding to our understanding.

Nevertheless, people can be hard to convince. Some who are sceptical of the methods of behavioural economics and social psychology modify Gary Becker's argument that market forces must drive out irrationality. They argue, similarly, that selflessness could not survive in competitive markets because selfishness would drive it out. Selfish people would keep on doing better than selfless people until the latter changed their attitude. As before, this argument is wrong. First of all, the evidence shows, simply, that selfless acts do occur in market economies. Second, the argument's idea of evolutionary forces is again too simplistic. Selfish people do not always make more money. It depends on the economic environment – as the following experiment shows.

Take a Public Good Game in which a group of subjects each get £10 to divide between themselves and "the pot", which will be increased and then split equally. Players, sitting at remote computers, are anonymous and identified only by numbers. As we know, players will contribute on average about half of their money to the pot. But suppose the game is repeated with the same players, such that in successive rounds they get more sums to divide, and that players are given feedback after each round. They can see on their screens who contributed what to the previous pot ("Player No. 1 put in £4", "Player No. 2 put in £7", etc.). What will happen in the second round?

In the absence of any communication between players, contributions to the pot usually decline. Although initial contributions are substantial, players resent those who put in less and tend to reduce their own contribution in the next round. Successive rounds produce a race to the bottom, as the *witt* instinct falls prey to selfishness and most contributions, though not all, fall to zero. The difficulty of this anonymous Public Good Game is that the only way a player can punish tight-fisted contributions is to reduce their own contribution in the next round, which punishes everyone. In this game, this particular economic environment, selfishness does drive selflessness out.

But two researchers in behavioural economics, Ernst Fehr from Switzerland and Klaus Schmidt from Germany, changed the game. After each round players could still see who had contributed what. But before the start of the next round they were permitted to punish other players, individually, if they wanted to. Meting out an individual punishment required some sacrifice. Players could pay, say, £1 of the money they had made to reduce the takings of another player by £3. Introducing individual punishment to the game completely changed the result. Some players selflessly sacrificed a bit of their takings to punish those few players who contributed less than the rest. The result was that contributions to the pot remained high. The race to the bottom became a push for the top, as in successive rounds the pot increased, until almost all the money was going in and everyone ultimately emerged better off. Instead of the *witt* instinct being undermined by a minority selfishly free-riding on the generosity of others, this mini-society rewarded the *witt* instinct, reformed offenders and reaped greater overall benefit.

Whether selfish instincts trump selfless instincts depends on the nature of the game. If it is possible to punish selfishness in some way, the selfless people can drive out the selfish ones, making us all better off. Once again, it is the interaction between the individual and the environment which matters.

This also suggests a different perspective on the Ultimatum Game. The *yucki* instinct may be operating like punishment in Fehr and Schmidt's repeated Public Good Game. Responders may be punishing selfish people on behalf of us all, as if the Ultimatum Game were an ongoing, society-wide Public Good Game, in which the public good is fairness. Greedy proposers will then be less likely to treat others unfairly. Each responder makes a sacrifice, trusting that others in their situation will do the same – as, in fact, others do. Proposers, meanwhile, mostly offer a fair share anyway, either because they believe in being fair, or because fairness is prized by enough people that being unfair risks punishment. If so, then it is selfishness which is driven out. When volunteers in Ultimatum and Public Good Games are asked to explain why they behaved as they did, "fairness" is mentioned as a primary influence.

Interestingly, the *endian* instinct can also act to drive selfishness out. We have already seen that donations are more generous when people identify with the group that benefits. But there is experimental evidence too. Something really interesting happens when group identity is allowed into the Ultimatum Game and Public Good Games. Social interaction between subjects in these experiments seems to strengthen the *yucki* and *witt* instincts. The effect is strongest if the volunteers are allowed to discuss the game – promises tend to be made and kept. But even if there is no discussion of the game, if subjects are part of a previously formed group, or if they socialise a little beforehand, or if they merely experience some silent time to get used to each other's company, simply placed in the same room, they increasingly feel as if they belong to a group. The *endian* instinct kicks in. Offers from proposers are more generous; or contributions to the pot higher. This matches what we observe in the real economy.

Honesty boxes are most likely to work when they involve groups of people who share an interest, such as hikers, music fans or lovers of a particular beauty spot; people who identify with each other.

Instead of assuming, wrongly, that selfishness dominates other economic instincts, we need to work out why instincts that can override selfishness have developed. Something about our economic environment must foster them. Transactions are risky and uncertain – we can be MISLED. As Muddletonians, we instinctively favour what is familiar, to reduce the risk and uncertainty surrounding economic exchanges. Familiarity, as the word suggests, applies to people too. Thus, one way to make the world more predictable is to nurture and exploit alliances. Alliances can be thought of as forming ever widening circles of decreasing strength, starting from an inner circle of family and friends, then going wider to colleagues, acquaintances, people who apparently share our interests or are similar to us, and finally complete strangers.

Mutual support between family and close friends involves large investments of time and money. Here, the *witt* instinct is strong. We make sacrifices and expect them in return. We offer support when times are bad, share useful experience and information. Sometimes we are let down; mostly we are not. But the evidence shows that we seek and exploit alliances far beyond our inner circle of family and friends. The *yucki* and *witt* instincts are manifestations of unspoken mutual alliances to support fairness, which although stronger between people familiar with each other nevertheless operate between total strangers. Group identity helps to cement these alliances. The *endian* instinct is so strong that we quickly identify others with whom we have anything in common and try to strengthen the alliance. This is the people equivalent of the "mere exposure" effect that we met earlier – even the slightest familiarity with someone else leads us in their direction.

These instincts help us to cope with an unpredictable economy, in which support, experience and information matter to us. In a society where our fellow citizens are prepared to punish people for unfair division of gains we are all less likely to be MISLED. Where gains from trade are fairly shared, people have more margin for error and can be more confident that each exchange will bring benefits. A society in which people form alliances is likely to be one in which exchanges are more predictable, because experience and information are shared and people have the benefits of mutual support and trust.

These are the rewards of selflessness in a market economy. They are not individual, but collective. We all have an instinct to be selfish, and it is stronger in some than others. But we are not Marketopians, for whom selfishness trumps all else. Our selfish instinct is held in check by instincts to form alliances with other people; instincts that help us all in an unpredictable economy. Muddletonians need other Muddletonians.

Economically literate outrage

At the height of the Irish Ferries dispute, one of Ireland's highest-profile economists found himself in hot water. Speaking on national television, Dr Dan McLaughlin would not condemn the slashing of wages and conditions proposed by Irish Ferries. "I don't quite understand what the problem is," he said. "It's a private company. It's decided to do this. You either accept it or you don't. If we live in a capitalist system, you accept it." Many angry phone calls from members of the public later, Dr McLaughlin, chief economist at Bank of Ireland, felt the need to stress that he was speaking in a personal capacity and not on behalf of his employer. Oops. To be fair, many of his fellow professional economists were saying the same thing. If you are trained to believe that the world works (or should work) like Marketopia, then you believe that people are selfish, at least economically speaking, and that companies should make as much profit as possible and not care about things like fairness. Many economists often talk as if the public simply fails to grasp such basic economic reality.

The problem is that mainstream economics may have basic economic reality wrong. The evidence shows that the majority of people are not motivated as economists have traditionally assumed, nor need they be for markets to work. Our selfish instincts are complemented by instincts to form selfless alliances with others. In the Irish Ferries dispute, workers' refusal to accept the company's exploitative offer, at a potential cost to themselves, was an example of the *yucki* instinct in action. Individual union members stuck together, as a group, to risk their redundancy pay in support of a better deal for all – the *witt* and *endian* instincts in action. Their decision was also of potential benefit to workers in other industries, whose employers might think twice about trying to drive down wages and conditions, as well as to the incoming foreign workers who ultimately got higher wages. The union's behaviour was consistent with all three of the economic instincts described in this chapter, which the majority of us who "live in a capitalist system" share. Mass support for the union was therefore understandable.

Importantly, nothing in this argument means that unions necessarily get it right and companies do not, for it is sometimes the other way around. The dispute at Irish Ferries is just one example. Unions have at times used the threat of industrial action to take so much revenue for the workers that companies could not operate properly. In such cases, it is the union which is being too selfish and undermining the principle of sharing gains fairly.

Believers in the perfection of Marketopia find this argument about selfishness hard to swallow. They claim that even though the majority of us have selfless instincts, the economy would nevertheless work better if we didn't. Logically, it is possible that if we all suddenly became Marketopians and stopped bothering about each other, it *could* make the economy more efficient. But I doubt whether it *would*. Because this is to forget how difficult it is to ensure that transactions are beneficial – how easy it is to be MISLED. If everyone in a capitalist economy behaved utterly selfishly, if we didn't seek alliances and make sacrifices to support them, if we didn't look out for each other, if we didn't punish selfish people, then trade would probably be more hazardous and less beneficial than it is. A world where people cared only for themselves would have more risk and uncertainty. It would deny us alliances with others, which through trust, mutual support and the sharing of experience and information make buying and selling more predictable and attractive. There is no natural association between mutually beneficial trade and selfishness. A market of selfless traders may be more efficient than a market of selfish ones. The irony is that those arguing for a more selfish worldview may actually be advocating something that would reduce the volume of mutually beneficial trade and make markets less efficient – hardly their aim.

If I am wrong and these selfless economic instincts are actually bad for us, then here is something odd: we pass them on to our children. For example, the Ultimatum Game has been played with kids. Little children behave quite selfishly, with proposers consistently offering less than 30% and responders accepting these small offers most of the time. But by the time they reach the age of eleven, most children reject offers of less than 30%, and once they are eighteen, almost all do. Similar results occur with Public Good Games. But, interestingly, if our children go on to study economics, they appear to lose maturity. A number of studies have found that when economics students are used as experimental subjects, they are more inclined to behave selfishly than students of other disciplines. This association between economic orthodoxy and childishness is fairly amusing to those of us struggling to open the profession's mind – patiently enduring the toddler-tantrums of the traditionalists as the evidence piles up. But it has a serious side. If we teach and argue for an economics based on the assumption that selfishness brings rewards for all, we may damage successful capitalism, not promote it. We have probably developed strong, selfless economic instincts for good reasons. Without understanding what those reasons are, it could be very unwise to assume that selfless instincts are detrimental to economic efficiency. Consideration of the unpredictability of our economic environment suggests selfless instincts may be a glue without which markets would come unstuck.

The *yucki*, *witt* and *endian* instincts, particularly the first two, are more often used as examples of the failure of conventional economics than as a basis for building new economic models. But this is no academic argument. The findings may, ultimately, prove to have controversial implications. They show that economic alliances are strongest between people with most in common. Meanwhile, globalization is forging economic relationships across cultural and national boundaries. It is no accident that the dispute at Irish Ferries, a clash between international competition and fairness, was a useful example for highlighting these instincts. It is interesting to consider other issues of globalization in the same context.

Take the heated debate about "sweatshops". Outrage is frequently expressed at the tiny proportion of the price of goods that goes to the workers in developing countries who make them, especially in the clothing industry. Many economists say this outrage is economically illiterate, because it arises from failure to understand how markets work. The two most common points they make are, first, that workers take jobs in sweatshops only if the work is better than the alternatives and, second, that if wages were pushed higher, the jobs would disappear. This, apparently, is how markets work. It is certainly how standard economics suggests they work.

But the *yucki*, *witt* and *endian* instincts affect how markets work too. When jobs pay low shares of the revenue they create, most of us find it unfair. In developed countries people seem to respond with the *yucki* instinct and so tell the company to raise its wage or keep its job. That very poor people don't suggests that wage deals in sweatshops are probably negotiated differently from wage deals in developed countries. This could be because the poor are desperate and so take unfair deals. But evidence does not support this view – the *yucki* instinct is strong among poor people too. More likely is that other forces are at work. The international supply chain is hard to follow, with goods marketed and sold far away. Workers mostly have no idea how much revenue their labour creates and often don't even know which company they are ultimately supplying goods for. The *yucki* instinct cannot operate without this information. Even where information is available, workers are frequently denied the legal right to organize and demand a fair share of revenue, or punished if they try. Where employers have superior information and employees lack rights, the *yucki* instinct is suppressed.

Workers' shares of revenue are often so low that increasing them would be a marginal cost to major multinationals and very significant to the lives of workers. Yet companies often argue that fierce competition means they have to drive labour costs as low as possible. Here, the *witt* instinct seems to fail where it could succeed. Competing companies could agree to meet more generous labour standards, provided they could trust each other to meet them and get redress when competitors did not. Why can't competing companies make the *witt* instinct work between them? And why do international organizations lack the teeth or motivation to help make it work? These are, of course, difficult questions. But it is not economically illiterate to raise them, nor to think that such challenges could be met.

In developed countries, where there is more organized labour and better information on industrial activity, the same companies cannot get away with it. Thus, there is also the suspicion that the *endian* instinct is working against people in sweatshops. If the workers shared nationality and culture with the people in the countries who ultimately buy the goods they make, would their conditions still be so bad?

Traditional economic theory assumes that the labour market in a sweatshop works just the same way as it does in an air-conditioned office in a rich country. This is probably wrong. Selfless economic instincts may not work in the sweatshop as they do in the office, nor as they did in the richer nations during the decades when they became rich. Back when times were tougher in developed countries, the fact that bosses and workers usually came from the same community, with shared information and a sense of identity, may well have led to better pay and conditions. Essential forces behind the success of markets in developed countries might, therefore, be missing in the market for sweatshop labour. It is not bad economics to express disquiet about this – indeed, it may be the very opposite. A better understanding of our economic instincts may make for economically literate outrage.

Going to work is arguably the biggest transaction we ever undertake. The exchange of our toil and sweat for wages seems simple enough, as does selling what we produce for the revenue that pays our wages. But, as you're probably beginning to suspect by now, and as the following chapters will show, workplaces turn out not to be as simple as that.

6

The elephant on the corner billboard

STARTING UP A COMPANY is, by turns, thrilling and terrifying – one of those things it's better to have done than to be doing. That, at least, was my experience.

We were a new radio station and the low point occurred just after the company's first birthday. We knew that many people who tried the station liked what they heard, but we were failing to get noticed. When the official listenership figures arrived, they were dismal. The advertisers who provided our income, seeing the same numbers we were staring at, would quickly realize there was little point in advertising with us. We were in deep trouble. Shareholders started to pull out, tempers were lost, teamwork and trust began to break down. I had personally recruited over forty journalists whose jobs were now in jeopardy. It was miserable.

The board of a struggling firm will often send in consultants; international specialists who know the market in many countries. They bring pet ideas and potential rescue plans. They also assess the day-to-day management and report back: time for a new top team? So it was no surprise when a confident stranger appeared in my office doorway, looking fresh off the plane. "Here's what you need to do, Pete, mate." He hadn't introduced himself, though he knew my name. "You need to understand your market, mate." Consultants are hardly famed for modesty, but this guy had the air of a man who thought he could market anything.

Without a flicker, he outlined his plan. First we should assign a dedicated researcher to find a kid dying of cancer. It would be important, apparently, that the child should not be merely suffering from cancer, but dying, and not too soon either. We should explain to the parents that the station wanted to set up a charitable fund to help families in similar circumstances, attracting donations from listeners. We should offer to name the fund after their child, provided the family was prepared to tell their ongoing story in regular interviews. After finding the "right" family, we should record and broadcast the, doubtless harrowing, interviews. We should then play tear-jerking extracts from them, throughout the day, every day, complete with emotional music and a voice-over describing one small family's extraordinary courage in the face of tragedy. "You know the kind of thing, mate." When the child died, we should broadcast extensive live coverage of the funeral and try to involve the newspapers.

As I attempted, with great difficulty, not to verbalize the screams coming from my conscience, the consultant pulled out an unfeasibly small laptop, fired it up on my desk, and clicked open a fancy piece of radio software. "Listen to this, mate." The same plan had, it seemed, worked wonders for a similar station in another country. He played me clips of an interview with the child, now deceased, then promotional extracts, complete with pleading, wrenching, seemingly compassionate script, delivered as only seasoned radio presenters deliver. This station had, he said, gone from hopeless case to market leader in a few short months.

The punchline was yet to come. Closing his laptop, the consultant, for the first time, smiled. "Mate, how many marketing guys do you know who got their logo on to a kid's coffin?" The answer was, and thankfully still is, just the one. As is doubtless clear, I didn't implement his scheme and, I'm glad to say, the radio station survived without it. Since then, more stations around the world may have adopted it, I don't know.

Few economists have ever spent time running a business. Most work in large organizations managed by others, like universities, government agencies or major banks. Spending time at the economic coalface increased my doubts about the orthodox economics I had been trained in. It also gave me insight into the power of marketing. For instance, two things now strike me about the episode with the consultant. First, he was better at making money than I will ever be. He did, indeed, understand his market. He knew how to orchestrate an intense relationship between the station and its listeners, who would then hear lots of adverts, making the station a pile of cash (some of which would handsomely reward the consultant). Second, the relationship between company and consumer he aimed to develop was an utter fraud. If listeners knew about the radio station's insincerity and the moral blackmail of a vulnerable family, many would object and end their relationship with the radio station by switching over. But the company controlled all the relationships, so listeners were unlikely ever to know.

Something to relate to

Modern marketing is all about understanding and manipulating the relationship between company and consumer. This doesn't mean all marketing professionals are out to deceive us. Like businesspeople generally, they can use their talents honestly, to market products they believe in, or ruthlessly, to market anything that will make money. "Relationship marketing" is just a way of thinking, developed through years of experience and research into how people decide what and what not to consume. While economists like me entertain theories about how people buy and sell, marketing professionals live or die by them. Marketing people are, therefore, very interested in our economic instincts. Economists, on the other hand, could pay much more heed to how marketing works.

Take the case of the unfortunate producers of Danish Butter

Cookies. Their product was sweet and buttery, presented in a traditional tin, featuring pictures of the Danish Royal Guard and Copenhagen's famous "Little Mermaid" sculpture. The cookies were high quality and selling well. Then the producers decided to supply direct to the cut-price German supermarket chain Aldi. Standard economic theory would tell you that, at Aldi's lower price, demand for the delicious cookies would be even higher. Sales should have risen. In fact, demand plummeted and the commemorative tins piled up.

In the marketing literature, this story has become a case study to explain the dangers of cheapening the brand. People bought Danish Butter Cookies when they were feeling a bit special; to mark an occasion, for visitors, or perhaps as a gift. Once the cookies appeared on discount supermarket shelves, though the taste was still buttery and sweet, and the tin still fancy, they ceased to be a bit special. The producers had thus mismanaged the relationship with their customers. With better marketing, involving more market research and feedback from customers, they might have realized that a primary attribute of their brand was that it was perceived as a treat. On cut-price shelves, it ceased to be so.

If "relationship marketing" still sounds like psychobabble, here's a contrasting example. As the UK economy grew in the 1990s, many more people wanted to buy BMWs. Standard economics says that BMW, facing increased demand, should have increased its price and supply of cars, thereby making lots more profit. BMW's response was different. In 1998 the company decided to limit UK sales. It actively prevented too many BMWs being sold, even though it could have supplied more cars for more profit. Why? Because the company understood that the relationship between BMW drivers and the company was based on exclusivity. It realized that putting too many BMWs on the road would damage the long-term relationship with loyal customers. As a company spokesman rather coyly put it: "This is a question of balancing our brand image." Unlike the producers of Danish Butter Cookies, BMW sacrificed an immediate opportunity for profit to protect a lucrative relationship with its customer base. That's good relationship marketing.

Relationship marketing involves researching and understanding the perceptions and behaviours of existing and potential customers. The knowledge gained is then used to strengthen the relationship. This technique, for all its simplicity, is the culmination of about two centuries of marketing activity; a history that tells us much about how marketing works.

While there is some dispute about when marketing as such first emerged, it seems to have begun in earnest during the Industrial Revolution. This, in itself, is telling. The Industrial Revolution delivered many more new products, much greater availability and the possibility of constant product development. Put simply, in countries where the Industrial Revolution took hold, innovation became a fact of life. From the Industrial Revolution onwards, firms therefore faced the problem of how to get the market interested in innovations. The first method they developed, still the biggest component of marketing, was advertising.

Until the early nineteenth century, trade cards and posters were the primary forms of advertising. Relatively expensive to create and distribute, they were largely used to spread the word about one-off events, such as big shipments, grand openings and so on. But with the advent of newspapers and magazines, firms began to advertise as a matter of routine, on a long-term basis. By the latter half of the century, a large number of companies, big and small, were advertising in the USA and Britain. Food, clothing and cleaning products, a major part of household spending in those days, were common advertised goods. The perception that emerged, clearly, was that advertising worked. *The Grocer*, a magazine launched in 1862 and still going today, told its Victorian readers to "advertise to keep alive".

The content of early advertisements tells us much about how companies perceived the problem of attracting customers. Most ads tended to quote prices, describe goods and explain where to get them. An early advertiser in 1860s New York was B.T. Babbitt, supplier of household goods, or "articles of everyday use", in Babbitt's words. By today's standards, Babbitt's ads were like reading an essay, with about fifty lines of text and a dozen listed prices. But, in a sign of things to come, Babbitt's soap powder was "celebrated", its unlikely promise was "washing without labor", and above the text was the tagline "to meet the wants of families". Nevertheless, the main emphasis was on supplying information to the customer, making them aware of products, prices and availability.

By the end of the nineteenth century, adverts had started to change. Less priority was given to information and more to persuasion, with images depicting lifestyles and emotions. Even in Victorian Britain, sex was used to sell, though it was fairly well covered up. Hudson's marketed a soap called "forget-me-not" – positively racy for the era. The turn of the century was a golden age of capitalism, especially in America. As innovation and mass production opened up new markets, good mass marketing was a distinct advantage. Large corporations began to research which ads worked best. King Camp Gillette, with his creative packaging and star endorsements, was a marketing pioneer.

By the 1920s, newspaper and poster ads had honed in on methods that have changed remarkably little since. Images were bold, colourful and eye-catching. Text was kept to a minimum. The aim was to deliver a crisp message with which the consumer might identify. Thus, posters for AutoMatic provided just one reason to buy their Model 20 washing machine: the working man should "Be a real Santa Claus to the wife". With appropriate updates to image and sexual politics, the same ad could appear today.

Any theory of what consumers are like, how we are drawn to purchase, should be able to account for this evolution of the advert, which is characterized by the steady extinction of product information, bettered by cleverness, punch and style. Why did advertising progress from extensive written information to simple, striking, emotionally charged images, rarely accompanied by more than a single phrase?

Marketing changed again, and radically, in the 1950s. By then, it was understood that consumer behaviour was not driven by price and product alone, but seemed to be more subtle. Marketing people tried to peer into the consumer's mind, using customer feedback forms, market research surveys and product trials. Advertising became only part of the marketing mix. Borrowing more and more techniques from social science, especially psychology, marketing also began to take off as a respectable academic discipline. "Marketing science" had arrived.

In 1960, Theodore Levitt of the Harvard Business School wrote a groundbreaking article: "Marketing Myopia". In it, he argued that the key question managers had to be able to answer was: "What business are you in?" The answer, said Levitt, should not be a good or service, but the want or need it satisfied. Those who thought they were in the railroad business were not – they were in the transportation business. Instead of a product focus, a company needed a customer focus; not a production orientation, but a market orientation. In fact, the story of Danish Butter Cookies is a classic case of Levitt's marketing myopia. The firm thought, wrongly, it was in the biscuit business. It was really in the treat business.

Once Levitt's message had sunk in, the profession was just one step away from relationship marketing. Marketing scientists began to discover that consumers didn't care only about the ability of the product to match their wants and needs. As consumers, it turns out, we constantly assess companies, brands and products, on just about every dimension possible. All kinds of dealings with a firm can influence the chance that we will do business with them. As well as the desirability and price of the product, consumers care about ease of purchase, whether the company meets its promises, the attitude and personality of company staff, the reputation of the company, the after-sales service – indeed, any aspect of a business you can think of. This matches our Muddletonian instinct to seek any social signals we can to reduce the uncertainty of exchanges. The whole relationship between company and consumer is what matters.

So here is an interesting thing: orthodox economics has paid hardly the slightest attention to any of these developments. Pick up a standard economics textbook and you will be lucky to find any reference to marketing. Yet, in the real world, successful companies have large, sometimes very large, marketing departments, and almost every transaction is preceded by numerous attempts to communicate the benefits of the product, even if only via its packaging. You can't go for a day in a modern economy without being exposed to marketing messages. They are on billboards and bus stops, packets and wrappers, TV and the internet. Even if you don't leave the house, brand names, logos and taglines are on products you already own. Unless you strip off and sit naked in the middle of a desolate moor, marketing people are constantly communicating with you – a ubiquitous presence in modern life.

Surely, therefore, despite being virtually ignored by traditional economics, marketing must have an important or essential role in the economy. In the area of economics, marketing is the elephant in the corner.

Advert your gaze

As one might expect from its 200-year pedigree, this elephant in the corner is no baby. Advertising is the largest component of marketing spend and the easiest one to compare figures for. Numbers compiled by *Advertising Age* show that, in 2006, total spending on advertising in the USA amounted to 2.2% of national income. That's getting on for $1,000 for every person in America. The biggest advertisers were Procter & Gamble, AT&T and General Motors. Procter & Gamble spent an incredible $5 billion on ads (including over $200 million on Gillette). Forty so-called "mega-brands" were backed by over $1 billion. The extent of advertising in other developed countries, while not quite so spectacular, is nevertheless pretty similar. Advertising is one of the world's biggest industries and marketing as a whole is, obviously, bigger still.

Why do economists avert their gaze and ignore the elephant? Because marketing, at first glance, shouldn't be there. It is not consistent with the view of our economic instincts that traditional economics has adopted, because it suggests that people's tastes and preferences might be manipulated, or in some way irrational. In Marketopia, for example, there is no marketing. There's no need for it. Marketopians know their own preferences and tastes, don't care about the reputations or opinions of others, spend their money rationally and are already aware of all available economic opportunities. So what would be the point of marketing?

Strictly speaking, then, marketing seems to violate standard economics by its mere existence. Marketing appears to have the ability to influence the simple transaction, to destabilize the economic atom. If we are persuaded to buy a certain product when, in fact, we would be better off buying a different one, or not buying one at all, then marketing results in people being MISLED. If transactions we freely enter into don't produce mutually beneficial gains, or if we don't opt for the transactions that are most beneficial to us, then some great economic totems tumble. A free market, with persuasive marketing, may be inefficient. The consumer might not be a true sovereign, but may really resemble a puppet king. If people akin to the consultant who visited my office are successful, then it suggests that companies do not make money merely by satisfying our tastes and preferences, but by distorting them and fooling us instead. Such implications, for many economists, are close to heresy.

Denial is always an option and, in this case, it's the one that my profession has traditionally taken. I am aware of two economic theories of advertising, which I will describe shortly. But they are not part of a standard economic education, which simply ignores marketing, in all its forms. You needn't take my word for this. As far back as the 1930s one of Harvard's top economists, Edward Chamberlin, thought that marketing raised such fundamental economic issues that he referred to "… neglect by economists of a force of such overwhelming importance …". In those days, economists often argued that advertising, in particular, wasn't effective enough to distort people's purchasing habits. If this had turned out to be true, then the rather odd implication would have been that almost all the world's major companies routinely wasted vast sums of money.

Besides, as more data became available, the idea that marketing didn't work became untenable. One simple method for testing the effectiveness of marketing is to compare sales before and after the onset of a campaign. The result is clear: firms tend to increase sales, occasionally substantially, although campaigns vary greatly in effectiveness. A second method is to look at data for all the firms in an industry and see whether companies that spend most on marketing also make higher profits. An issue with this method is that it is difficult to separate alternative explanations. Marketing may increase profits, but profits may also increase marketing – it is hard to tell which is causing which. Nevertheless, firms that spend on marketing do, indeed, make greater profits. It is also possible to study individual consumers. Researchers have attached devices to televisions to record which adverts we watch, then compared the data with our purchasing habits. Sure enough, TV ads make us more likely to buy what's advertised. Denial is not an option – there really is an elephant in the corner.

In defence of the profession, Chamberlin was not the only economist to point towards the corner, aghast, and try to get his colleagues to acknowledge the vast beast he could see. The career of the great English economist Alfred Marshall, arguably the inventor of the concepts of supply and demand, spanned the late nineteenth and early twentieth centuries. Observing the evolution of adverts during this period, he was troubled. Billboards didn't seem, to Marshall, to provide consumers with real information on which to base product choices, but rather to be persuasive. He therefore considered advertising to be a competitive weapon, a way of transferring custom from one business to another, yet of no benefit generally. Once one firm in an industry spent on it, so must the rest, meaning higher costs, higher prices and tough times for new businesses trying to break into a market. Marshall concluded that advertising was wasteful. The elephant wasn't only there, but unwelcome.

It wasn't until more recent times that some economists decided, finally, to square up to the intruder. Their aim was somehow to fit advertising into the framework of orthodox economics. This was a considerable intellectual challenge and, perhaps unsurprisingly, it was taken up at the University of Chicago, where Marketopia's champion, Gary Becker, was again involved.

The two economic theories of advertising accept the incontrovertible truth that adverts make us buy things we would not otherwise buy, but they maintain nevertheless that ads do not change people's tastes and preferences, nor result in irrational consumer decisions. That is, the two theories attempt to preserve the orthodox view of our economic instincts, while accounting for the existence and effectiveness of marketing, specifically advertising.

Let's look first at the more radical theory of Becker and his colleague Kevin Murphy. The argument goes like this. When consumers buy more of something after it is advertised, this is not because adverts persuade them to change their preferences, but because the combination of "product plus advert" appeals more than the product alone. This might be, for example, because the advert creates a positive image or cachet associated with the product. Instead of simply buying a pair of trainers, we *prefer* to buy a pair of trainers associated, via adverts, with some cool imagery – we like "trainers plus imagery" more than just "trainers". If so, then the ads do not change our minds or manipulate our preferences, they just *improve* the goods, as judged by stable personal preferences that are unaffected by the ads. So we need not worry that advertising causes people to select one product when another may have been better, because when an advert leads us to buy a particular product, the ad has done so by making it the better product. In effect, we consumers are still sovereign, but we have ordered our court jesters to tell attention-grabbing, exaggerated and repetitive tales about the wonders of our kingdom because, after all, royalty often likes that sort of thing.

The argument is ingenious, but is it right? There is at least one major problem with arguing that we prefer "product plus ad" to "product". Quite simply, people don't like advertising. Surveys routinely show this. We consider adverts to be a nuisance and an eyesore. Even those few ads that are clever or funny struggle to be clever or funny on tenth viewing.

Aware of this problem, Becker and Murphy argue that this dislike of ads doesn't *necessarily* prove them wrong. We sometimes consume things we don't like which complement things we do. For instance, we might spend money on vaccinations, which are positively painful, because they allow us to visit exotic locations we must otherwise avoid. Perhaps adverts are like jabs – painful at the time, yet more than compensated for by how they improve our enjoyment of the products we subsequently buy. But there remains a crucial difference that ruins this analogy. We don't enjoy vaccinations, yet, unlike adverts, we nevertheless actively seek them. Put another way, jabs are painful, but we are glad they are there. We know some people prefer "jabs plus exotic travel" to "non-exotic travel", because they will pay for vaccinations. If we really prefer "product plus ad" to "product", then we should be glad the ads are there, which surveys show we are not, and also willing to pay for them, which we are not. In fact, we have to be compensated for having them foisted upon us. Television and radio ads are surrounded by programmes we want to watch or hear. Billboards are placed between us and where we want to go.

Here's another way to think about it. Marketing companies frequently find a well-marketed food or drink product is preferred to its rivals despite the fact that blind taste tests show it to be inferior. There is a particular British brand of tea that is famous for this in marketing circles, yet which benefited from a particularly striking and long-running ad campaign.* This makes sense from the

---

* I would love to be able to reveal the brand, but I promised my source in the marketing industry that I wouldn't and, in any case, I am scared of the company's lawyers. Of course, a few blind tests in your own kitchen are likely to give you the answer.

perspective of Becker and Murphy's theory, because as consumers we might rationally be willing to sacrifice our taste buds to be associated with the striking ads. But here's a question: how do people react to knowing the results of the blind taste tests? If it really is a rational choice to buy inferior but better-advertised tea, we shouldn't care that the tea is inferior. But if, instead, we had merely been persuaded by the marketing, the results of the test should mean we feel duped and switch to the better tea. Of course, what actually happens is that we realize we've been fooled and switch brands.

In fact, marketing people frequently try to capitalize on this reaction by using it as the basis for adverts, especially those aimed at taking market share from popular brands. The famous example is Pepsi, which invited people to compare its cola in a blind test with a certain other brand. There would have been little point asking us to "take the Pepsi challenge" if our reaction to discovering that our preferred brand tasted inferior had been: "I don't care, I prefer the ads ..." In fact, the campaign was very successful.

Becker and Murphy's theory may on occasion be right, perhaps when a product is associated with a particularly funny, dramatic or spectacular advert, or one that makes something especially fashionable. But, in general, we just don't like ads enough for this theory to apply. Something else is needed to explain the presence and effectiveness of the humdrum mass of irritating marketing that, day after day, we routinely do our best to avoid.

Invisible Inc.

There is something intrinsically exciting about hidden communication. Secret messages, code-cracking, invisible ink, all conjure up images of audacious deeds and clandestine romance. According to the leading economic theory of advertising, if you can bring yourself to believe the conspiracy, adverts actually contain hidden signals, received and decoded by consumers. If this is true, marketing is not really the relentless repetition of tacky taglines, but a cryptic connection between consumer and company.

There is no one author of this theory of advertising, but perhaps the best statement of it is a paper by Evan Davis, John Kay and Jonathan Star at the London Business School, before the former became economics editor at the BBC. The theory accepts that the Marketopian ideal of individuals possessing perfect information is wrong and claims that adverts act as a kind of sticking plaster for this problem. By improving our information about products, ads help the world to function more like Marketopia. The twist in the theory is the claim that product information is not transmitted through overt pictures and advertising copy, but through two types of covert signal. Overt product information is not precluded; the idea is to explain why most ads seem to contain so little, or even none at all.

The first type of hidden signal is the company's very willingness to advertise. By spending large amounts of money advertising their product, a firm has sent a signal that it sincerely believes the venture will be a success. It has put its money where its mouth is. Furthermore, in order to afford the campaign, either the firm has convinced its financial backers that the product is worth the outlay, or it has already persuaded other consumers to buy in considerable numbers. Hence, this signals that other people sincerely believe in the product also. The primary message, then, is not the content of the ad, but the expense incurred in producing it. When this code is deciphered, it says: "People know our product is good enough to get back the money this ad cost and more." Thus, a rational consumer can infer from an expensive ad campaign that the product is likely to be good quality.

The second signal concerns what is known in marketing jargon as the product's "market position". The type of advert, the characters and situation it depicts, or any celebrity endorsements, can all signal that the product is aimed at a particular section of the population. This may be based on social class, gender, age, personality type and so on. A signal of market position is useful to consumers, because among the ever-expanding range of available products, it helps us to find the items most suitable for us. Advertising that signals market position improves the efficiency of the market by helping to match products to appropriate customers. Thus, if a celebrity appears on an advert and you have to ask your teenage daughter "Who's that?", instead of feeling old and out of touch, comfort yourself with the thought that you weren't supposed to recognize them – the ad is just efficiently signalling that the product is for her, not you.

Both of these signals, expense and positioning, are possible ways in which an advert can be of use to both company and consumer, increasing sales while guiding us to products that are both good quality and suited to us. Neither persuades us to change our preferences or tastes, nor elicits any irrational response to the advert. Furthermore, the hidden signals theory adapts easily to marketing activity other than adverts, including promotions, sponsorships, even packaging, all of which can be designed to convey expense and market position.

There is an important assumption, though, which is that consumers can believe the signals – that the secret messages are not luring us into a trap. The key issue is whether the company has any incentive to deceive us. With respect to market position, it is hard to see why a firm would not aim to attract the clientele most likely to enjoy their product. So there is no problem of deception there. But with the signal of expense, the story is more subtle, because whether expenditure on advertising is a reliable signal of quality depends on the type of product. Suppose, as with shampoo or packeted food, it is possible for consumers to assess quality reasonably soon after purchase – your dandruff vanishes, or the sauce does wonders for a sausage sandwich. With such a product, a company that heavily advertises a poor product will get caught out fairly quickly and potentially, therefore, fail to recover the cost of the ad campaign. Thus, a company has the incentive to back this type of product only if it genuinely believes in it. But what about a product where it could take years for any deception to become apparent, such as a private pension or a dishwasher? The company may have an incentive knowingly to advertise a poor product, because it will make plenty of profit long before customers discover that the fund managers were useless or the knob was inclined to fall off.

This distinction between types of product leads to a prediction that can be used to test the hidden signals theory. If this is how adverts work, then the level of advertising should be highest for products where the signal is believable, where the company would get caught and suffer fairly promptly if it spent heavily pushing a dodgy product. Davis, Kay and Star tested this by comparing advertising-to-sales ratios for different products. They found that goods consumers could assess in a reasonable period of time were, on average, more heavily advertised. So maybe it's true that we consumers expertly assess hidden signals, finding some adverts reassuringly expensive, others a natural fit to our social position.

There are, however, findings that are harder to square with the hidden signals theory. If the theory is good, companies that spend heavily on advertising should be keen for this to be public knowledge. It should be a commercial peacock's tail; a signal of pedigree, nothing to be shy about. But this is hardly the case. Firms do not strut their stuff, but are notoriously coy, embarrassed even, about the size of their advertising budgets. Also, a number of studies have examined whether the perceived expense of ad campaigns is linked to their effectiveness. Consumers are less convinced by cheap ads, in line with the theory, but we are also distrustful of particularly expensive-looking ones, feeling that the company is perhaps trying a bit too hard.

While the jury is still out on the evidence, most economists seem to be inclined to believe the hidden signals theory. It fits the general pattern described earlier. The conventional assumption that people have perfect information about products (and all other economic opportunities) is the one economists are most willing to give up. Marketing, which at first appears to be a violation of standard economics, can then be seen as a rational way to make our world more like the standard model, improving our information about products and so making mutually beneficial transactions in free markets more likely. What, at first, looked like evidence against the theory actually just shows what a good theory it is – a sort of theoretical jujitsu. In this way, all the other assumptions of Marketopia can be maintained. But, by now, the problem with this logic should be familiar. Once we accept that our economic environment is not like Marketopia, then it is likely that our economic instincts have adapted to cope, and that we are therefore not like Marketopians. Sure enough, the world of marketing provides a wealth of examples.

Two things can be true

Now for something completely different. Suppose, momentarily, that the weird sightings in the sky, most commonly reported in desert regions, are not sunlight reflecting brilliantly off small aircraft, but really are flying saucers, and that inside them are alien social scientists sent to study the human race. The data they collect contributes to a debate that is raging in the little green social science community. One group of researchers is convinced that the purpose of the bicycle is to get from A to B. They cite observations of humans leaving their homes in the morning, clearly atop a bicycle, spending the day completing menial tasks by alien standards, then returning home on the bicycle in the evening. Nevertheless, a rival group of little green scientists disagrees. It has spotted riders leaving their homes and cycling long distances, without stopping, only to return to exactly where they started. This, they say, refutes the theory. The purpose of the bicycle cannot be to get from A to B. Their alternative hypothesis is that bicycles are machines to improve the function of the human heart, which unlike little green hearts frequently malfunctions and destroys the organism. The argument rumbles on, as the Little Green

Research Council funds additional intergalactic data-collection missions aiming to resolve the issue.*

I am very grateful to an old boss of mine who first pointed out the fallacy of assuming that alternative theories, designed to explain the same phenomenon, are necessarily in opposition to each other. After watching champions of different ideas trade blows across a meeting room, he would gently point out that, as he put it, "two things can be true". A bicycle is a vehicle powered by people, and so can be used for transportation or exercise, or a mixture of the two. Marketing is a vehicle for selling products, and so can inform rational consumers, or persuade irrational ones, or a mixture of the two. In other words, even if the hidden signals theory (or, less likely in my view, Becker and Murphy's theory) has some truth in it, this does not logically imply that adverts don't also alter our preferences and tastes, or appeal successfully to irrational instincts. What does the evidence say?

Marketing professionals take it as read that their job involves persuasion and that their target audience is not rational. One of the top marketing textbooks stresses that it is a mistake to treat consumer decisions as rational.† It advises businesspeople to undertake market research because: "Customers often do not judge product values and costs accurately or objectively. They act on perceived value."

So far, so superficial. Let's dig deeper. There is now a very large body of research that addresses the issue of which marketing techniques work best and why. One of the most consistent results arising from this research is that emotional marketing, on average,

---

* This trick of viewing the world from the perspective of someone who approaches it knowing nothing, but draws some conclusions from what they observe, can be surprisingly instructive. There is a more serious example in Chapter 7.

† For an economist trained in orthodox theory, Armstrong and Kotler's *Marketing – An Introduction*, now in its eighth edition, is almost a horror story. It teaches marketing students, most of whom go on into business, to ignore just about every assumption economists make. At various points throughout the text, it advises that consumers are not independent, rational or selfish, that they do not have stable preferences and that they are often poorly informed.

works better than non-emotional appeals to logic. Thus, an advert that lists reasons why a product is better than its rivals tends to be less effective than one that, say, places the product in a family context where it appears to be popular with some healthy-looking children. A similar finding emerges with the use of drama in television commercials. Studies have found that ads employing a character and a plot are less inclined to induce counter-arguments regarding the quality of a product than adverts using a narrator to argue the product's case. The most effective emotional or dramatic ads portray scenes that associate a simple and consistent image with the brand. This trumping of meaningful information by meaningful imagery, reported in marketing science journals, mirrors the evolution of the advert up to the 1920s.

Such research has led to refinements of marketing techniques. In particular, brand managers have learned to create and reinforce "brand attributes" – simple associations with the brand in people's minds. For instance, Lucozade was a declining British brand with steadily falling sales – an old-fashioned drink for ill people. Then, in the mid-1980s, it was turned around by clever brand management. The owner, Beecham's, now part of one of Britain's biggest companies, GlaxoSmithKline, hired a firm of marketing experts called Ogilvy and Mather. They realized that Lucozade was associated in people's minds with something negative, sickness, and looked instead for positive associations they could use. They came up with "energy". Lucozade, the same drink, was reborn. Everything about it now said energy: the bottle depicted bursting bubbles, its size was reduced, enabling it to fit in sports bags, the colours were brightened, and a new ad campaign featured Olympic gold medallist Daley Thompson. The formerly sick brand sprang to life.

Lucozade's rebranding was effective, if hardly subtle. Yet branding can be both. One technique is to invite members of the public, perhaps through a focus group, to say what comes to mind when they think of the brand. In relationship marketing terms, the marketing team tries to understand how consumers relate to their brand. They then select between one and three words that encapsulate the positive feelings – the "brand essence", in the jargon. Thus, when competition ate into sales of Guinness in the 1990s, the company's research found that people's most positive associations with Guinness were watching sport, the beer's reputation for high nutritional content, and tradition. They distilled a new brand essence: "power, goodness, communion". Advertising was commissioned to give life to these concepts, featuring determined characters who performed feats of strength, often involving swimming, before a coming together at the bar, to down the swirling black goodness that seemingly inspired the feat. The same brand essence formed the heart of many quite different ads. You wouldn't know how they were conceived from watching them, but the message was consistent, subtle and effective. Sales began to rise again.

In the relationship between company and consumer, as in all relationships, deception is possible. Brand attributes can be purposefully selected to hide the truth, to strip away the negative and promote only the positive. As health concerns increasingly made a burger in a bun a negative image, McDonald's devised ads featuring trendy, skinny, carefree young people "just loving it" – an attempt to induce self-denial among a clientele that hardly resembles this image. Similarly, ads for beauty products use only people who don't need them; ice cream and chocolate ads feature people who love chocolate yet have more sex than the rest of us; and buying sensible financial services products apparently turns your grandchildren into adoring angels.

The conclusion to draw from marketing research and practice is that marketing strategies differ greatly in effectiveness. In short, content matters. Good campaigns consistently associate brands with positive attributes, usually preconceived, perhaps factual, often inaccurate, but especially emotional. And good campaigns work.

Lastly, for anyone who is still unconvinced, here is a study that provides almost irrefutable evidence of the power of marketing. Belgian economist Marianne Bertrand and some colleagues recently conducted a field experiment in conjunction with a company offering consumer loans in South Africa. The firm sent mailshots advertising loans to over fifty thousand former clients. The interest rate offered was randomized and other aspects of the mailshot were manipulated to gauge their effectiveness. Men were so susceptible to a photograph of a female employee on the mailshot that it increased their likelihood of taking up a loan by the equivalent of several percentage points of interest *per month*. Another interesting finding, consistent with our desire to avoid being MISLED, was that take-up was increased by limiting the number of available options to make the product appear more simple. These effects were as strong for more educated clients as for less educated ones.

Is it really possible to cling to the position that marketing, including modern brand management, is powerless to change our preferences and tastes, and that we consumers respond to it rationally? Covert signals of the company's expenditure can't explain why different marketing strategies that cost the same produce radically different results. One could try to argue that all marketing content signals market position, but what group within the population is defined by emotion, drama, the gender of an employee, or "power, goodness and communion"? Besides, the market position of many brands, especially older ones, is already well known.

If it looks like an elephant, walks like an elephant and sounds like an elephant, it's an elephant. It's time for us economists to face it. Marketing persuades.

Transacting on instinct

Actually, speaking as an economist, I can say that once you face the beast, it turns out to be much more friendly than you might fear. Obviously, you have to accept that marketing violates the orthodox economic model, and that our economic instincts are not those of Marketopians. But once this increasingly common perspective is adopted, the world of marketing, especially modern relationship marketing, is a great place from which to observe more about our real economic instincts.

Recall the economic instincts we have met so far. Because transactions are unpredictable, we are biased towards what is familiar and we actively seek any social signals from others about how they value products we might buy. To help us in our unpredictable economic environment, we seek to form alliances of mutual trust. The *endian* instinct leads us to seek them with people from our own social groups or, failing that, people with whom we have something, anything, in common. We are often selfless. We will make sacrifices in the hope of reaching the best common solutions – the *witt* ("we're in this together") instinct. We will also make sacrifices to punish those who betray our trust, by not contributing, or not sharing gains fairly, as in the *yucki* ("you can keep it") instinct. Now, here is an interesting thing: every one of these instincts can be found operating in the world of relationship marketing. Good marketing people understand that these are instincts we possess and tailor their dealings with us to suit.

Let's start with familiarity. The most obvious use of familiarity as a marketing tool is the endless repetition of logos, jingles and taglines. It's also why company representatives are taught to repeat your name. But our bias towards the familiar can be exploited more surreptitiously. Studies of drama and emotion in adverts show that, while these work generally, they are particularly effective if the ad manages to get us to identify with the emotion, situation or aspiration. Hence car adverts depict the pleasure of the open road, mortgage ads feature a happy couple, and shaving and make-up ads have people talking to the mirror. The more familiar it feels to us, the more effective the ad. Here's a more devious one. Have you ever played the game of trying to recognize the voice on an advert? Ads are more effective when voiced by famous people. You might think celebrity endorsement is behind this. But then why do the advertisers use the voice but not identify the person? What the advertisers are really after is a feeling of familiarity.

They also understand that we are influenced by the opinions of others. There is a whole genre of adverts designed to give convincing evaluations of products from seemingly ordinary people just like you and me. In the business, they are referred to as "testimonials". The aim is to make it as clear as possible that these are not actors, but real people. So TV footage is usually shot in the street with a slightly wobbly hand-held camera. Quotes on the billboards are very positive, but not so slick as to arouse suspicion about authenticity.

The *endian* instinct is a staple of the marketing menu. At its crudest, it involves little more than stamping the national flag on packaging, which is frequently done for all kinds of goods, from footwear to power tools. One of my favourite examples is to be found in my local supermarket, back on Leonard's Corner, where you can buy "100% Irish" chicken – how a chicken could be 70% Irish I'm not sure. Some companies like to suggest that by choosing a brand we are in effect joining a club. The US car company Saturn has even held social events for "Saturn owners". More intriguing is the relationship between the *endian* instinct and the logo. Branded clothing, bags, watches and so on offer the opportunity to show off our social status. But, through sporting particular logos, people also signal membership of many other sorts of social groups. Bands develop logos for albums, allowing free ads via the T-shirts of true fans. Logos can be used to associate products with political causes, such as drug legalization or gay rights. That said, a logo needn't stand for anything other than being the one worn by your social group. Our strong instinct to identify with groups, and to form them based on fairly arbitrary criteria, including brands of everyday items, is well known in the marketing world. Perhaps it's time we Little Endians developed our own logo?

The *witt* instinct is both exploited and feared in marketing. Most obviously, it is exploited in guilt-trip advertisements for donations to good causes which stress how many other people are contributing – we're in this together, are you doing your bit? Other cause-related marketing aims to reinforce the *witt* instinct by imploring you not to drop litter or waste water. Meanwhile, companies fear that they will be punished if they're seen not to do their bit, so they employ defensive marketing to avoid it. The best example is environmental claims, which now feature on the packaging of a vast range of products. Environmental contributions even form the basis of whole campaigns to promote oil and energy companies, for most of which renewable technology is a mere sideline.

The various ways in which prices are set tell us interesting things about the instincts of companies, which must wait for a later chapter. But marketing people often worry that setting prices too high might induce the *yucki* instinct and damage the relationship with consumers. This provides an explanation for a finding that has often puzzled economists: why do the prices of some products in extremely short supply not rise? Examples include tickets for major sporting events and concerts. Popular bands can fill venues many times over. Standard economics says that, faced with such demand, promoters should set much higher prices. But, for the most part, they don't. The same applies to toy shortages at Christmas, when excess demand leaves frantic parents unable to satisfy crazed offspring, as the toy behind the craze rapidly sells out, but at the usual price. Despite massive excess demand, marketing people know that if a company charges way above what most of us regard as a fair price, thereby inducing the *yucki* instinct, there may be long-term consequences. We may punish the company in the future, or be less inclined to believe the firm provides value for money generally.

Thus, each of the economic instincts we have met so far turns up in the world of marketing. The one I haven't yet mentioned, the most obvious, is self-interest. Of course, marketing often appeals to our self-interest, promising that parting with our money to own the product will make us better off. Value is a key part of many marketing messages. Yet, once you start viewing marketing as indicative of our economic instincts, it is interesting how much marketing plays on instincts other than self-interest.

Furthermore, the way in which much marketing appeals to our

self-interest suggests that the conception of selfishness embodied by Marketopians is inaccurate. Recall the independence of Adam and Eve. The pleasure Adam gets from what he owns is independent of what Eve owns. Marketing people understand that this is not true because, even in our more selfish moments, we instinctively evaluate much of what we own relative to what other people have. Keeping up with the Joneses provides a theme for a huge number of adverts, depicting people getting ahead of the crowd, while receiving praise from or incurring the envy of others. By my count, at least as many ads are based on social aspiration as on the material benefit of the product they push.

Interestingly, this observation matches a finding in a relatively new strand of the economics literature. Self-reported happiness research is as simple as it is controversial. For the past few decades, a number of routine surveys that collect demographic information have also asked people to rate their happiness on a scale. Researchers look at responses over time and at who is happier, on average, according to gender, income, employment status, race, age, and so on. Some economists are very sceptical of this data, because it is so subjective. Perhaps the studies tell us only who is best at lying or eliciting sympathy. But responses do tend to be in keeping with major life changes, such as bereavement, promotion or illness, and to match the assessment of friends and family. They are also correlated with the likelihood of suicide and the frequency of smiling. Whether you decide the research is flaky, fine or somewhere in between, it is interesting to note one of the main findings that emerges. Our happiness depends as much on how our income compares with those around us as on the level of our income itself. We are, of course, self-interested, and what we have matters to us. But so does how it compares with what others have.

The marketing people don't need studies of self-reported happiness to tell them this, they've been exploiting this instinct to sell stuff for years. Once technology has made a basic product sufficiently cheap that it is available to pretty much everyone, producers seek to add an element of exclusivity. The result is that rather ordinary things, such as toasters, pens, kettles, door knockers, vacuum cleaners and all manner of items of furniture, are turned into designer goods and status symbols. Of course, there is genuine value in design – we like to be surrounded by things that look and feel nice. But there is status too and, where there isn't, clever marketing people create some. It's not only the sleek and elegant design, or even the comfort and reliability, which matters, it's what your car says about you. (Actually, that last sentence is lifted straight from a car ad.)

Finally, there is one other finding of marketing science that is suggestive of a basic economic instinct. Research shows that marketing is more effective if it makes the company likeable. There is no obvious link between being able to produce a funny advert and a good product, but we are nevertheless more likely to buy brands with amusing ads. Other likeable personality traits also sell. This, once again, emphasizes the additional power of relationship marketing. Brand management, the creation and nurture of positive brand attributes, is effective. But it is possible to go further. Brand managers now try to give their brand, not just attributes, but a likeable personality. For instance, Virgin is a brand successfully applied to a whole range of different products, with no obvious common link, other than the brand's irreverent personality. Intel's jaunty audio logo, that "ding ... da-ding-da-ding", suggests that its microchips are bursting with the kind of liveliness you crave as your PC churns, grumbles and endlessly rotates that irritating little hourglass. As of now, I don't know of any behavioural economics experiment that has tested whether we are more inclined to trade with people with likeable personality traits, such as irreverence and liveliness. But I'd bet that we are.

Value Ad Tax

Marketing activity is designed to make people buy certain products and in that, as is now widely agreed, it succeeds. The question is how it achieves this aim. Marketing science has shown that different marketing techniques vary in effectiveness, irrespective of expense and market position. While consumers may rationally infer useful information about products from an ad campaign's cost or positioning, good marketing is straightforwardly persuasive. Interestingly, "persuade" is arguably even a synonym – the word "advert" is from the Latin *ad vert*, which means "turn towards". Marketing makes us buy things we would not otherwise buy, for reasons that are not necessarily rational.

Marketing science has developed the idea of relationship marketing, which mirrors findings regarding our real economic instincts and exploits our Muddletonian need for communication in an uncertain world. Indeed, understanding the instincts that govern whether we reach into our pockets for one thing rather than another is almost a job description for a marketing professional. Marketing people research and then appeal to our economic instincts, including our self-interest, our concern for relative social status, our bias towards the familiar, our strong tendency to identify with groups, our selfless desire to support common solutions and fair shares, and perhaps also a bias towards dealing with likeable personalities.

Yet why do people generally not like marketing, especially advertising? For one thing, we are wary of its power. Brand managers spend 40 or more hours a week thinking about how to get their message across, while we might spend 40 seconds absorbing or trying to ignore it. Companies market-test campaigns on small groups, sometimes employing eye-movement monitors, response boxes or galvanometers (machines that pick up skin responses) to measure what excites or grabs attention. While we might not know all this, we do perceive the huge effort that goes into persuading us to buy. The instincts that help us to trade with each other in an unpredictable world were not developed to cope with trading partners so sophisticated and powerful. People are not rational Marketopians, but we are far from stupid. We know the power of marketing, we know that we are susceptible to it, and we know that it is a battle not to be taken in. Of course we don't like it. We live with the constant suspicion that we are being fooled. Almost certainly, as the consultant who knocked on my door demonstrated, we often are.

Companies, on the other hand, have no choice. To survive in the modern economy, whether your product is good or bad, you have to market it. Consumers don't like marketing, but it works nevertheless.

There is too much marketing. We don't like marketing. We have no way to avoid marketing. Marketing wastes resources, as Alfred Marshall suspected nearly a century ago. These wasted resources include some of our smartest people, who use their considerable talents to convince us that switching shampoo will make our hair silky, who dream up unattainable aspirational images that make us feel inadequate, and who compose jingles scientifically proven to get stuck in our heads.

Given all this, here is an obvious question to ask: shouldn't marketing be taxed? A tax on marketing activity would not suffer from some of the negative things taxes tend to suffer from. It is almost impossible to have a black market. Nor can the industry relocate overseas to avoid the tax, which could be levied where the communication takes place.

Because we know that marketing persuades, new entrants in markets could be exempt from the tax for a period, to give them a chance to compete with established brands. Part of the revenue raised could go to fund objective information sources, such as research to test the quality and reliability of products, to verify marketing claims, or to protect consumer rights. Thus, any firm trying honestly to push a good product would be happy to pay the tax.

Of course, many people have criticized marketing – hardly surprising given how little we like it. When the criticism gets loud enough, the marketing profession sometimes defends itself. At one point in recent history, the American Association of Advertising Agencies decided it had to act. Its argument was that adverts don't persuade us what to buy, because only we decide what to buy. How did it try to persuade us of this? Without a hint of irony, it turned the message into a series of adverts.

7

When in company

IF YOU ARE READING these words then, statistically speaking, it is quite likely that your job involves sitting at a desk with a telephone and a PC on it. Chances are that the work you carry out at this desk involves a variety of tasks and is supervised by a boss. If you have never been an office worker, then my apologies – simply imagine for a moment that you are one.

Bosses, as we all know, vary in quality. There are bosses who inspire you, who stimulate you and who give encouraging and constructive feedback. There are also bosses who undermine you, who pick at your work and who undervalue your efforts. Pause for a moment and try to recall, or imagine, working in an office for a boss of each type.

Let's start with the bad boss. Suppose you are summoned to their door. A new project is summarily thrust into your hand, accompanied by the curt comment that it would be appreciated if you could do it a bit better and more quickly than last time. You leave the office carrying the file. Now imagine the same scenario with the good boss. You are asked to pop into their office when you have a moment. The new project is handed to you, accompanied by the sincere statement that although it represents a challenge, it is one they are confident you can meet, and that you should come back to them if you experience any difficulty. You leave the office carrying the file. Which of these characters would most inspire you to launch straight into what you were asked you to do, as opposed to quietly spending half an hour researching your next holiday on the internet? Which boss would lead you immediately to communicate the requirements of your task to colleagues, rather than sneaking away for coffee with your closest confidant for a gossip? In which scenario, when disturbed by a forwarded email containing a link to an internet video of a celebrity making an idiot of themselves, would you be most likely to delete such trivia straight away, instead of turning up the speakers, playing it a few times, using it as an excuse to start a conversation with your neighbour, then forwarding it to your address list of friends? In which environment, at the end of the working day, would you be more likely to discreetly slide a pile of office paper into your bag to restock the home printer? And, when it comes to your assigned task, for which boss would you be most likely to do the job just well enough to get by, rather than putting in a few extra hours to provide a touch of polish?

If you are anything like me, your productivity is strongly linked to who you work for. Similarly, my work-rate depends on who I am working with – the abilities and attitudes of colleagues. How interesting and challenging the work is matters too. What I'm paid is important, insofar as I get a fair wage relative to those around me, but the money I earn is not what gets me out of bed in the morning. Contrastingly, standard economics assumes that we are motivated, not by the nature of the work and the people we work with, but solely by what we get paid in return. Furthermore, fairness doesn't affect what Marketopians are paid, for in a competitive free market for labour, wages precisely match each individual's productivity.

The exchange of work for wages is the most important transaction in the whole economy. It is central to modern economic debates, such as what causes unemployment, inequality or inflation. But this simple concept, trading what we do in return for reward, is much, much older than that. It is no less than fundamental to human organization itself.

From prehistoric tribes to multinational corporations, from ancient civilizations to modern governments, people's willingness to work for others has been, and remains, the driver of human society. And evidence is emerging to challenge the traditional economic view of what motivates us to work.

You scratch my hairy back and I'll scratch yours

Our ability to form effective organizations and the instincts behind this economic behaviour probably run very deep. Humans have exchanged goods with each other for tens of thousands of years and possibly hundreds of thousands. We know this from archaeological evidence surrounding the movement of objects; the locations and depths of ancient articles found in the ground. But humans trade more than goods. Consider again the non-exhaustive list of resources we exchange, from the opening chapter: work, time, protection, ideas, shelter, promises, access, risk, skills, knowledge, rights, transport, experiences, potential, space, data and responsibility. Most of these resources are not objects, but actions or promises of actions – what we do, not what we have. It is likely that we have traded actions, not for thousands of years, nor even hundreds of thousands, but millions. Evolutionary scientists refer to this as "social exchange": an individual does something for another and gets a favour in return. We have probably traded favours with each other for far longer than we have traded goods.

How do we know we have traded favours for millions of years? First, social exchange is a universal human behaviour. Highly complex social exchanges between non-relatives take place in every human culture, including the few remaining hunter-gatherer tribes. Second, other primates also undertake social exchange. Our closest living relatives, chimpanzees, with whom we parted genetic company some

5–10 million years ago, trade favours too. It is, therefore, highly likely that our ability to benefit from social exchange has evolved through a process of natural selection. While humans are not unique in trading favours, our ability to do it is one of the defining features of our success as a species.

Throughout this book, I refer to economic "instincts" because, while the word is suggestive of evolutionary influence, it retains ambiguity – instincts can be innate or learned. Our economic instincts may be strongly influenced by natural selection or mostly handed on to our children via direction, interaction and imitation. Yet, as our understanding of evolutionary processes advances, it is becoming clearer that the debate about nature versus nurture largely misses the point. Trying to decide which of nature or nurture is the stronger influence is like searching for the very first chicken or egg – the question has no sensible answer, because it is the relationship between them that counts. Natural selection has adapted our minds to interact with our environment. Our nature is to exploit the opportunities offered by nurture.

Because our instincts result from this complex interaction between our genetic make-up and our environment, whether an individual behaviour is strongly influenced by natural selection is hard to tell. But not necessarily impossible. Evolutionary psychologists try to identify human abilities that seem to have adapted to solve a specific challenge of our environment. They look for skills that stick out from other human abilities because they are highly specialized – specific to a particular environmental context. If we locate a universal human ability that is closely matched to a specific and enduring challenge of human life, it is likely that evolution has adapted our instincts to meet the challenge.

Try this test, invented by the British psychologist Peter Wason. Placed in front of you are four cards, just like playing cards, except that each has a letter on one side and a number on the other. The four on the table before you read: A, B, 4 and 7. Your task is to test the truth of the following statement: "If there is a vowel on one side, then there is an even number on the other." You must turn over only those cards necessary to test the truth of the statement. Which cards would you turn over?

Once you have come up with your answer, try this. Again, there are four cards in front of you. This time, written on one side is a statement regarding whether a job is complete, on the other a statement about payment for the job. The cards you can see are: "job finished", "job not finished", "paid", "not paid". Your task, as before, is to turn over the cards necessary to test the truth of a statement. This time it is: "If the work is finished, then the company pays." Which cards would you turn over?

The overwhelming majority of people, 80 to 90% in some studies, get Wason's original letters and numbers task wrong. Interestingly, highly educated people are about as likely to get it wrong as less educated people. The two most common responses are to turn over just the A, or both the A and the 4. The correct answer is to turn over the A and the 7. If there is an odd number on the other side of the A, or a vowel on the other side of the 7, it disproves the statement. Contrastingly, the statement can still be true whatever is on the other side of the B or the 4.

As is doubtless obvious, the vowel-number and job-payment problems are logically identical. The statement you have to test is of the form: "If P, then Q", while the cards represent "P", "not-P", "Q", "not-Q". The correct answer is to turn over P and not-Q. Thus, the correct answer to the second task is "job finished" and "not paid". Now here's the interesting part. This time, around 80% of us get the answer *right*.

The general result, as discovered by American evolutionary psychologists Leda Cosmides and John Tooby, is that we usually get it right when the statement being tested refers to a social exchange, meaning a rule of the form: "If you take the benefit, you must pay the cost." We instinctively check the case where someone has benefited, to make sure they have paid the cost, and we also check the case where someone has not paid the cost, to be sure they haven't nevertheless taken the benefit.* We find it much easier to reason in this context of social exchange than when performing the logically identical task with letters and numbers.

Why? Cosmides and Tooby argue that humans have evolved specialized mechanisms for dealing with social exchanges. In simple terms, we have an instinct for detecting cheats. We are experts at spotting when someone takes but does not give, because getting mutual benefit from trading favours would have been very important for human survival. Experiments show that we are actually better at reasoning with a completely unfamiliar social exchange in an unknown tribe ("If you eat duiker† meat, then you must have found an ostrich egg") than we are with a familiar statement about modern life that is not a social exchange ("If you go into town, then you take the train").

Higher performance on reasoning problems that involve cheating on social exchanges has been recorded in every country where it has been tried, including in isolated tribal cultures. Cosmides and Tooby have also shown, using magnetic resonance imaging (MRI), that people use different parts of their brain to reason about social exchanges. It appears that the brain has a highly specialized method for policing social contracts. If you don't scratch my back, after I've scratched yours, I'm very likely to notice.

Social exchange is just one of a number of functions our brains perform so naturally and easily that we simply take it for granted. We can hear attitudes in slight changes in people's speech. We can detect beliefs from tiny eye movements. We can predict what people will do based on their personalities. Spotting when someone takes but does not give is another such function. We trade favours so instinctively,

---

* Actually, while the cost involved in a social exchange usually requires effort, it doesn't always do so, but can instead be a different kind of social requirement. For example, we also reason well with statements like "If the person is drinking alcohol, they must be over eighteen." Thus, more generally, social exchange fits the template: "If you take the benefit, you must meet the requirement." As we are interested here in the implications for economics, for simplicity I stick with "cost".

† For the curious, a duiker is a small African antelope.

it is such an ingrained part of how we relate to each other, that we hardly notice ourselves doing it.

What has all this to do with being a worker? A huge amount. After generations of social exchange, between distant and close relatives in tribes, we have learned to trade favours so effectively that groups of complete strangers can divide up tasks and achieve remarkable degrees of coordination and organization, in order to reach a common goal. Our ability to form large organizational structures is the most impressive and unique manifestation of our ability to trade favours. In modern society, within small companies, large corporations, agencies, institutes, charities and governments, social exchanges occur throughout the day, every day, not just between workers and bosses, but also between fellow workers, many of whom may hardly know each other. We are so skilled at social exchange that we don't seem to realize that, at one level, it is simply remarkable that a group of strangers can come together in an organization, dedicate a substantial proportion of waking hours to it, and work together to tackle whatever unique challenge it faces.

Given this, a crucial question arises. What stops people from cheating on each other? What prevents us from reaping the benefits of organization, the efforts of others, but not putting in the work ourselves? You might think that powerful figures, once chieftains, now chief executives, keep us in line by dishing out benefits only if they see effort put in. But this is only a small part of the story. In organizations, people don't merely do just enough to get by without incurring punishment from the powerful. The overwhelming volume of trade in favours between people is not on pain of punishment from some all-seeing overlord. It is voluntary.

To realize how much organizations rely on voluntary social exchanges, in a modern setting, try to imagine the damage you could do, if you really wanted to, by ceasing to trade favours at work unless you had to. What would it do to the productivity of the group you work with if you stopped passing on to your colleagues all information unless specifically asked for it? What if, every time your boss suggested doing something you had reason to believe wouldn't work, you just said "absolutely, no problem" and went ahead? How much slower would the organizational wheels turn if you suddenly became a stickler for the rules, reading all relevant company documentation on health and safety, IT practice, record-keeping and accounting practice, before following it to the letter? How much havoc would you create by prioritizing your work, not by who needs what when, but by "first task in, first task out"? What would happen to morale if you were to tell the boss whenever a co-worker left a bit early, made a long personal phone call or admitted struggling with some work? How would the corporate engine tick over if you purposefully assigned tasks to subordinates randomly, without taking account of what they particularly enjoyed or disliked doing? Lastly, what if every time you overheard a colleague or boss ask someone a question to which you knew the answer you simply stared quietly and passively ahead at your PC screen?

Unless specifically ordered not to do any of these things, none would be in breach of your contract, even if it were possible for your boss to detect what you were up to. People's willingness to offer information, to prioritize what is important to others, to gently bend rules and to be generally helpful to colleagues is all voluntary. Legally enforceable contracts between workers and employers agree wages, set official hours and specify some aspects of workplace behaviour, including references to such contestable catch-alls as "bringing the company into disrepute". In terms of how people actually behave at work, however, official contracts say little, if anything, about the bulk of mutually understood exchanges that occur in almost every organization. Of course, being an uncooperative colleague may not make us popular. But how cooperative we are is nevertheless up to us. Because contracts do not determine how willing and hard working we are, economists refer to the "problem of incomplete contracts". This is a misnomer. Contracts are not merely incomplete, they specify a tiny fraction of the rules of the game.

The real rules are unwritten. If we work hard for our employer, we anticipate a reward in the long term. If we do the minimum to get by, we do not. Our employer understands that there should be rewards for loyalty, effort and being a team player. We know this. We share information and advice with colleagues, and expect them to do so with us. But we understand that we can get burned if we help a colleague who does not return favours. We judge our colleagues by their attitudes, past behaviour and reputation. Often these are people with whom we are competing for promotion. We know it, they know it, and most people manage to separate the trusted colleagues from the few devious back-stabbers. In this environment, our ability to trade favours and spot cheats, honed over millions of years, is what makes organizations work. Co-workers share and trade information, effort, skills, time and the organization's resources. Bosses and workers rely on their perceptions of other people's actions, their understanding of mutual obligations and their expectations of reciprocation. Every day, in every organization, the degree of trustworthiness, honesty and common understanding that surrounds these exchanges determines how effective the organization is, how fairly its workers are treated, and how enjoyable or frustrating it is to work for. None of this is written into our contract – it doesn't have to be.

When voluntary, as opposed to contractual, cooperation between colleagues breaks down, collectively or individually, the effect can be severe. This is why a "work to rule" is a damaging form of industrial action and why, when a manager says that, if they could, they would happily pay a particularly difficult member of staff to stay at home, they usually mean it.

There is a large body of research into what makes some organizations more successful than others. While it would take an entire book to do justice to this sizeable literature, there are certain themes that emerge indisputably. The organizations that are most likely to achieve their goals and to induce high productivity from their workers, be they profit-making or not-for-profit, share certain characteristics. One is good communication between workers. Another is the openness and accessibility of bosses. A third is possessing simple management processes. Less obviously, the most successful organizations manage to maintain a culture in which change is not feared, through trust, loyalty and a sense of pride in the organization.

Notice that every one of these characteristics of successful organizations is likely to create a better environment for voluntary cooperation, either between workers and bosses, or between co-workers. When organizational theorists try to summarize the findings, the buzzwords and phrases they come up with are things like "culture of trust", "corporate team spirit", "motivational capital", "the knowledge sharing company", "culture of openness", "corporate social capital", and so on. These phrases do not describe a Marketopian world of competing selfish individuals, but a Muddletonian one of communication, mutual trust and interdependency.

It is interesting to contrast these consistent findings about the *characteristics* of successful organizations with findings regarding their *structure*. While there is perhaps sufficient evidence to conclude that, on average, flatter structures work better than more hierarchical ones, there are no particular organizational structures that emerge as being superior. The relationships between organisms matter more than the relationships within organograms.

Human organization is based on our unique ability to trade favours. Effective organizations create a good climate for such social exchanges. This is the defining characteristic of successful organizations, just as it is of successful human societies.

Gather your *witts*

When Alfred Tucker "discovered" Prisoner's Dilemma, his insight was considered to be a highly abstract piece of "game theory". It has taken decades for social scientists to see the everyday importance of what Tucker had hit upon. In fact, countless everyday social exchanges have a similar basic structure to Prisoner's Dilemma.

Recall your adapted Prisoner's Dilemma game with your

anonymous fellow player, "Manikin". Both of your computer screens present a choice between two buttons, A or B. If both of you click on A you each get £5. If you go for A and Manikin clicks on B, you get £1, Manikin gets £7. The other way around and you get £7, Manikin £1. If you both hit B, it's £2 apiece. Whatever Manikin clicks, you get more money by clicking B. But if you both click B then you get the worst common outcome. Individual incentives are at odds with the selflessness and trust needed to reach the best common solution.

When two people trade favours, the same is true. Each person would be better off if they could get away with accepting the favour but not returning it; cheating on the exchange. But if both people behave this way, both end up worse off. The *witt* ("we're in this together") instinct, therefore, is not the preserve of some complex laboratory game involving a hypothetical scenario. It is no less than fundamental to human social organization. For all the seeming complexity of Tucker's original problem, you and Manikin are, at a simple level, just trading a favour: each accepting slightly less money to make you both ultimately better off. In fact, we face repeated decisions like this, about whether to cooperate or compete with our fellow citizens, every day of our lives. Such situations rarely involve numbers, but nevertheless require us to trade favours to reach the best solution, which in turn requires mutual selflessness and trust from each party.

If, as evidence suggests, we have traded favours for millions of years, learning to reach the best common solutions and getting good at spotting cheats, then our instincts for coping with situations like Prisoner's Dilemma have been adapted over millions of years too. We process and deal with these dilemmas so effortlessly, so naturally, that we are mostly unaware of them. The long and tortured route that scientists had to take, from a mathematical problem on a blackboard, through Tucker's far-fetched story of imprisoned suspects, to laboratory experiments with anonymous players at computer terminals, is testimony to how we take our largely automatic and unconscious ability to conduct social exchange for granted.

In most cases, however, there are three important differences between a social exchange and Tucker's original problem. Recall our two workers stuck in a Prisoner's Dilemma about what time they leave the office. The best solution is for both to leave each day no later than six o'clock, which is all the job demands, but each has an incentive to stay a bit longer, thereby appearing to be more hard working. The workers can selfishly compete and be worse off, or self-lessly cooperate, trust each other and end up collectively better off. For these gender-neutral times, let's call one worker Nicky, the other Sam. The first difference between Nicky and Sam's office scenario and Prisoner's Dilemma is that one person must act first. In the original problem, both prisoners had to decide what to do without knowing what the other had done. In Nicky and Sam's case, either Nicky gets to watch Sam leave, or vice versa. Somebody goes first.

The second departure from the classic Prisoner's Dilemma is that Nicky and Sam do not face a one-off decision, but an ongoing situation. The dilemma arises day after day. The consequence of this is that each worker has the opportunity to respond to the previous behaviour of the other. With luck, the *witt* instinct will triumph and roughly half the time Nicky will watch Sam pack up and leave before six, while half the time Sam will observe Nicky do the same. On the other hand, the *witt* instinct may succumb to competitive self-interest. Suppose, after a few weeks, Nicky concludes that Sam is consistently waiting for Nicky to leave first, wanting to appear more dedicated. Nicky can begin to respond in kind, so both workers watch the clock turn past six and well beyond. If Nicky prizes free time more highly, Nicky can punish Sam by not cooperating in other ways, refusing requests for help or withholding useful information. Nicky and Sam are in Prisoner's Dilemma, but the decision to cooperate or compete can be reviewed on a daily basis.

We'll find out shortly whether the *witt* instinct works when people take turns to act, or when the scenario is repeated. But the third difference between the worker's dilemma and the prisoner's one may be the biggest: other people are likely to be watching. Let's introduce a third colleague to the office, Pat, who is more senior. Suppose Pat happens to perceive, accurately, that Sam is trying to gain an unfair advantage over Nicky by staying late, appearing to go the extra mile. Now, there are people in such situations, even some bosses, who decide it's none of their business what silly games junior colleagues play. There are others who, instead, understand the importance of team-building, of reinforcing the *witt* instinct, and will intervene. Suppose Pat, casually walking past Sam's desk, at twenty past six, makes an apparently generous offer: would Sam like Pat to relieve some of the workload, seeing as it seems to be taking Sam longer to finish the work than others, who have already headed home for dinner? As a manager, I found that, if I spotted someone pretending to go the extra mile, the suggestion that they appeared to be running the same number of miles more slowly was usually sufficient inducement to end the charade. That a third party, be it the boss or otherwise, may take exception to selfish behaviour and get involved is a further difference between Nicky and Sam's situation and that of the prisoners.

We know the result of anonymous Prisoner's Dilemma experiments for money. For around half of us, the *witt* instinct is strong enough that we try to cooperate to reach the best common solution, although orthodox economics predicts that we would all selfishly do otherwise. So, what happens if we change the experiment? What happens when one person has to go first, or when such dilemmas are repeated over many consecutive rounds, or when a third party gets involved? Behavioural economists have looked at our instincts in each of these situations.

It's you and Manikin at your terminals again. Suppose you are given £10, while Manikin is given nothing. You have two choices. You can either keep it, or you can give a proportion of it to Manikin by electronic transfer. Any amount you give to Manikin is to be tripled. Assuming that you give at least some money, Manikin then gets to decide how much of the tripled sum to return to you. This is entirely up to Manikin, who might return all of it, half of it, exactly the amount you gave originally, or he might simply walk off with the lot. How much would you give? Once you've come up with an answer, try switching roles. Suppose Manikin is given the £10 and decides to give £5 of it to you, which is then tripled to £15. How much, if any, would you give back?

This is, perhaps unsurprisingly, referred to as the "Trust Game".* As you may have realized, the game is very similar to Prisoner's Dilemma. In the case where you decide how much of the £10 to give, the best common solution is that you give it all to Manikin, who returns enough of the resulting £30 that you both make a nice profit. But if Manikin is selfish, nothing will be returned. And your decision must be taken before Manikin's, so you have to place your trust in Manikin, who only has to decide whether to reward your trust.

When this game is played for real money, even large amounts of real money, many people, including completely anonymous strangers, trust each other enough to hand over significant sums. The favour is usually returned, such that a substantial proportion of the money is handed back. Once again, there are selfish types who neither trust nor repay trust, although they are in a minority. Hence, in games similar to Prisoner's Dilemma, but where one player goes first, the *witt* instinct performs as it does in the classic experiment.

What about if the game is ongoing? When people play repeated Prisoner's Dilemma games for real money, with the same individual, over many rounds, it turns out that more people manage to reach the best common solution and reap the mutual rewards. The main reason for this seems to be that, once the game is repeated over and over, even selfish types find it is in their own interest to cooperate. Most of us start off trying to cooperate, but if we find that the other person behaves selfishly, we punish them by retaliating in subsequent rounds. Thus, really selfish players are likely to end up worse off and many initially selfish types, anticipating retaliation, realize that they

---

* It is also occasionally called the "Investment Game", although this label captures far less of what the game is really about.

are better off pretending to be a generous type. Overall, in repeated games of Prisoner's Dilemma, the *witt* instinct becomes stronger and mutually beneficial cooperation is more common.

Perhaps more surprising is what happens when a third party is given the opportunity to watch two people play a Prisoner's Dilemma game, and to intervene if they wish. In completely anonymous experiments, if a third party is given the power to take money away from either player, after each round, they tend to punish selfish players. They will do this even if it costs them some money to mete out the punishment.* Note that this is somewhat different from the Public Good Game described earlier, where many players could contribute to the pot and allowing punishment improved the level of contributions, because in this case the third party who punishes isn't a player themselves. Even if punishment changes the future behaviour of the two players, the third party stands to neither gain nor lose, and could simply keep their nose out of it. Nevertheless, around half of us spontaneously intervene. Many people seem to be motivated to force selfish types to cooperate with others, even when there is no reward for doing so. The result, as in the Public Good Game, is that selfish types are coerced into begrudgingly supporting the common good.

From all this research emerges a picture of human instincts surrounding the trading of favours. Most of us have sufficient generosity and trust to spontaneously trade favours with strangers, even if we have to perform our favour first. When the relationship is ongoing, trading of favours is more reliable, because even the minority of selfish types find it is in their interest to behave like a cooperative type. Furthermore, where trades of favours are watched by others, enough people are willing to intervene in support of a fair outcome, that selfish types can once again be forced to behave like nicer people.

---

* Usually, the third party has been allocated some money at the start of the experiment, and gets to keep whatever they don't expend dishing out punishment. Subjects often play a whole series of anonymous games for real money in a session, as players and third parties, having been given an endowment right at the start. In fact, the contextual details of these experiments make remarkably little difference to results.

All of this is underpinned by the fact that we are highly skilled at detecting selfish types; those who cheat in social exchanges by taking and not giving. The *witt* instinct is fallible, but it is strong enough and has enough supporters that selfish types are, for the most part, outnumbered and kept in line.

Sticks, carrots and donkey-work

Whether such simple experiments involving economic dilemmas genuinely reveal deep economic instincts that operate in the work-place is obviously contestable. They do not take place in a work context and, after all, they are just simple experiments. They would be more convincing if they involved employers and workers, and if results were backed up by evidence from real workplaces.

With various other behavioural economists, Ernst Fehr, who devised the Public Good Game we met earlier, has also designed experiments in which people act as bosses and employees. The aim is to create different artificial labour markets and compare how people behave. One basic set-up is as follows. A group of people are randomly assigned to be employers or workers. Each employer can offer a wage, from within a possible range, and specify a desired quality of work. Just as in a real business, the higher the quality of work done for them, relative to the wage they pay out, the more profit the employer makes. Workers, for their part, can choose to accept one of the offered jobs or not bother. If they accept a job, they then decide how much effort to put in. Putting in higher effort determines the quality of work done, but also costs the worker more.

In this experimental design, note that employers have no control over the amount of effort workers ultimately put in. They can only offer a wage and then hope that whichever worker accepts it actually puts in the effort to deliver the associated quality of work. Nevertheless, something very interesting occurs. Employers offer wages above the minimum and ask for effort levels above the minimum too. The result is that workers who accept jobs don't do as little as possible, but instead put in higher levels of effort the higher the wage. Workers do this even though it costs them to do so and despite the fact that there is no penalty for taking the higher wage yet doing the bare minimum. Thus, this miniature labour market works like the Trust Game described above. Employers offer a high wage and trust that workers will respond by putting in an appropriate amount of effort, which they seem to do. In completely anonymous circumstances, with no sanctions for lack of effort, employees appear to think it would be unfair to take the money and not do an appropriate amount of work, even though they could get away with it.

This is known as the "gift-exchange" experiment. Employers offer gifts of decent wages and receive corresponding gifts of quality work. It is a selfless and trusting trade of favours, with the employer acting first. The findings go against standard labour economics. If employers assume that workers are Marketopians, always choosing minimum effort for maximum reward, they should offer the lowest possible wage, knowing that workers would put in the minimum effort anyway. In fact, at least in these experiments, employers don't assume workers are like Marketopians and workers don't behave like them either. Employers make fairly generous offers and workers repay their trust. The result has been replicated many times, including once in Russia, where the experimental subjects earned up to three months' income in a two-hour session.

More impressively, making a few changes to the experiment alters behaviour. Fehr, together with Austrian behavioural economist Simon Gächter, compared the outcome in a gift-exchange experiment with an almost identical miniature labour market in which employers could monitor effort levels and alter wages accordingly. The process of job offers and acceptances was identical, but employers were allowed to administer a degree of performance-related pay. Where they detected any shirking on the job, they could reduce the wage, and workers knew this. The outcome was fascinating: job offers were less generous and the quality of work lower than in the gift-exchange scenario. That is, when the exchange of work for wages was based on mutual trust, wages were higher and more work was done, meaning greater gains from trade, than when it was based on direct monetary incentives. The labour market based on trust was hence more efficient. Interestingly, as if to underline the social nature of the exchange, the outcome was also affected by how the performance-related payment structure was described. Wages and quality of work were better when it was called a "bonus" for good work than when it was called a "fine" for shirking, even though the deals involved were identical in monetary terms.

The implication of these artificial labour markets is that where workers have any leeway regarding the amount of effort they put in, an exchange of favours between employer and employee, based on mutual trust, may induce better work and higher wages than an explicit link between pay and productivity. Is there any evidence that real labour markets work like this? Yes. In fact, thinking about the employer–worker relationship as an exchange of favours involving a degree of mutual trust helps to explain a number of phenomena that have puzzled economists for some time.

We have already come across one phenomenon in which productivity and pay diverge greatly. Workers of equal productivity get paid more if they happen to work in more profitable industries. Earlier, we related this to the Ultimatum Game. Our *yucki* ("you can keep it") instinct is such that we are prepared to make considerable sacrifices to punish people who don't give us a fair share. Thus, we may not accept a higher-paid job if it means working for an employer who doesn't give us a fair share of the revenue our work creates. This explanation stresses the worker's motives, but the gift-exchange experiment suggests that wage differentials may suit firms too. What orthodox economists find so puzzling is that very profitable firms don't seem able to reduce their wages. Standard theory says they should drive wages down to match what less profitable firms pay for the same work. But if a key component of the relationship between employer and worker is mutual trust, such that employers trust workers to respond to a good wage by putting in reasonable effort, firms might worry about trying to force wages down. Even if they could get past the *yucki* instinct and find sufficient people to take the jobs, imagine what such behaviour might do to mutual trust and levels of effort.

An even more straightforward puzzle for conventional labour economics is why so few companies adopt performance-related pay schemes. If workers really were like Marketopians, then they would respond only to monetary incentives and it would be most efficient for employers to pay them according to their productivity, just as the standard economic model suggests. In fact, studies show that few companies directly link pay to productivity. Furthermore, when they do, there is very little evidence that the incentive schemes work. Only in certain low-skilled jobs where output is easy to measure, such as tree-planting or windshield-fitting, have such schemes been shown to be effective.

Money appears to be only one incentive among many. Studies of self-assessed happiness suggest that work status and job satisfaction have a bigger impact on our well-being than how much we earn. A recurring finding in labour economics is that, while higher wages may induce some people, especially women, to join the labour force, it is very difficult to find a reliable relationship between wages and the amount people want to work. On average, more productive people do tend to be paid more, but individual productivity is just one factor among many that determine wages. Not only are people not paid according to their individual productivity, employers don't even try to match pay to productivity.

They are probably wise not to. When they try, it often seems to backfire, because by prioritizing monetary rewards employers can damage other motivations. Part of the problem is that, with most jobs, it isn't possible for the employer to measure accurately how productive individuals are. The rather ironic upshot of trying to relate pay to productivity is that workers devote time to being seen to be productive and thereby become less so. Performance-related pay schemes give workers incentives to spend time sucking up to the boss, to cooperate less with each other, and to timetable more impressive work to coincide with assessment periods. Furthermore, research shows that assessments of performance by managers are subject to strong biases. Studies have located a "centrality bias", whereby bosses are unwilling to differentiate fully the good from the bad, and "leniency bias", whereby managers tend to mark up poor performers.

Why does this happen? Let's return to the Muddletonian view of the workplace, according to which we are intensely social creatures who interact constantly with each other, in organizations that rely extensively on voluntary social exchanges, or the trading of favours, both between fellow workers and between the worker and the employer. In such an environment, which is so dependent on team spirit and mutual trust, can you imagine anything more damaging than introducing a pay scheme that, first, implies that workers care only about money and, second, values individual productivity above the productivity of the team as a whole? It could be managerial suicide. This is why firms don't usually try to match pay to individual performance, why their managers don't actually implement the schemes properly when they do, and probably why they spurn my profession by hiring consultants with degrees in organizational behaviour rather than economics.

In fact, the predominant link between performance and reward in organizations has remained the same for centuries. It is promotion. The bulk of differences in wages results from job changes, as people move up to more senior posts. This process, as anyone who has been forced to compete for a job against a good friend and colleague will know, can be painful and damaging to working relations. But promotion is infrequent instead of ongoing, often rewards team players rather than individual performers, and usually results in only one or two members of a work group being differentiated from their colleagues. For effective organizations, promotion may therefore be the least worst way to reward ability and effort.

Before moving on from individual incentives, the following research finding, for me, says more about how workplaces operate than perhaps any other. It seems that there is one kind of incentive scheme that consistently improves productivity, by something in the region of 5%, according to a number of studies. This most reliable incentive scheme is profit-sharing. It works even among large companies with hundreds or thousands of employees. From the perspective of standard economics, this finding makes no sense at all. The additional profit produced by any extra effort one individual puts in is split between all the workers, so the return to the individual who puts in the extra effort is but a tiny fraction. In a company of 500 employees, 5% extra productivity by one individual equates to an increase in their own pay packet of 0.01%.

If you can see why profit-sharing schemes work, then you understand the labour market of Muddleton. By bringing in profit-sharing, a firm effectively introduces a pot, just as in the Public Good Game, to which every employee can contribute. If all workers put in extra effort, and trust each other to do the same, then they all get the benefits. The logic, for workers, is straightforward: "we're in this together". What better scheme could you introduce into an environment already dependent on the selflessness and trust required to successfully trade favours?

Prejudice about prejudice

Of course, the world is not full of enlightened companies that build great teams, tackle shared goals by spreading knowledge through their flat-as-possible structures, create a culture of change to meet the latest challenge, and then share the profits. Still, we would all be better off if there were more of them. Back in the real world, every workplace has selfish types who are a pain to work with, as well as valued colleagues who may become lasting friends. There are good bosses and bad. Sometimes those skilled at self-promotion are those the bosses choose to promote too, while talented, diligent team players are overlooked. Organizations and people can also be simply unlucky; in the wrong market or the wrong job at the wrong time.

Nevertheless, the downsides of office politics notwithstanding, here are some interesting findings from the USA, compiled for a paper by George Akerlof and Rachel Kranton. In a representative survey, 90% of employees agreed that they were proud to work for their organization, 86% were moderately or very satisfied with their jobs, 78% agreed that their values were similar to those of their organization, and 82% disagreed with the statement that they felt very little loyalty to their organization. Similar surveys in other developed countries record similar results. This means, of course, that a significant minority of people dislike their jobs and just turn up for the pay cheque. But they really are a minority. Akerlof and Kranton contrast the orthodox view that money is the sole incentive with survey results, evidence on incentive schemes, research on successful organizations, and modern management theory, which stresses the need for workers to be involved in setting their own goals and linking them to the organization's mission. They conclude that the degree to which people identify with the organization they work for is a key aspect of motivation at work and, thus, of performance across the organization.

This idea fits well with the view of workplaces as reliant on effective trading of favours and the mutual trust that such social exchange requires. One of the most consistent findings in behavioural economics is the impact on economic behaviour of manipulating group identity. In Prisoner's Dilemma games, Ultimatum Games, Trust Games and Public Good Games, the more strongly players are made to feel part of a group, the greater the degree of cooperation between them. The instinctive response that "we're in this together" depends on how strongly an individual feels part of the "we". The *endian* instinct and the *witt* instinct reinforce each other.

This possibility brings another of the lasting puzzles of labour economics into play – one that is highly sensitive and needs very careful consideration. There has long been a belief among economists that market forces are a weapon against discrimination. The logic is straightforward and many people find it compelling: the market gives employers a strong incentive to hire the best people, so the market should naturally reward hiring and promotion policies based on people's abilities, not their gender, skin colour or any other superficial characteristic that may give rise to discrimination. According to orthodox economic theory, the market is blind to gender and race.

The trouble is, evidence consistently suggests otherwise. In the 1998 *Journal of Economic Perspectives*, American economists William Darity and Patrick Mason reviewed over three decades of work on discrimination in the labour market. Times, most certainly, have changed. Looking back to US newspaper advertisements of the 1960s, Darity and Mason found examples such as this one, from the *Chicago Tribune*:

> WHITE married men who
> can furnish and opr.
> late air cond. Cadillac
> Limo. – Good
> opportunity. ID 2–4864

This ad, not untypical of the era, discriminates on three dimensions in a single line. At the time, workers routinely declared their own gender and race in the "situations wanted" section too. Studies show that, following the Civil Rights Act of 1964, discrimination declined. Indeed, evidence from a number of countries suggests that equality legislation reduces discrimination. Nevertheless, even since the passage of strong equality legislation, numerous organizations, including major multinationals such as Texaco and General Motors, have been successfully sued or forced to settle discrimination cases for large sums. This is all very problematic for standard economics, based on the idea that firms have an incentive to hire and pay only according to productivity. Why does it take legal action to prevent firms damaging their own profits?

Attempts to solve this puzzle have produced over forty years of academic effort, in which economists have come up with various reasons why companies that care only about profits might nevertheless discriminate. Most have argued that discrimination is related to differences in average productivity within social groups. The strongest standpoint is to suggest that there isn't actually any discrimination, but that where women and non-whites are, on average, less productive, there simply appears to be discrimination. Another theory holds that, because it is hard for employers to know how good candidates are, they use gender or race as a rough indicator, such that in individual cases there is unfair discrimination, but because the practice selects more productive workers, on average, it persists.

Let's leave aside the issue of whether men and white people actually are, on average, more productive. For even if we concede this clearly contestable and, doubtless for some, offensive assumption, the evidence doesn't stack up. Recent techniques for studying discrimination have involved a most unusual phenomenon in economics: real-life experiments. Researchers send matched applications in response to real job adverts, where the only difference between two applications is the race or gender associated with the candidates' names. This kind of study has been done in the USA, Europe, Australia and elsewhere, and the result is always the same: there is substantial discrimination. Males and whites get more requests to attend interviews. Hence, the claim that there is no discrimination, but only appears to be, looks to be plain wrong – candidates of apparently identical ability are discriminated against. What about the idea that employers use gender or race as a statistical indicator? Another interesting finding of these studies with matched applications is that for traditionally "female" jobs, such as being a secretary, discrimination against men is found. Is it possible to argue that men are on average more productive, except when it comes to administration?

There is one study in the literature on the economics

of discrimination, by Claudia Goldin and Cecilia Rouse, that I find compelling. These economists studied data on orchestra auditions. In the 1970s and 1980s, most major US orchestras changed their audition procedures, by introducing a screen to hide the player's identity. Having obtained the data on who was subsequently hired, Goldin and Rouse found that substantially more women got positions once the screen was introduced. This result is very hard to square with a statistical theory of discrimination. Why would orchestras have used gender as an indicator of how good the player was when they could actually hear for themselves?*

The standard theories of discrimination, based on pay for individual productivity, do not account for the data. Instead, here is a plausible, if discomforting, alternative. There is a growing volume of evidence that organizations are more effective if they create an environment in which people successfully trade favours. Meanwhile, experiments show that where people belong to the same group they are better at finding the best common solutions, across a whole range of scenarios. Mutual trust is usually stronger when people share an identity – the *endian* instinct reinforces the *witt* instinct. Could it therefore be that bosses like to hire people who belong to their own social group and to have teams that belong to the same social group, because it tends to improve how effectively people cooperate and work together?

For anyone who doesn't object to being called "liberal", this is a very troubling theory. It is, however, consistent with evidence. It would explain why markets don't drive out discrimination, but may actually reinforce it, until legislation creates a financial penalty. It would explain why people sometimes discriminate against

---

* One possibility is that audition committees marked women down because they believed women would take more leave of absence than men, in particular to have children. Careers in major US orchestras tend to be very long, however, and, in fact, the data contained no significant difference in overall time off taken by male and female musicians. The more likely explanation, then, is that audition committees perceived something else negative about hiring women.

a candidate even when they know them to be the best individual performer. Productivity is not the sole preserve of the individual. The workplace is a social place – a fact that has upsides and downsides. On the one hand, we are not, as standard economics would have it, competing rats on treadmills being paid for the number of rotations we clock up. On the other, negative and pervasive social forces such as discrimination are unlikely to leave their influence at the corporation gates.

If discrimination is partly caused by smoother trading of favours between members of the same social group, then we may need to change how we tackle it. For one thing, this theory suggests that discrimination is more subtle than is generally thought. There is a tendency to believe that getting rid of discrimination is about stamping out hostility towards certain groups. While laudable, this may be too simplistic.

Take this experiment, by behavioural economist Lorenz Goette and some colleagues in Switzerland. During obligatory national service in Switzerland, those selected for four weeks of officer training are randomly assigned to platoons. Goette's team conducted an experiment in which national service trainees who had been in platoons for three weeks played anonymous Prisoner's Dilemma games, for real money. The usual result occurred, whereby about half the subjects selflessly tried to reach the best common solution, while the other half acted selfishly. They also found the usual effect of group membership. When trainees were told that the other player was a member of their own platoon, cooperation rose from 50% to 70%. The experimenters also tried a Prisoner's Dilemma game in which an anonymous third party was allowed to observe the game and could pay to punish either player by having their takings reduced. Selfish types were often punished – the standard result. But the dishing out of punishment turned out to depend on group membership in a distinctive way. Willingness to pay for punishment was significantly greater when the victim of the selfish behaviour was from the third party's own platoon. Thus, the trainees made greater sacrifices to defend members of their own platoon. But when it was the selfish player who was from their own platoon, rather than the victim, third parties showed no favouritism. They punished fellow platoon members for being selfish just as severely as members of other platoons.

The experiment is clever because it separates two kinds of discrimination: favouritism towards members of your own group and hostility towards members of other groups. The conclusion Goette's team draw is that, at least in their experiment, discrimination is an attempt to improve cooperation within people's own group, not an attack on other groups. Of course, as with all these experiments, whether the finding reflects life in the real economy is not clear. But the finding is consistent with the idea that discrimination may, at least to some degree, result from the attempt to use common identity to increase successful cooperation within social groups, rather than being driven by hostility to people from other social groups.

Finally, it is worth remembering the optimism of Henri Tajfel, the social psychologist who revealed the power of group identity. The negative side to the *endian* instinct, discrimination, is counterbalanced by a positive side, the solidarity that results from shared identity. The ease with which group identity forms, our instinct for it, may cause discrimination, but it may also act as an antidote. For while it is true that, initially, people who belong to the same social group cooperate with each other more successfully, it is also quite easy to establish new group identities. The trainees in the Swiss platoons had been complete strangers until just three weeks before the experiment, yet their new group identity had a strong effect on behaviour. One possible way to tackle discrimination based on social background might therefore be to create a stronger sense of identity that overcomes it. In an organization that builds a sense of team spirit, loyalty and common purpose, workers may be more inclined to ignore their different backgrounds. Similarly, a society that takes pride in being multicultural, making diversity itself part of its identity, may find it easier to be diverse.

The job to be done

Human beings have evolved to be highly skilled at detecting selfish behaviour – spotting and punishing those who take but do not give. This skill is fundamental to our ability to organize ourselves. Most of us overcome selfish instincts to engage in successful voluntary social exchanges – mutually beneficial trading of favours. We act to reinforce the mutual trust required to do so, even at a personal cost to ourselves. In modern society, these instincts extend to how we deal with people we hardly know, in the workplace. Organizations, be they profit-making companies or public agencies, whether providers of widgets, financial services or a police force, rely extensively on workers' ability to trade favours with colleagues and bosses. How well organizations manage to create a climate of trust and teamwork, in which social exchanges thrive, determines society's ability to provide goods, services and government. It is, therefore, at the heart of economic activity.

Yet the selfless instincts behind the trading of favours run counter to orthodox economic thinking, which is based on the idea that we are solely motivated by money. Sure, workers expect a fair reward for their efforts, and a greater reward for increased seniority and responsibility. But the prevailing economic wisdom that people do only what they are paid to do, that our aim is to take what we can and give as little as possible, is not supported by evidence and certainly not by wisdom. It is highly damaging and there is a job to be done to change it.

Most pressingly, there is a drive across the developed world, and beyond, to reform public services. Many aspects of these reforms, such as the spread of best practice, the incorporation of modern accounting systems, the removal of promotion systems based merely on seniority, the rewarding of talent and effort, are to be welcomed. Making public services more flexible, incorporating good ideas from the private sector, getting more feedback from service users, all these reforms make sense. But alongside these beneficial changes there is an ideological view of public services that has its ultimate genesis in orthodox economics. It takes as given the idea that people work only for money. Its effect is to see the forced introduction of performance-related pay systems, or targets combined with monetary incentives to meet them, both in individual pay packets and in the budgets of schools, hospitals, local authorities, and so on.

Evidence suggests that the assumption that people only work for money is wrong. The assumption that the most efficient way to pay people is according to their individual productivity is probably wrong too. The assumption that this is the way the private sector operates is certainly wrong – wages, quite simply, do not match individual productivity. There is very little, if any, evidence that trying to force wage structures to match individual productivity improves organizational performance.

These findings match what we can all observe. During my time in journalism, I met many people who had chosen to work in certain vocations, fully aware that they would earn less than they could elsewhere. The most striking example of this was a prison officer. A huge and gentle man, he had volunteered to work with sex offenders. His own personal morality led him to believe that while society had to be protected from these individuals, they also deserved protection from vengeance and a chance to reform. For generations there have been people who take such decisions, in caring professions, education, local government, various other parts of the civil service, and also in parts of the private sector, where many people work in a particular line of business because they believe in the benefits of the good or service they provide. Such people demand a fair wage, relative to what their organizations can afford, but they do not work primarily for money.

As is clear from the list above, people who choose to work for the greater good, when they could earn more elsewhere, often work in areas that are emotionally demanding, where team spirit and mutual support are particularly necessary for job satisfaction and for people's continued willingness to expend effort. Forcing monetary incentives and productivity targets into these kinds of workplaces is the sort of ideological approach to economics that gives my profession a bad name. It is based on assumption, not evidence, and it is poor economics.

Understanding the instincts of workers, creating an environment that motivates, is an important part of running an organization. But success requires looking beyond the walls as well as within them. Organizations operate in an environment too. How decisions taken by an organization interact with this environment can determine the success of the organization, with consequences for workers and owners. So, what are the instincts of the executives who must take these decisions?

8

Business is big ... very big

HUBERT HENDERSON was a practical sort of chap. A distinguished career in Whitehall, advising the prime minister on economic matters, had led him to value facts more than theory. When, in 1934, he became a fellow at Oxford University, Henderson wanted to study the economy, not by theorizing, but by finding out how real companies worked. This was not easy, as businesses did not necessarily want to spill their secrets. Undeterred, Henderson devised a unique methodology in keeping with his practical nature. Tempting invites were sent to leading businessmen, requesting the pleasure of their company for high-table dinner at Oxford's All Souls College. Tempting too was the fine selection of aperitifs, claret and brandy on offer. The target businessman's tongue was thus lubricated by high-class truth serum, and the conversation continued to flow even as members of the Oxford Economists' Research Group gathered round and quietly took out notebooks.

Henderson's researchers expected the executive outpourings to confirm their theories, once suitably translated into the drier language of economics. Instead, these oak-panelled research evenings startled the economists, who discovered that firms did not behave as standard economics predicted. In fact, the businessmen expressed puzzlement at the economists' questions, which assumed that the commercial world was similar to Marketopia. When deciding what products to offer, how much to produce and what to charge for it, captains of industry did not appear to skipper their vessels the way Maurice Mule runs Mule's Muffins.

As an economist reading about Hubert Henderson's innovative research group, I find it impossible not to be struck by how little has changed in over seventy years. Empirical methods have, alas, moved on. Instead of a bow tie and access to a cellar full of excellent alcoholic beverages, modern researchers require powerful computers, fluency in the latest statistical software, and the patience to trawl through enormous sets of data that record such exciting things as the productivity of tyre factories. Nevertheless, as we will see, the principles and practices that poured forth from the boss class of the 1930s foreshadowed the findings of painstaking statistical analysis done decades later.

You might think that in order to understand how firms start up, operate and respond to the business environment around them, learning something about the instincts of businesspeople would be a sensible strategy. It might be insightful to visit some firms and ask questions of the managers who take decisions that determine success or failure. Yet most economists have remained deeply sceptical of what businesspeople have to say.

Behavioural economics is changing the way we think about individual economic behaviour. Its insights are beginning to alter our understanding of consumers and workers. But firms, it transpires, have instincts too. After all, they are owned and run by people. Arguably, there were a few behavioural economists working in industrial economics decades before the description was invented – Hubert Henderson could be regarded as one. As with individuals, behavioural studies of firms can explain some findings that orthodox theory cannot, and they are challenging the traditional economic theory of the firm. Behavioural findings and ideas imported from evolutionary theory can change one's perspective regarding how capitalism works.

Understanding the economic instincts of executives and firms is an issue not only for those naturally interested in the world of business – the readers of pink pages. In our globalized age, the behaviour of companies, especially large companies, is receiving unprecedented scrutiny. This is as it should be. The developed nations of today undoubtedly have the most successful economies in human history, and most of the economic activity behind this success is carried out by private firms, each making their own autonomous decisions. To understand how these economies have thrived is to understand economic development. If we want to enhance that development, get more benefits from it, do less damage through it, and perhaps offer its opportunities to those living in parts of the world yet to experience it, understanding the behaviour of private companies is vital. Meanwhile, what happens when the activities of firms cross national borders is a defining economic debate of our times. Good economics requires a good "theory of the firm".*

The traditional theory of how firms operate needs to change. It contributes to an understanding of competition that overvalues cheapness and undervalues quality. It leads consumer groups and competition authorities to worry excessively about prices, but insufficiently about excess profits and the fortunes of new firms. More importantly, it leads us to view successful capitalism as a mechanical process, when in reality it is an evolutionary one.

Maurice Mule's Mega Muffin Monopoly

Join me back on the outskirts of Port Friedman, the capital of Marketopia, to carry out a case study of our own. Let's examine Mule's Muffins,

* Economists usually use "firm" rather than "company" (or "business") because there are precise legal definitions of companies, which often exclude, for example, sole traders or partnerships. "Firm" is a catch-all for private production, covering everything from the Coca-Cola Company to an artist selling home-made bracelets on the street. Here, I use "firm", "company" and "business" interchangeably.

a little company that embodies the traditional theory of the firm, which makes specific assumptions about firms' aims, capabilities and the environment in which they operate. Once we see how Mule's Muffins works, we can compare it to firms in the real world.

The inviolable objective, the overriding concern, of Mule's Muffins is to do whatever it takes to make as much profit as possible. This assumption, profit maximization, is central to orthodox industrial economics. It is the commercial equivalent of the standard assumption that individuals are selfish. We have already seen that organizations and their workers develop relationships of mutual trust in which selfless behaviour produces common rewards. And, as we know, evidence shows that the assumption regarding individuals is wrong – we are routinely selfless and our economy would not work as well as it does if we were not. Nevertheless, it is possible that with a firm, rather than a person, the equivalent assumption may be more reasonable. Executives face pressure from shareholders and threats of takeover from those who think they can do better. So, for now, let's treat profit maximization as a hypothesis to be reckoned with.

You may recognize the following argument: "… given natural selection, acceptance of the hypothesis can be based largely on the assumption that it summarizes appropriately the conditions for survival". These are the words, not of Gary Becker, but of his one-time colleague at the University of Chicago, the late Milton Friedman. This argument, published in *Essays in Positive Economics* in 1953, expresses a logic almost identical to that Becker invoked half a century later to dismiss evidence from behavioural economics, which shows that people are not independent, rational and selfish. The idea is that a profit-maximizing firm will always do better than a non-profit-maximizing one, so we can assume that only the former will exist. It is an evolutionary argument, based on market selection rather than natural selection, for the ultimate domination of a single trait. As we know, it exemplifies the fallacy that evolution follows an inevitable path towards a perfect specimen. We'll return to this in the light of evidence shortly.

Being a Marketopian firm, however, Mule's Muffins does maximize profit. It also makes independent decisions in a "rational" manner. Obviously, we now have a wealth of evidence that people have other economic instincts. But, for now, in the context of firms rather than individuals, let's allow these assumptions about the nature of firms a new lease of life.

Standard theory also assumes things about the business environment, including that firms have perfect information about economic opportunities. But the business climate in Marketopia exhibits another form of perfection, which economists call "perfect competition". This means that prices and wages are set entirely by supply and demand. Recall that when Maurice was setting up the business, he took a tour of Marketopia's cafés to check the price of muffins, and he also checked the going wage for workers with a bit of catering experience. He needed these two pieces of market information in order to calculate how many workers to hire. The assumption here, which defines "perfect competition", is that Maurice has no power over the price of his muffins or the wages he pays. Both are determined by market forces. If his price were higher, no one would buy his muffins because they would buy other people's. If his wages were lower, no one would work for him because they would work for other firms that paid more. Under perfect competition, prices and wages are set by supply and demand – you can't buck the market.

There is one more key assumption in the traditional theory of the firm, which limits how the firm can interact with its environment. It relates to size. Maurice employs 23 workers and bakes just over ten thousand muffins a week. Because Mule's Muffins maximizes profit, it must be the case that hiring the 23rd worker added to profit, but hiring a 24th would not. That is, the extra muffins baked by the 23rd worker must make the company more in revenue than it costs to employ the worker, but the 24th must cost more to employ than the revenue from selling the extra muffins they would bake. This logic conforms to the final, crucial assumption in the standard theory of the firm: if firms get too big they become inefficient.

At this point, before we turn to the evidence, it is enlightening to adopt the approach of the inquisitive toddler towards the idea that firms face limits to their size. That is, keep asking: "But why?" So, apparently, a 24th worker at Mule's Muffins would make a loss. But why? The conventional explanation is that Maurice faces rising "marginal costs". Beyond a certain number, each extra muffin costs more to bake. There will therefore come a point at which extra workers can bake muffins only at a loss. The most efficient size for a firm will vary from industry to industry; different for muffins, insurance contracts and cars. But in every industry, as firms get bigger they always, ultimately, face rising marginal costs. But why? Economists think of a firm as a system that creates output (its product) from two inputs, labour and capital. "Capital" refers to buildings and equipment – physical stuff the firm possesses.* The standard theory assumes that in the short term a firm's capital is fixed – Maurice bought a bakery of a certain size. This in turn limits how many people can efficiently work for it, because there is only so much space and equipment to go round. Hiring more and more people eventually becomes inefficient, because the amount of capital they share is fixed. But why? Standard textbooks give two reasons. They say that, first, it would require inefficient, bureaucratic layers of management for a firm to own lots of capital in different places, and second, that because firms initially set up on the most efficient site, expanding to new locations would itself become increasingly inefficient. Meanwhile, any increases in efficiency that might come with getting bigger will eventually run out. But why? Like the toddler, you will never get a satisfactory answer. What prevents Maurice from acquiring more capital: a bigger bakery, several replica bakeries, or even a massive chain of bakeries on the

---

* The word "capital" is probably the most confusing piece of economics jargon – no mean feat. It has at least two separate uses. It refers to durable stuff (machinery, tools, factories, offices, etc.) that is used to make other stuff, i.e. products. But it is also used to refer to a sum of money raised for investment. This gets especially confusing when the sum borrowed is used to pay for durable equipment or space, because "capital is being raised" to "acquire capital". (Don't shoot, I am only the messenger.)

outskirts of every town in Marketopia? Why can't he aim for domination, as Maurice Mule's Mega Muffin Monopoly?

The real reason why economists stick by the assumption that expanding firms ultimately face rising marginal costs, and why they invent ad hoc justifications for it, is because otherwise the mathematical equations don't work – they provide no solution regarding how big firms will get. In fact, lack of confidence in this assumption about efficient size is one reason why industrial economists throughout the last century have been obsessed by the potential "problem" of monopoly – the domination of an industry by one large firm. The problem, for orthodox theory, is that if a firm gets so big it has few competitors, then unlike Mule's Muffins it won't have to accept market prices and wages, but may be able to decide them for itself. More specifically, there is reason to believe that a firm that enjoys a monopoly will restrict supply and raise prices.* As with asymmetry of information, standard theory accepts monopoly as a potential market failure – less trade may take place than if more companies competed in the market. The formal proof of this proposition, that monopolies will supply less and charge more, is a standard exam question in undergraduate economics. But it can be understood fairly simply.

When I was at primary school, one member of my little gang had the good fortune, as we saw it, to have parents who allowed him to visit the sweet-shop on the way to school. Paul used to buy Black Jacks – aniseed-flavour sweets that made our tongues go black. Back in the 1970s, Black Jacks cost just one pence each. We loved them; some of us more than others. Mark couldn't resist them, I liked them a lot, and Gary quite liked them. Paul used to sell some of his Black Jacks to us in the playground. He was the sole supplier – lax parenting had created a monopolist. At playtime, each of us wanted a sweet.

---

* There has been a recent resurgence of interest in the idea that firms may have partial monopoly power arising from distinctive products, but which is limited by competition, because if they raise prices too far people would eventually buy from other firms. This so-called "monopolistic competition" is also seen as less efficient than "perfect competition".

Suppose Mark was prepared to pay 4p for a Black Jack, I was willing to pay 3p, and Gary 2p. Paul was in a position to make a sweet profit. But at what price should he sell his Black Jacks? If he asked for 4p, he'd sell one sweet, to Mark, and make 3p profit. At a price of 3p, Paul would sell two sweets, to Mark and to me, making 2p on each, increasing his total profit to 4p. Selling at 2p, he'd sell three sweets, one to each of us, reducing his profit back to 3p. To maximize his profit, he should therefore sell at 3p. This would mean, of course, that Gary would get no sweet. Note that Paul can only do this because he faces no competition. If he sold Black Jacks at 3p and another seller appeared in the playground, they could charge 2p and take all his business at a decent profit.

Provided some people are prepared to pay more than others, a profit-maximizing monopoly will restrict supply and charge more than the market rate. In actual fact, this was not what happened in the playground at all. Paul sold us sweets at 1p each. We knew the fair price for a Black Jack and so did he. Maybe he just liked us. But he also knew that there were three of us, one of him, and that we would probably have pinned him to the ground and shoved grass in his mouth had he tried anything else. Apparently, even little boys understand the need to regulate monopolies.

The standard theory of the firm and the problem of monopoly it raises have dominated industrial economics for decades. The theory offers some predictions about what we should in the real world: firms taking decisions that maximize profit; in competitive industries, firms being forced to accept market prices; in each industry, firms tending towards a most efficient size; where they manage to dominate an industry, firms restricting supply and charging high prices. The theory also acts as a guide for competition policy. Where firms get too big, it provides an argument for trying to increase competition, by breaking them up or changing regulations to encourage new firms into the market. It suggests positive benefits from globalization, as more competition from foreign firms should increase supply and lower prices. But, more fundamentally, the orthodox theory of the firm offers us a version of what has made capitalism successful. The profit motive and competition drive firms to produce what people want as efficiently as possible.

So, does this theory match what we actually see in the real world? Does it describe the instincts of real businesspeople?

Flaws of supply and demand

It wouldn't be everybody's idea of a rip-roaring Friday or Saturday night out, but back in the dining hall of All Souls College, Hubert Henderson's research team was discovering the truth about prices. Between sips of spirits, the tipsy tycoons were serving up surprises. For a start, they seemed to be unconcerned by market prices. Instead, they appeared to suggest that they could set their own prices as they saw fit. They described how, for each product, they would establish a level of output they could produce, work out what it cost to deliver, and then set the price a little higher to make a bit of profit. The economists were baffled. How could it be that the instincts of successful businessmen were to ignore the competition? Then there was an extra surprise. It wasn't that the industrialists were unworried about prices – far from it. But what they were most worried about was how customers might react if prices were changed.

Of course, the instinctive reactions of half-drunk 1930s businessmen are hardly the most reliable form of evidence. But it is noteworthy how accurately their responses match statistical evidence that has emerged since.

The American economist Frederic Lee is a self-proclaimed "heterodox" economist.* Inclined to the careful examination of data, he

---

* I am indebted to Lee for introducing me to the exploits of Hubert Henderson. His book, *Post Keynesian Price Theory*, is an explicit attempt to do economics by looking first at empirical findings from the real world and then trying to produce a theory to explain them. Lee argues that this simple scientific method is, in itself, enough to make him a "heterodox" economist.

has painstakingly compiled results from over one hundred separate pricing studies. The conclusion is inescapable: most firms actively set their prices, rather than accept market rates. Costs of production are totted up and an amount added for profit. The precise method for calculating costs and deciding on mark-up is not universal. For instance, General Motors calculated its prices over many years by adding 15% to the total cost of producing each model, while others might use a different rule. The key point is that firms don't simply accept market rates.* Furthermore, rather than changing prices in response to market conditions, most firms try to hold them steady for an extended selling period. Comparing these pricing studies with what Henderson's team were told 70 years ago, the data matches the description.

Although little known, these findings should give every economist pause for thought. The most fundamental of economic concepts, the most widely known, the usual conclusion to the opening chapter of an introductory textbook, is the law of supply and demand. It states that prices naturally adjust towards an equilibrium, to match supply and demand. But if firms generally ignore market prices, the law of supply and demand could be routinely violated. Prices may deviate from the law for months or even years. Do they?

Even in our modern, barcoded and bleeping economies, the law of supply and demand is very hard to test. Researchers can of course observe how much of a particular product is bought in a week, and at what price. The problem is, how do we know whether the price recorded does, in fact, match supply and demand? "Demand" refers to how much people would buy at each different price, while "supply" relates to how much firms would be willing to produce at each price. Thus, these essential economic concepts exist only inside the heads of consumers and company managers. They are hypothetical – impossible to measure directly.

---

* There are of course some products that have become standardized commodities, such as certain metals, oil, some agricultural produce, and so on. Prices in these industries are set by the market.

This fact has profound consequences for the science of economics. Consider a toy that bounces on the end of a spring. When finally it stops moving, with the spring somewhat stretched, it always returns to the same height. A physicist will tell you the toy is caught in equilibrium between the force of gravity pulling it down and the force of the extended spring pulling it up. At its resting height these forces are equal. The physicist's theory can be directly tested. Each force can be measured separately, by weighing different toys or by stretching the spring to different lengths. Now, prices are supposed to be in equilibrium too, caught between consumers pushing them down and suppliers holding them up, matching supply and demand. But we can't weigh supply in our hands, nor playfully stretch consumer demand. The most fundamental economic law cannot be tested directly.

It can be tested indirectly, by looking at how prices change. If they are controlled by supply and demand, then when supply or demand changes, so should the price. After a cut in supply, say when flower-growers are hit by bad weather, the price of a bloom should rise; while following a fall in demand, perhaps caused by the launch of an alternative product, such as the electric razor, the price of razor blades should fall.

These simple predictions frequently do not hold. The issue was first examined even before Hubert Henderson's soirées in Oxford. In the 1920s, the American economist Frederick Mills found, as others have since, that some product prices are "sticky"; that is, they don't move when supply and demand change. Roughly speaking, industries tend to fall into two groups: one in which prices change frequently with supply and demand and another in which they hold steady, sometimes for years at a time. The law of supply and demand appears to apply only to the first group of industries. But it might not even apply to those, because this test is indirect. It shows only whether changes in supply and demand move the price in the predicted direction, not whether the price actually matches supply and demand.

There is, in fact, one way to test the law of supply and demand directly. Suppose I give you a token to take into a room where people are buying and selling tokens. I guarantee that if you choose not to sell it, I will exchange the token for £10 when you return. You are like a firm supplying a product with a production cost of £10. If you can get more than £10 in the room, you should supply your one token and make a profit. Now suppose instead that you are a buyer in the room. You enter the room with no token. I guarantee that if you buy one I'll give you £12 for it when you come out. Obviously, you should buy one for as little as possible, but not bother if they cost more than £12. If you, as buyer, met your selling alter ego, a trade at £11 would clearly benefit you both.

This is the world of artificial markets. It allows researchers to know things they cannot know about the world at large. A group of sellers going into the same artificial market can be given different guaranteed amounts for returning their token. This means experimenters know exactly who profits from supplying their token at every possible price – the very information it is hard to get from firms in the real world. Similarly, buyers can be given varying guarantees, so researchers can know exactly how many buyers would benefit from buying at each price – again, impossible to measure in reality. Effectively, experimenters can vary supply and demand and observe what happens to sales and prices, like the physicist weighing toys and stretching springs. They can predict precisely where the equilibrium price ought to be if the law of supply and demand works. They can also set the rules in the trading room. They can keep exchanges private, or require sellers to display prices. They can run the market just once, or repeat it until the price becomes steady. So, what happens?

It turns out to depend on the rules in the trading room. If buyers and sellers are permitted to haggle, sales usually converge on a price that matches supply and demand.* But if sellers decide on the prices

---

* Technically speaking, they don't exactly haggle but rather participate in what

they charge, as most firms do, prices do not adjust to match supply and demand, but remain higher. Some sellers fail to sell their tokens, even though there are buyers present who would pay more than the seller's guaranteed return. The result has been replicated many times. Exactly why the law fails is an ongoing research area, but it is as if sellers build in some sort of margin for error when they decide their price.

One of the most interesting aspects of research with artificial markets is that the results remain virtually unchanged when the experimental subjects are businesspeople. The best that can be said about the law of supply and demand, based on evidence from genuine price data and from artificial markets, is that it is very approximate. It may operate as the textbooks say in some industries, but in many it is inaccurate, while in others prices only adjust with a significant time lag. All of which goes some way to explaining why bosses who decide pricing policy, presumably based on years of experience, pay it such little respect. What businesspeople seem to respect more is the reaction of customers to changes in prices. They are right to.

One bad Apple

"We apologize for disappointing you, and we are doing our best to live up to your high expectations." These were the words of Steve Jobs, chief executive of Apple, to all those who had bought the new iPhone for $599, in summer 2007, before seeing the price plummet to $399 in September, just two months after the product's launch. The company was bombarded with emails complaining about the price cut. Mr Jobs didn't only apologize, but gave each customer a $100 voucher and added that Apple needed to "do the right thing for our valued iPhone customers".

---

economists call a "double auction", meaning that buyers and sellers offer prices to the market until sales are agreed.

Apple was engaged in what's called "price discrimination" – charging different types of customer different prices for the same product. Very early adopters of the iPhone were charged more and they felt unfairly discriminated against. The fact that they presumably wanted an iPhone more than people who bought one later did not alter how they felt. We expect prices of high-tech products to fall substantially with time, but not that fast. When those who had already bought realized that Apple could knock a third off and clearly still make a profit, they felt ripped off.

As we saw earlier, we have a concept of a fair price. Studies show that most people instinctively find price discrimination to be unfair. There are other pricing practices we don't like either. Try for yourself:

How would you react to a hardware shop that substantially raised the price of its snow shovels the morning after a big snowstorm? What would you think of a grocer that, when informed that a shortage was about to raise the wholesale price of its next batch of tinned tomatoes, immediately put up the price of the ones it already had on the shelves? Would you think it reasonable for a supermarket chain to charge considerably higher prices in a particular town where it had no competitor?

These examples are adapted from a paper by behavioural economists Daniel Kahneman, Jack Knetsch and Richard Thaler. In each case, over three-quarters of us consider the firm's behaviour to be unfair. The first two examples show that most of us don't think increased demand or reduced supply are necessarily good reasons to raise prices. The third suggests my gang in the playground were not atypical. We dislike what we see as abuse of a monopoly position. Now compare with these:

What would you think if a grocer raised the price of a lettuce by 30p to cover a 30p increase in the wholesale price caused by a local shortage? How would you respond to a landlord who passed on increased costs of upkeep by raising the rent, knowing that it was likely that the tenant couldn't afford it and would have to move? In both of these examples, even though the consequences in the second one are quite severe, more than three-quarters of us think the behaviour is fair. It seems that we believe that a fair price is related to the cost of production.

These findings are consistent with the previous ones connected to the *yucki* ("you can keep it") instinct. In these latest examples, whether customers would or wouldn't continue to do business with the firm was not asked. But some of the behaviour we encountered earlier – the marketing of sell-out events, toy stores handling the latest craze, people's different degree of willingness to pay for beer from grocers or hotels by the beach – is consistent with these attitudes about fairness. Interestingly, it is also in line with the pricing policies of Hubert Henderson's well-oiled industrialists, and of companies involved in pricing studies. People think a price should fairly reflect costs of production, not an equilibrium between supply and demand. And this is what firms generally seek to achieve. Whether they do this because they think they should, or because they expect the bad Apple treatment from customers if they get caught doing otherwise, is harder to say.

One size fits few

Perhaps it was the brandy, but business leaders dining in finest Oxford tradition were not only spouting heretical pricing theories. They also seemed to be completely unaware of rising "marginal cost". If it was limiting the scale of their operations, making further expansion unprofitable, then it was doing so without their knowledge. The economists thought each manager should be carefully watching their marginal cost, squeezing out every last drop of profit, but being sure not to over-expand, become inefficient and so produce at a loss. Not only were the businessmen not watching it, they had no idea what it was.

The rising marginal cost of conventional economics was

apparently not uppermost in Sam Walton's mind either, when he decided to open a Wal-Mart on the outskirts of just about every town in America.* From a single discount store in Arkansas, opened in 1962, Wal-Mart has grown, and grown and grown, until by 2004 it was the world's largest company, with one in every eleven dollars Americans spent while out shopping going into its cash registers. If Wal-Mart faced limits to its size from rising marginal cost, the effect certainly didn't kick in at the 23rd employee – nor, it seems, the one million and twenty-third.

Massive corporations don't thrive only in the retail sector. Britain's largest company in that same year, 2004, was BP, which recorded post-tax profits of £16 billion – higher than the national incomes of 46 sub-Saharan African countries. In the mid-1980s, the US workforce of General Motors was greater than the population of seven US states. Coca-Cola executives like to quote a survey that found "Coke" to be the second most recognized word in the world. (Presumably it is a bizarre coincidence that removing its first and last letters gives you the most recognized one.) These giant firms do not, to say the least, resemble Mule's Muffins. Corporate giants are, of course, exceptions by definition, but it is not just household-name companies which are large. Around half of all American workers are employed by companies with over five hundred staff, while a quarter work for corporations with over ten thousand. Corporate America, cheerleader of world capitalism, does not dance to the tune of traditional economics, with competing firms kept small by rising marginal cost.

The American political scientist Herbert Simon, who was part economist (another Nobel Prize winner), part psychologist, part organizational theorist – indeed, one of life's true polymaths – found

---

* Marginal cost is usually described as the cost of the last item to roll off a production line, such as a muffin, but the concept applies equally to a retailer like Wal-Mart, or to services generally. Effectively, Wal-Mart produces "purchase opportunities", for the price of the mark-up on what it sells. Standard theory says Wal-Mart should keep opening more stores for more hours until providing another hour of purchase opportunities costs the company more than it gets in mark-ups from the hour's sales. It appears that the company has yet to reach that point.

another way to put it. Writing in the 1991 *Journal of Economic Perspectives*, Simon tried to imagine what initial observations an alien social scientist approaching from space might make of the way humans organize society. He envisaged the alien scientists using a particular kind of telescope, which could automatically map human social structures. Through this telescope, each firm could be seen as a solid green area, with interior contours dividing departments, and faint blue lines within them corresponding to lines of authority between bosses and workers. Market transactions could be seen as red lines between the green areas. Simon's thought experiment led him to form a few conclusions about what the aliens using this special telescope would report. Given the size of the green areas, the initial map transmitted back to their home planet would probably show "large green areas interconnected by red lines", not "a network of red lines connecting green spots". Given this and the complexity of the internal structures of the green areas, the aliens would be far more likely to call what they observed an "organization economy" than a "market economy". Furthermore, they would see that the richest countries on the planet contained by far the largest green areas. At first sight, successful capitalism appears not to negate massive firms, but rather to require them.

This view, that the growth of large corporations is an essential component of successful capitalism, receives further support from historical studies of the growth of corporations. For example, the late nineteenth century saw a revolution in transport and communications, with the commercialization of railroad, steamship, telegraph and cable systems. It propelled a period economic historians call the "second industrial revolution", which lasted until it hit the buffers of the Great Depression. It was a foretaste of modern globalization; a time when two-thirds of all industrial goods were produced by the USA, Britain and Germany. The foremost expert on this era is Alfred Chandler, Professor of Business History at Harvard. His detailed historical research documents how successful firms realized that changes in communication had removed any limits to size, offering economies of scale in organization, marketing and distribution. Big firms faced *falling* marginal costs – the more they produced, the *cheaper* each unit was to make. Mass production permitted expansion into new markets, including foreign ones. Many household-name brands, some of which remain dominant today, established positions as giants of their industries during this period, including: Heinz, General Electric, AT&T, Siemens, Del Monte, Quaker, Coca-Cola, Singer, Wrigley, Monsanto, Ericsson, Du Pont, Colgate, Allied Chemical, Procter & Gamble, Union Carbide, Philips and, of course, Gillette.

Chandler, writing in the *Journal of Economic Perspectives* in 1992, urged economists to note what little insight into this heyday of capitalism orthodox theory gives, and to look for alternative explanations of how it came about. During this period, Herbert Simon's little green scientists, looking through their social structure telescope, would have sent urgent reports home about human economic development, as they watched the green areas on their maps expand at an unprecedented rate. The success of massive corporations suggests that, at least in some industries, getting bigger and bigger allows firms to keep pushing their marginal cost *down*, producing more goods more cheaply the bigger they get, until they are a dominant player in their target market.

Modern data on what economists call "industrial concentration" shows that industries are often dominated by a small number of big players. According to the latest US Economic Census, the largest four firms in any given industry account for, on average, a market share of about 40% (that is, they make 40% of all sales in the industry). But this is just an average; there is plenty of variation. The four largest makers of breakfast cereal gobble up 83% of the market, while America's four big breweries swallow a 90% market share. Yet the four largest manufacturers of heating equipment have just 20%. Variation aside, the key message is that many sectors are "oligopolies" – the jargon for an industry dominated by a small number of large companies.*

---

* Figures for the EU are broadly similar, but less clear, because as industries have adapted to the European Single Market, it is hard to decide whether the appropriate

Faced with such data, traditional economists often argue that there are actually limits to the size of firms, but that the most efficient size just varies between industries. A favourite example is aircraft manufacture. The factory space, technology and systems required to make a single jet aeroplane cost millions, so it would be very inefficient having invested in all this capital not to use it to make a lot of planes. The most efficient size for an aircraft manufacturer will therefore be a trade-off between the massive scale of investment needed to make planes and inefficiencies caused by getting too large. This explains why the world market has room for only two major players, Boeing in America and Airbus in Europe; although there is still some competition. Compare this to the handmade jewellery trade, where the tools required are cheap and matter less than the skill of the craftsperson. The result is a world market of thousands of competing small jewellery operations. Many economists believe this logic explains why the standard model is right, even though there are many very big corporations. Size limits kick-in at a different scale in different industries.

This story sounds reasonable, though it is harder to see how the theory explains the dominance of major breweries or breakfast cereal companies, neither of which make big, expensive products. Furthermore, although Wal-Mart is the dominant player in retail, there are still some very profitable small supermarkets. But we can do better than anecdotal evidence. If the theory is right, then it predicts that there should be an ideal company size in each industry – massive for aircraft companies, tiny for handmade jewellery. If firms go beyond the ideal size for their industry, they should be beaten by leaner, meaner competitors. In short, it should be possible for firms to get too big for their boots.

What does the data say? In most industries, both large and small firms can be successful, as measured either by increased sales or

---

measure of market share is the national or EU-wide one. Nevertheless, oligopoly is just as common in Europe.

profits. Size does not determine whether a company gains market share. That said, averaged across a wide range of industries, corporate giants make slightly higher returns than local minnows; that is, for every dollar invested in them, they return slightly more profit. But, crucially, evidence for an ideal, advantageous size in each industry is weak, as is any obvious penalty for being bulky. (Some data suggests an individual plant can be inefficiently large, but big companies simply build separate plants to avoid the problem.)

The standard theory of the firm, which Hubert Henderson's team found to be at odds with the instincts of businesspeople back in the 1930s, cannot account for the way firms expand, nor how they make decisions about prices. What business instincts can?

Survive and thrive

Here is a brief history of a hugely successful and yet extremely simple modern product. Almost certainly, you will have used it.

In 1968, Spencer Silver was working in a research laboratory, trying to develop a strong adhesive. He failed. Instead, he produced a glue so weak that the objects it bound could be ripped apart with the slightest pull. Although he looked for a use for his invention, its potential lay dormant until one Sunday morning in 1974. Art Fry, another scientist who worked for the same company, was a chorister in his local church. A peaceful pastime, you might think. But on the morning in question Fry was getting increasingly irritated. The bookmark in his hymn book kept falling out. For whatever reason, Fry's irritation turned into invention. He thought of his colleague's failed glue, and wondered whether it could be used to make a bookmark that wouldn't fall out. Like King Camp Gillette 80 years before him, Fry had chanced upon a marvel among the mundane.

The US firm that Silver and Fry worked for, 3M, had a policy called "bootlegging", under which technical staff were encouraged to spend 15% of their time on pet projects. The scientists used this time to adapt Silver's light adhesive to the task, so that it stuck well enough to stay fixed to the paper, but not so well that lifting it off would rip the page or leave a sticky mark. It took three more years for the product to be developed so that it could be manufactured. By 1977, nine years after the discovery of an unremarkable glue, the world had its first batch of a remarkably successful product: the "post-it" note.

One year later, the workforce at 3M HQ were pretty well hooked on post-its. But the firm had a problem – a marketing problem. Market testing showed that people realized how useful post-its were only once they had actually used them. The standard solution to such a problem is to offer free samples, but if the strategy fails it can prove costly. So 3M launched what they called the "Boise Blitz". They piloted the marketing of post-its in Boise, Idaho, saturating the office supply industry with free samples. The office workers of Boise, once they'd tried them, became hooked too. Finally, in 1980, the strategy and the post-it went national, and in 1981 international.

The moral of the story? If King Camp Gillette were still alive he'd doubtless quote his mentor, William Painter's, advice: create something people find useful but throw away. The bigger message, however, is about the environment in which firms operate, which is overwhelmingly characterized by two things: uncertainty and change. Industry, like individuals, must operate in Muddleton too.

With all due respect to its inventors, the post-it is hardly a cutting-edge, high-tech invention. Yet even with a small, simple manufactured product, firms don't know how effective it will be, don't know the level of demand for it, don't know whether someone else is developing one too, don't know whether someone else is developing something that will make it obsolete, don't know what years of development through trial and error will ultimately deliver, and don't know how successful years of marketing through trial and error will be.

The reason the standard economic theory of the firm doesn't match what we observe in the real world is that it fails to identify the most important issue firms face. Their principal problem is not to decide on a scale of production and a price, in order to maximize profit. If only running a business were that simple. If only successful entrepreneurship were as straightforward as running Mule's Muffins – obtaining easily observed market information and doing a few sums. None of us would be workers; we'd all be making a fortune instead. The principal problem facing the firm is much, much more difficult. The firm has to decide how best to survive and thrive in a changing marketplace of great uncertainty. And, at the risk of being repetitive, it is how the individual (in this case a firm) and the environment interact which counts.

This statement is informed by more than an anecdote about the invention of the post-it, instructive though the anecdote is. Instead, it is derived from a collection of evidence, including surveys of businesspeople, data on industrial structure, business history and case studies of how firms operate.

In developed economies, between 5 and 10% of businesses fail every year, depending on how you define an existing business. Failure is a fact of commercial life – a constant threat of significant but uncertain magnitude. Success and failure are driven by change. Firms must respond to changes in their environment: tastes, business practices, policies, technology, confidence. They must also manage internal change: strategies, staff, investment, information, structures. Each decision, taken in the face of change, or in the anticipation of future change, can increase or decrease revenue and raise or lower costs.

The availability of bigger and better data-sets in many countries has allowed economists to look at which firms are most likely to survive and which to fail. There are certain regularities in this data. Small and young firms are more likely to fail than large established ones, but there are major companies that go under too. Regardless of age and size, though, firms are more likely to survive if they are innovative. This doesn't just mean if they develop new products. Innovation comes in many forms. Studies show that, as well as product innovation, survival is linked to finding more efficient ways to supply existing products, or "process innovation". Survival is also linked to innovation in marketing. Indeed, given the evidence of its effectiveness, it is not a surprise that one of the most persistent findings of industrial economics is a link between profitability and marketing. Nevertheless, the overriding message is that, to survive, firms must keep looking for ways to do things better. In short, to survive and thrive, you need to change.

Yet timing matters too. Data on the number of firms within individual industries, both modern and historical, reveals a pattern, often referred to as the "product life cycle". When a new type of product appears, such as the domestic light bulb, anti-wrinkle cream or the digital music player, there is an initial rise in the number of firms that produce it, which pretty quickly reaches a peak. During this early period, there can be many competing versions of the product, or different designs, combined with a similar variety of marketing techniques. There also tend to be a lot of early business failures, although until the peak is reached failures are outnumbered by new firms trying to get in on the action. After the peak, even though the volume of sales within the industry as a whole continues to grow, the number of firms declines. More popular versions of the product survive; less popular ones vanish. Business failures continue, while fewer new firms appear. Winners emerge, who take larger and larger market shares. There are fewer innovations in design and marketing. But innovation continues, concentrating on process – making more and better for less cost. The industry stabilizes, usually with a few leading, large firms, surrounded by smaller firms that may have established significant niches within the market.

This kind of dynamic process explains why there is no ideal efficient size for a firm in each industry, because it depends on timing, on which segment of the market the firm is targeting, on the maturity of the industry when the firm started up, and so on. It may also explain a long-standing economic puzzle. When the same industries are compared across different countries, the pattern regarding dominant firms tends to be similar. For instance, there are particular industries in which a small number of large firms tend to dominate, albeit different companies in each country. Examples are cigarettes, bottles, fridges and batteries. Economists have wondered why the pattern repeats, especially for industries making simple products where there is no obvious advantage for large firms. The answer may lie in the fact that while the industry includes different companies in each country, its evolution benefits from the same innovations everywhere, and so the pattern of successful firms associated with them replicates.

The crucial difference between this perspective on how capitalism works and the perspective of traditional economics is that in an environment of change and uncertainty, each firm is likely to tackle the same challenge in a different way. The orthodox view sees one "rational" way to operate in each industry, because every firm has the same information, must pay the same prices and wages, and so there is one "rational" solution to the problem. The reality of business life is nothing like this.

For instance, researchers have studied the way executives tackle business problems. They find they tend to opt for innovations in keeping with their own expertise. Those with a marketing background are inclined to see new marketing ideas as the way forward; those with a production background look for possible product changes. Different business brains looking at the same problem opt for different solutions. Consistent with this, variation in the way firms tackle the same market has been carefully documented in industrial case studies. Competing firms differ in strategy, structure and core capabilities. Because firms are run by people with differing backgrounds, and because the outcomes of decisions are so uncertain, the innovations firms choose to back are bound to vary.

The result of this plurality of approaches is a plurality of products, prices and marketing within each industry. The standard theory that competition forces firms to accept the market price assumes they sell the same product. In reality, the offerings of different companies in most industries differ considerably. Firms that enter an industry without at least one key innovation don't survive. Even where products are similar, distinctive marketing means consumers treat them otherwise. One of the key principles of good marketing is distinctiveness. Marketing professionals know that, within limits, most consumer decisions are based not on price comparisons, but on desire for the product. To attract a new customer or make someone switch brand, the product has to be seen as distinct. This is another reason why firms can price according to cost, not competition.

Successful capitalism requires this plurality of approaches. The uncertainty of the market is too great for even the smartest and most visionary entrepreneur to second-guess it reliably. Trial and error by companies, trial and error by consumers, feedback from customers: all contribute to more product, process and marketing innovation.

In among all this change and plurality, are there general business instincts that emerge? Yes. As we have seen, in an environment of constant change, successful firms innovate. But how much? How does the successful businessperson decide which innovations to back? Orthodox economics says firms take decisions that maximize profit. But this is to ignore the second salient characteristic of the business environment: uncertainty. It may initially seem odd, but in an uncertain market, aiming to maximize profit may be a poor strategy.

Here's an analogy. On Friday nights during the winter, my family likes to watch our local team, Leinster, play rugby. Getting to the game is, invariably, a rush, involving fast preparation of food, picking clothes to match temperamental Irish weather, finding tickets, and so on. Then, short of time, we have to decide how to get there. Games usually kick off at 7.30 p.m. The fastest way is to drive, which is usually about twice as fast as walking. But if we always drove to the game we would miss more kick-offs than if we always walked. Why? Uncertainty. Although it takes, on average, about twenty minutes to drive, there are odd occasions when Friday night Dublin traffic turns the main roads into car parks. It can happen that the journey eats up over an hour. If we walk, it takes about forty minutes. Always. Driving is the fastest option, walking is the option less likely to result in a missed kick-off.

In many decisions, the option that produces the fastest, best or strongest outcome, *on average*, may nevertheless be more likely to fail completely. If there are business decisions like this, where the option expected to deliver the highest profit is also more risky, aiming for maximum profit may be a poor strategy.

There is evidence to suggest that decisions of this sort are common in business. Surveys of managers' attitudes consistently report that many bosses do not regard profit as their top priority. They are likely to say that the long-term survival of the company is the top priority. Others, particularly but not only Japanese executives, give innovation higher priority than profit. Innovation, as we have seen, is linked to survival. Meanwhile, many executives also say market share is more important than profit. Larger companies have better survival prospects too.

Sometimes, surveys make the tension between survival and profit more explicit. In recent times, particularly in the USA and Britain, the so-called "shareholder value" movement has placed greater pressure on companies to return higher profits. Shareholders may care less about the firm's survival and more about profit than executives, because most hold shares in many firms – their eggs are in more than one basket. Indeed, surveys of CEOs show that many believe this pressure for higher returns poses a threat to the company. Studies of managers' attitudes to risk show that 90% say that they would not take risks where a failure could jeopardize the survival of the firm. More generally, managers show greater concern about taking any risk that could result in a loss.

Still, let's be sceptical for a moment. Surveys are subjective, so perhaps the top brass tell lies when researchers appear with clipboards, because they don't wish to appear ruthlessly profit hungry. So let's look at a more objective measure, such as how executives are rewarded. If profit is the ultimate aim of a firm, then the bosses who make most profits should be the best paid. Yet they are not. Boss-class pay is linked more to the size of companies than to profits. It seems that the bottom line is, perhaps, not actually the bottom line.

All of this suggests that Milton Friedman may have been wrong. In a changing and uncertain market environment, maximizing profit may not be the best survival instinct. Market selection, far from weeding out those who don't maximize profit, may penalize those who do. The profit motive matters, but other instincts matter too, and probably more.

Beating the competition

If a good business consultant were to pass through the bakery gates, they would probably react with horror to the way Maurice runs Mule's Muffins. For a start, they wouldn't be able to see the firm's "unique selling point", or USP. They would immediately stress the need to differentiate the product from other muffins. Maurice would be advised, perhaps, to make the muffins a little spicy and work on a distinctive tagline – "only a Mule's Muffin kicks". Perhaps he should bake a chocolate muffin aimed at kids, with a little grinning plastic mule embedded in the top. The consultant would worry about the lack of strategic thinking. With all the workers engaged in churning out very average muffins as efficiently as possible, competitors would be sure to get a step ahead. Maurice would be told to take his smarter people off shift for a while, even if it meant lower short-term profits, to rethink company strategy. Perhaps a second product line? Maybe Mule's Marshmallows? Are there any new developments in baking technology on the horizon? What are younger people eating with their morning coffee? Any new flavours to market-test?

In a changing and uncertain environment, the instincts of successful businesspeople are to gather information about their market, to look for innovations that improve products, processes and marketing, and to decide which innovations are most likely to benefit the long-term prospects of the company. In addition, they need to be good managers – to organize the firm to get the most from its workers. Prices are generally set to make a reasonable profit over and above costs, being careful with customer perceptions of price. Traditional theory conceives of the main problem a firm faces as selecting its optimal size and price to maximize profit, given market rates and available technology. Within each industry, each firm faces the same problem. This misses the driving force of modern developed economies. The business environment and the instincts necessary to survive in it mean that successful capitalism is characterized by plurality. Each firm has a separate history, employs workers and teams with different capabilities, is run by executives with various backgrounds, and arrives in the market at a different time. Thus, a defining feature of capitalism is that firms develop different traits, through trial and error. The market determines which survive. The traditional theory fails to capture the essence of capitalism, with implications for the understanding of economists and decision-makers.

First, our conception of the importance of competition needs to change. The mantra that competition means lower prices and better value for consumers is now firmly embedded in Western economic and political culture. But this is only one form of competition and it coexists with others that may be more important to economic development. Sure, we want to pay a fair price for what we buy. But constant consumer pressure to drive down margins has the potential to stifle innovation. Process innovation, performing the production process more efficiently to lower costs, is not the only way we want firms to compete. Firms also need the time and space to improve products, to look for advantages from new technology, to get feedback from consumers, to engage in development by trial and error. Where there is competition between firms, it should not be measured only by prices, but by innovation and progress. Indeed, there is evidence that price wars can damage investment in new ideas, as firms sacrifice long-term development for short-term survival. Consumers may actually benefit if prices are slightly higher but investment in better products is higher too. This is not simply because people with higher incomes may prefer better to cheaper, but because tomorrow's better products become the day after tomorrow's cheaper ones. What consumer lobbying should perhaps aim for is not cheapness, which has a downside, but curbing excess profits (relative to turnover). Where there is insufficient competition to innovate, revenue may be sucked out in large profits rather than reinvested. In these circumstances, consumers have a legitimate complaint that prices are not fair. We should worry more about excess profit, less about prices.

Second, the domination of some industries by large corporations is not necessarily a sign of insufficient competition and monopolistic practices. The nature of certain industries, especially those that require long-term investment in innovations of uncertain benefit, may mean that large corporations are desirable. The sheer financial muscle of larger companies allows them to take chances smaller companies cannot, without risking their survival. Large companies with multiple product lines are often able to take innovative risks with one product, knowing that there are others to fall back on in the event of failure. The ability to shoulder greater risks and spread risks means that larger companies tend to be more profitable and more likely to survive. Massive and successful corporations are a hallmark of developed economies, not a symptom of inefficiency.

That said, there are negative sides to corporate giants. Some maintain market share primarily through massive spending on advertising and brand management. Others flood the market for a single product with similar brands that pretend to be distinct, yet are all owned by the same company. Such wasteful marketing tricks could be taxed, or regulated to allow consumers to see through the trick. Meanwhile, like consumers, competition authorities place too much emphasis on prices. Sure, where there is evidence of price-fixing there are likely to be unfair prices and excess profits, so competition authorities should be tough. But the bigger potential problem associated with an industry dominated by a few very large firms may be monopoly of ideas, not monopoly pricing. Competition policy should focus more on supporting innovation and new firms trying to break through.

Third, there is a more subtle implication in understanding capitalism as a process of trial and error in response to uncertainty and change. Orthodox economics, with its emphasis on rational behaviour and the efficiency of markets, tends to make us think that the market is largely meritocratic, rewarding ability and effort.* Where an honest business succeeds, we are inclined to think that it must have made insightful decisions and efficiently provided people with products they wanted. Where a business fails, we tend to assume that it must have made mistakes, misjudging the market or being poorly run. There is some truth in this, in the sense that better decisions lead to better outcomes. But only some. Where there is such uncertainty, there is also luck. King Camp Gillette chanced upon a lucrative marketing trick long after he risked thousands of dollars and years of his life on the disposable razor blade. Art Fry might have possessed a high-quality leather bookmark and so never become so frustrated by losing his page that he dreamed of a sticky one. It is possible to make the best business decision on the information available, yet be unlucky; take a mediocre one, yet get lucky.

Psychologists will tell you, because studies show it, that it is in our nature to explain success or failure as the consequence of decisions, not random events. But in an uncertain and changing capitalist economy, there is probably much more luck involved than is generally believed. The market is far from meritocratic. It is a matter of political preference how one responds to this insight; how much we think those who get lucky owe those who suffer ill fortune in both senses.

Finally, our understanding of the way firms operate is a crucial

---

* No textbook I have ever read states this. It is more that it is an implication that follows from a theory that does not take account of uncertainty and so downplays the role of luck.

component of our understanding of the controversial changes that are occurring in the international economy. Traditionally, economists have tended to be strong supporters of free trade, because of the mutual benefits of trade itself and the effects of opening up markets to foreign competition. Some of this reasoning is clearly valid. Opponents of trade often fail to see the broader picture that accompanies the opening of markets. It is true that some industries in developed economies, especially traditional manufacturing, do decline in the face of foreign competitors. But this is compensated for by growth in other industries, often more lucrative ones, which enter the new foreign markets and expand. It is a fallacy to think that nations compete with each other for market share the way companies do. Companies in the same industry compete for the same customers; they don't trade with each other. But nations do trade with each other, meaning that when one country does well, others can benefit. A fast-growing country, such as China or India, can both produce more products we might wish to buy and earn higher income, which in turn makes it likely to buy more of our better products. Countries get mutual benefit from trade that competing companies don't.

Nevertheless, this optimistic picture about the potential benefits of trade needs serious qualification. In a market economy characterized by uncertainty, mutually beneficial trade is not assured. When trade crosses borders, the degree of uncertainty is higher. Moreover, the degree of common identity and the relationship between the parties is less strong, at least initially. Companies, especially multinationals based in developed nations, may capitalize by taking unfair shares of the revenues generated by foreign workers, or unfair shares in deals with smaller, less informed traders – shares they could not get away with in their own countries. Furthermore, if trade barriers are reduced quickly, the speed at which workers must transfer from less successful to more successful industries can be painfully rapid, creating unemployment and associated problems that potentially outweigh the gains from trade. The speed of adjustment is also subject to great uncertainty.

In this context, consider the instincts of businesspeople suggested by the evidence. Firms aim to establish a distinctive product that captures a dominant market share within an industry. They then seek to develop new product lines, to expand further. Size brings security. It allows a firm to spread risk and makes it more likely to survive in uncertain markets. Because global markets are characterized by even greater uncertainty, we would expect the advantage of large, established corporations to be bigger still. Developed, as opposed to developing, nations have many more such companies, capable of spreading risk, funding trial-and-error innovation, and devoting resources to market research in many countries simultaneously. It is therefore very likely that it is these massive companies which will be most cushioned from the bumpy ride of globalization, while the smaller companies of developing nations suffer the real bruises. This is another reason why people in poorer nations, who in principle could gain from greater trade, are right to be sceptical of pressure to open up their markets quickly.

9

Governing principles

THE COLCA CANYON is, as the Peruvians like to tell visitors, twice as deep as the Grand Canyon. Climbing from the Rio Colca up to the canyon's edge is an exhausting yet fabulous experience. The guidebooks say that to tackle the snaking, rocky, vertiginous path, fully exposed to the Andean sun, you need high-quality walking boots, light equipment and frequent rest stops for water. This last instruction is easy to follow. Rests not only ease the pounding of heart and lung, but also allow you to savour wondrous sights. Hundreds of metres below your feet, the river dashes over rocks towards the Pacific, while thousands of metres above, amid a full horizon of snow-capped Andes, the Sabancaya volcano puffs smoke. Occasionally, a condor or an eagle circles up towards you on a thermal, hardly seeming to move, yet soaring far above in just a few seconds. The sheer beauty of the canyon, isolated but vast, ancient yet alive, is humbling.

It's humbling too when, as you grit your teeth and place one boot purposefully ahead of the other, a girl of maybe eight or nine skips past in a homemade dress and a flimsy pair of sandals, carrying a basket full of water and snacks to sell to foreign hikers. Judging by her nimble negotiation of the path, she probably does the 1,000-metre descent to the campsite at the bottom, then back the other way, most days. Her village, perched on the canyon's lip, is characterized by a curious mixture of the antiquated and the modern. It is ringed by authentic Inca terracing; layers of tiny levelled fields, still ploughed by oxen and harvested by hand. Some children clearly work from a young age, herding livestock into the hills by day, returning at dusk. Large families live in two-room houses. Yet the local school appears positively first-world – a good size, well built, a pristine basketball court in the playground. A small hotel has state-of-the-art solar water heating. Most striking of all, the square has an internet café with half a dozen fast PCs. It bustles with sophisticated teenagers, including one who runs it and has the relaxed air of someone who knows his networks. The village is on the superhighway, but its physical connection to the outside world is a dirt road. It is a puzzling scene.

We flew to Peru from Chicago, where my family spent a year, and where there are other puzzling scenes. Chicago is testimony to human enterprise. Some of its downtown streets have three layers, while others carry elevated trains. There are warm winter walkways underground, connecting the main buildings and shops. The layout is the culmination of over a century of urban invention and architectural innovation. Through a system of locks, Chicagoans reversed the flow of their river. They raised the level of the streets over ten feet by lifting the buildings and inserting new foundations, sometimes even while people were sleeping above. They built their homes up into the clouds. Yet a substantial number of Chicagoans live surrounded not by the steel and glass of a skyscraper but by the paltry insulation of a cardboard box. The lower levels of the streets, where the service vehicles and waste trucks come and go, are home to hundreds of people.

One day in Chicago we boarded a bus going the wrong way. Realizing our error, we got off, no more than a few blocks from our intended route. A friendly man took one look at us and ran over. "You shouldn't be here," he said, "this place is dangerous." He helped us to flag down a cab. "Normally they won't even pick people up here." We sped back downtown.

I have visited rough areas of many cities in developed and developing countries, but this remains the only time a local came running up out of fear for my safety. My family and I loved Chicago. But a year there left me wondering how and why a society with such enthusiasm for life, with such drive and inventiveness, had also managed to create such extreme deprivation and violence.

A few years earlier, we spent some time in Copenhagen. I cannot imagine a less threatening city. We journeyed through Denmark, crossing spectacular bridges on the cleanest train I have ever seen. We hired bikes and pedalled on perfect cycle paths. When we looked at the houses, shops and cafés, the whole country appeared to be middle class. Yet here and there were cracks. Copenhagen felt old somehow. Its beauty and tradition were not balanced by lively youth or the buzz of diversity. The few poorer people we did encounter were quite likely to be immigrants. I wondered whether Denmark's comfort and cohesion could survive what an increasingly interconnected world might throw at it.

When people describe and compare countries, the economic decisions of governments feature prominently in their explanations. Whether in Peru, the United States or Denmark, indeed in all countries I have travelled to, developed and developing, the lives of the people and the cities, towns and villages they inhabit bear the imprint of power. People's economic opportunities, the threats they face and the environment that surrounds them, are determined by leaders and decision-makers, current and past, elected and unelected; powerful people acting on particular theories of how society should be, or at least of how they would like it to be. Economics and economists exert a strong influence on these people. In recent decades, the thinking behind what is now orthodox economics has had a profound effect on economic policy in most, perhaps all, countries.

The instincts of individuals and firms are not, however, as orthodox economics assumes. "Microeconomics", the study of individuals, firms and markets, is being revolutionized – a revolution that is in its youth. It is an indication of how profound the revolution may be that it is already exerting an influence on "macroeconomics" – the picture that emerges when all the individual economic lives of an economy are added up. One reason that economic life differs so much between nations is that different societies harness economic instincts in different ways, rewarding or punishing different instincts. The classic issues of macroeconomics, such as the causes of growth, unemployment and inflation, are beginning to be influenced by behavioural findings, which are also featuring strongly in debates about how governments should respond to the current crisis. The behavioural revolution in economics has begun to penetrate the world of politics and government. And to change it.

Making a difference

At various points, when describing experiments that suggest we have particular economic instincts, I have commented that the result seems to be universal – the outcome of the experiment is the same wherever it has been tried. In broad terms, this is true. For instance, I have read results from Ultimatum Games played in over twenty countries on all continents bar Antarctica. In every case, the study has recorded the *yucki* ("you can keep it") instinct in response to ungenerous offers. Nevertheless, there are smaller but potentially significant differences in the results between different cultures.

The American anthropologist Joseph Henrich, together with a long list of fellow anthropologists and behavioural economists, set out to measure just how big these differences can be and what might cause them. They arranged to conduct experiments, including Ultimatum Games, Dictator Games and Public Good Games, in fifteen societies with radically different cultures. The experiments covered twelve countries on five continents. The cultures ranged from the Quichua of Ecuador to the Sangu of Tanzania. The games were all played anonymously, except that players knew that the other player in the game was another member of their society. The money involved in each game was considerable – roughly one or two days' wages.

In qualitative terms, the results were all standard, suggesting that universal human instincts were at work. Most people behaved self-lessly. They shared gains and cooperated with other players to reach best common solutions. Some people behaved selfishly and people made sacrifices to punish their selfishness. In not one of these societies did anything other than a small minority behave like Marketopians. Still, in quantitative terms, there were some differences observed. For example, the average offer in the Ultimatum Game among the Orma of Kenya was 44% of the stake, while among the Torguud of Mongolia it was 35%. Differences were similar in the other games.

Henrich and his colleagues then sought to explain these differences. They estimated the degree of routine cooperation in each society, by looking at how many non-family members individuals usually worked with. Thus, societies in which men went out fishing together had high routine cooperation, while those in which individual families worked their own crops had low cooperation. They also estimated the number of market transactions within each society – how often individuals routinely exchanged goods or money with each other. Their fascinating result was that these two measures accounted for two-thirds of the differences in behaviour between the societies. Those with high routine cooperation and larger numbers of transactions behaved less selfishly. These large effects could be contrasted with the fact that they found no difference in behaviour by gender, age, wealth, the population of the village or the size of the stake being played for in the game.

For anyone who still doubts the relevance of these experiments for understanding economic life, this result takes some explaining. It suggests a strong relationship between the organization of the economy in which people live and their economic behaviour. Of course, none of the participants in these experiments was a member of a large modern economy. The aim of the study was to visit remote societies to see how universal our economic instincts are and to obtain as much variation in behaviour as possible. Generally speaking, between nations, the differences in behaviour in economic experiments are much smaller.

But here is an interesting thing: they still matter. Two behavioural economists, Colombian Juan Cardenas and American Jeffrey Carpenter, have analysed results from the Trust Game, in which one player can choose to hand some money to another, which will be tripled, before the second player decides how much, if any, to give in return. Again, in all countries the results are qualitatively similar – there is trust, and that trust is usually rewarded by returns. But even with the relatively small amount of data available, there is a clear correlation between the degree of trust found in this simple laboratory game and various aspects of the economy in which players live. Specifically, Cardenas and Carpenter show that more money is entrusted between strangers in countries with higher economic growth, lower poverty rates, more equality and less unemployment.

There are many questions raised by these results. Is the build-up of trust an important ingredient in economic progress? Does living in a poor economy erode trust? How robust is the result anyway? The effects appear to be pretty strong, but as of now the data is sparse. We also don't know whether or not other experimental results correlate with economy-wide phenomena. It may well be that the way a national economy is organized can have important effects on individual economic behaviour, and perhaps vice versa. Some economists respond to these results by saying they show that lack of trust is symptomatic of underdeveloped countries. Maybe. But there is evidence that economic behaviour varies between developed economies too.

Marketopian myths and woolly thinking

Marketopian thinking has dominated macroeconomics as it has microeconomics. As repeatedly stressed, the Marketopian perspective is not based on scientific evidence, but on assumptions about people's economic instincts that turn out not to match scientific evidence. Nevertheless, it informs the way people tend to compare the relative economic fortunes of countries.

The poor performance of some European economies in recent decades has led to a spate of unfavourable comparisons from those who believe that Europe's departures from Marketopian principles simply must have an adverse effect. A parallel is often drawn between Europe and the United States. Before discussion of the present economic crisis began to dominate the airwaves, you would often hear economic commentators, or politicians of certain persuasions, say that European economic growth is lower than that of the USA because European taxes are higher and European governments are too large. If you look at recent decades and compare the USA with all fifteen pre-expansion EU countries (the so-called EU-15), then it is possible to provide statistics to back these claims up. Similarly, you frequently hear it said that European countries tend to have less inequality between rich and poor, but that such equity comes at the price of efficiency, resulting in lower economic growth. Again, choose the comparison carefully and the claims can be backed up with statistics. Economists are inclined to believe these claims because they are consistent with the Marketopian view of our economic instincts, which implies that governments are naturally inefficient and that taxes reduce incentives.

The claims are misleading because the comparison works only if you group together very different European economies, dragging the performance of the best down by grouping them with the worst. There are huge differences between the economies of Europe. Arguably the best way to group them is into four categories or "models", usually labelled "Anglo-Saxon"* (UK, Ireland), "Continental" (Austria, Belgium, France, Germany, Luxembourg), "Mediterranean" (Greece, Italy, Spain, Portgual) and "Nordic" (Denmark, Finland, Sweden). The Netherlands perhaps fits least well, falling between the

* For some reason my profession has adopted this phrase to cover the economies of English-speaking nations. In doing so we have bought into a myth of nineteenth-century British historians that propagated a very narrow view of genealogy. English-speaking people are not primarily descended from Anglo-Saxons. Even the white English population is a mixture of Celts, Vikings, Normans, Saxons and a good few others.

Continental and Nordic categories. The categorization is based on a combination of economic history, the level of taxes, how the social welfare system works, the way wages are negotiated, and the protection offered to workers.

Now, take Denmark, Finland and Sweden, which have big governments and tax burdens of 49%, 44% and 50% of national income respectively, compared to just 27% in the USA. They also have a much narrower gap between rich and poor. Calculated over a substantial period, 1960–2004, average annual economic growth in the Nordic nations was 2.2% in Denmark, 2.9% in Finland and 2.1% in Sweden. In the USA, it was 2.4%.* If big government, high taxes and equality make for lower economic growth, then there must be something very special going on in the Nordic nations to compensate for such handicaps.

Sometimes people insist that the world has changed, that the global economy has become more competitive and that, while it may have been possible to get away with big, generous governments in the past, it isn't any more. Let's change the period and focus on 1980–2004. Average annual growth is then 1.6% in Denmark, 2.1% in Finland, 1.7% in Sweden, 2.0% in the USA. Still there is no clear difference. The real fun starts when you include Norway too. It has a tax burden of 44% and grew at 3.0% per year for 1960–2004 and 2.5% for 1980–2004. Norway is a high-tax, big-government, low-inequality country that, relative to America, kicks economic ass.

The truth is, if you select the comparison countries and time period carefully, you can quote support for most economic principles you happen to believe. Perhaps a better test of a macroeconomic theory is to look at the impact of economic reforms. Indeed, for anyone who doubts the impact that economic theory has over our lives, there are numerous examples of countries that have undertaken "textbook" economic reform.

---

* I'm using economic growth figures for GDP per capita based on what is generally accepted to be the best source, the Penn World Tables.

The failure of free-market reforms in Russia and elsewhere in eastern Europe, following the fall of the Berlin Wall, has been well documented.* Apologists often put the failure down, not to the theory on which the reforms were based, but to how quickly they were brought in, the sequence in which they were enacted, or the problems of introducing markets to citizens who lived under communism. Another hotly contested set of reforms occurred in Chile, when the economy was redesigned by a group of young Chilean economists who trained under Milton Friedman in Chicago. There is no consensus on the legacy of the "Chicago boys", in Chile or outside. These examples are suggestive, but difficult to draw firm conclusions from. It is debatable whether the impact of reform in countries emerging from communism or living under an oppressive dictatorship, as Chile was at the time, amounts to a fair test. Macroeconomics rarely throws up anything close to a controlled experiment.

Nevertheless, there is one developed country that has arguably done more than any other to reform itself to match the standard textbook model. Beginning in 1984, this nation spent over a decade trying to become the closest thing to Marketopia the world had seen. In doing so, it received praise from international agencies such as the International Monetary Fund (IMF) and the Organisation for Economic Cooperation and Development (OECD). It was the subject of special articles in economics journals, mostly praising the reforms and enthusing about the efficiency gains they would surely bring. Step forward and take a bow, New Zealand.

By all accounts, the New Zealand economy was in poor shape in 1984 – hit hard by recession, suffering record unemployment and high inflation. All were agreed about the need for reform. Orthodox economics offered but one route, along which New Zealand set off with determination and speed. The governing principle was,

---

* Joseph Stiglitz, former Chief Economist at the World Bank, provides a detailed and vivid account of the role of the international financial institutions in these reforms, and draws the link to the traditional theories on which they were based.

ironically enough, to decrease the role of government. That entailed a greater role for markets, reducing regulations and increasing competition. Over the next decade, New Zealand deregulated its markets, lifted restrictions on international capital, reduced or removed subsidies and tax incentives, privatized billions of dollars' worth of public assets, and slashed import quotas and tariffs. All these reforms were driven by the belief that markets are naturally efficient. To assist efficiency, New Zealand also became the first country, in 1989, to make price stability the sole aim of monetary policy (an issue to which we will return). The country took seriously the Marketopian idea of what motivates people. To provide greater incentives to workers, New Zealand cut income tax, reduced welfare payments and forced unions to negotiate pay at an individual level. Where state agencies couldn't be privatized, they were reformed to make them more like private companies. Managers were given explicit targets and held accountable for them with individual incentives.

How should we judge what happened next? Comparison of economic performance in the decade or so before and after the reforms is little use, because the international economic environment changed. As we will see shortly, the 1970s, in particular, was a peculiar decade in economic terms. Moreover, we can never know what would have happened had New Zealand chosen another path. Still, fortunately for our present purposes, the country comes with a handy yardstick a mere thousand miles or so to its north-west: Australia.

The comparison is good because the countries share a similar history and their economies are very similar. They had grown almost in parallel until, in 1967, a crash in the price of wool had a disproportionate impact on New Zealand, which has lots of sheep – lots and lots of sheep. This allowed Australia to nose ahead in terms of income per capita. When the reforms began, almost two decades later, it was still faring slightly better, but the similarity remained good for comparison. Moreover, the two countries had a free trade agreement and free movement of capital and labour between them. Another point to bear in mind is that, after 1984, Australia underwent some free-market reforms of its own. This was, after all, the 1980s. But the scale of the New Zealand reform programme, particularly its reduction in the role of the state, was very much greater.

So, in the Marketopian beauty contest of the 1980s, New Zealand chose to sport an especially skimpy government bikini. The sight certainly pleased many economic judges at the time, but how did it feel to be New Zealand? Pretty exposed, I suspect. Twenty years on from the reforms, New Zealand has not aged well, and can only regard its much healthier-looking neighbour with envy. A genuine economic gap has opened up between the two countries, where previously there was near parity. On average, Australians are now more than 20% richer than New Zealanders, even on a conservative estimate.* Analysis of the period reveals more. New Zealand's "efficient" free markets and greater incentives were supposed to increase employment and productivity. In fact, unemployment grew sharply following the introduction of the reforms. Then, in the 1990s, the productivity of New Zealand's workers began to lag behind. Finally, while other developed economies, including Australia, rode out the ripples from the Asian financial crisis, market-driven New Zealand went into recession in 1998. Slower economic growth was not the only outcome. The country also experienced a dramatic widening of the gap between its rich and poor.

For many economists, Marketopia is an ideal. New Zealand, a successful developed democracy, embraced this ideal more fervently than any other country, only to discover that the embrace was cold.

The economic performance of New Zealand was doubtless the result of a complex set of factors. But the relative decline in workers' productivity, in particular, is very much in keeping with the behavioural evidence on workers and firms. Contrary to conventional theory, increased monetary incentives, greater price competition and

---

* There are different published estimates of the size of the economic gap between the two countries. It depends on the precise definition of national income used (GNP or GDP, purchasing power versus dollars, etc.). On a less conservative estimate, the gap is now over 30%.

a less regulated labour market may have damaged motivation and stifled innovation in New Zealand, by undermining trust and forcing companies to slash margins rather than invest in innovation. An inquiry by New Zealand's Treasury in 2003 suggested this, concluding that investment by private firms was stronger in Australia than in New Zealand.

In 2002, I met two successful radio journalists who had left New Zealand, partly in response to changes in their industry. It had been "deregulated", allowing many more stations to start up, with much greater competition between them. From the perspective of traditional economics, these developments sound good. I asked one of them what had happened. "I worked longer hours for less pay to produce cheap crap," was the reply. Translating this into economics-speak, you get almost what standard theory would predict. Competition drove cost saving and reduced prices. Unfortunately, you then get to the word "crap".

The contrast between New Zealand and Australia is telling, because of the scale and textbook nature of New Zealand's reforms, the similarity of the economies, the timing of New Zealand's transition to less impressive performance and, most importantly, because the negative outcome makes perfect sense from a behavioural perspective. By trying to make their country like Marketopia, the New Zealanders damaged some essential components of Muddleton.

That's priceless

The experience of New Zealand provides yet more evidence that the fabled efficiency of free markets is greatly exaggerated. In an uncertain economic environment, mutually beneficial transactions don't just happen by magic, but require familiarity, communication and mutual trust. Even the most ardent believers in markets, who don't recognize this, do recognize that markets sometimes fail and that, when they do, a degree of government intervention may help.

Asymmetry of information and monopoly are two of the potential market failures recognized by orthodox economics. As we have seen, behavioural economics has something to say about each. There is a third.

Consider, for a moment, your nearest park, or equivalent piece of green space where locals like to walk. Suppose that a developer wants to buy it and turn it into a housing estate. One day, a letter from the local authority lands on your doormat. It explains that the authority will permit the development to go ahead provided local users are compensated to the degree that they would rather have the compensation than have the park. You are invited to give a figure for compensation that you would be willing to accept in return for losing the space. What price your park?

Sometimes, when two parties trade, third parties are affected. The classic example in textbook economics is pollution. A company makes a product to sell to customers, but causes pollution in the process – burdening people who have nothing to do with the company or its product. In economics jargon, pollution is an "externality", meaning that it has an impact on people external to the market transaction. If the developer buys the park and is allowed to build on it, you lose some valued public space, even though you are not involved in the transaction. Externalities can be good, as when the arrival of a company helps to regenerate an area, or bad, as when excess packaging causes a waste problem.

Externalities are part of basic economic theory, as is the standard response, which is to "internalize" them. According to standard economics, the solution is to get everyone affected involved in the transaction. Thus, a local community may allow a company to pollute to a certain level in return for compensation – the community, effectively, sells the right to pollute. If compensation is sufficiently high that the community prefers the combination of pollution plus compensation to neither, then the community is happy. If the company can still make a profit once it must pay the compensation, it is also happy. And if the customers are prepared to pay the inevitably higher price for the company's product, they are happy too. The market has provided the most efficient solution. So the theory goes.

This is why the local authority wants to know the level of compensation you are prepared to accept for the park to be turned into a housing estate. Once it has determined the total level of compensation, the developer will decide whether the venture remains profitable given the compensation bill it must pay. If so, everyone is supposedly better off. The exercise of finding out how much people value something they don't themselves buy or sell is known as "contingent valuation". Because so many externalities are linked to our environment, it is a central concept in environmental economics. It is used in many countries to assess environmental damages, although it is probably most widespread in the USA. The World Bank also uses the method to assess externalities associated with projects in developing countries.

Contingent valuation is perhaps the ultimate manifestation of Marketopian thinking. Initially, it seems that externalities (at least the negative ones) are a failure of the free market – damage caused by unregulated commercial activity. But, in another act of theoretical jujitsu, orthodox economics says the problem is not too many free markets, but too few. There just needs to be a market for pollution, public space, disposal of packaging, or whatever the externality is, and we can all live efficiently ever after.

But traditional economics takes beneficial exchanges for granted, because it assumes we will not be MISLED. Transactions are much more uncertain than orthodoxy assumes for the main protagonists, let alone third parties. How do the instincts we have developed to cope with this uncertainty operate when the thing we are supposed to value is like our local park – something we have never traded ourselves, will probably never trade, and has value for us now and well into the future? Does contingent valuation work in uncertain Muddleton?

The answer is: not very well. In the process of contingent valuation, the endowment effect can become exaggerated out of all proportion. When people are asked to put a price on the value to them of an existing local park, they find the task almost impossible. They will price it many times, often hundreds of times, higher than if asked to value an identical new park. Some people simply refuse to price it at all, saying there is no level of compensation they will accept.

The degree of uncertainty surrounding the value of environmental resources is such that answers differ greatly depending on how the question is asked. In one behavioural study, Amos Tversky and some colleagues asked people to choose between two options for cleaning up a local beach. They could elect to pay either $250,000 out of local taxes for a limited clean-up, or $750,000 for a clean-up that would make the beach suitable for swimming. These figures produced a split of about 50–50 between those who went for the expensive option and those who preferred the cheaper one. But when people were told first about the $250,000 option, then asked what price they would be prepared to pay for a better clean-up that would allow swimming, only 12% put it as high as $750,000. The results were therefore completely contradictory. Similarly, a study asked people to put a price on the impact of reduced visibility resulting from pollution at the Grand Canyon. The values people gave were five times higher when the question was asked in isolation than when it was asked together with other questions requiring valuations. Indeed, when people are asked to value several environmental resources at once, they give completely different answers when the questions are asked in a different order, and if they are asked to value a number of sites together, they will quote less than the total when asked to value each separately.

We find it impossible to put a realistic price on our environment. We have no familiarity with buying and selling it. We know that our attitude to it might change as we get older or when we have children. We know that if we happen, by design or fate, to become familiar with a beautiful place, the value we place on it will change utterly. In an uncertain world, contingent valuation, the idea that everything has a price to everyone, is Marketopia gone mad.

A recent contingent valuation study was carried out in Ireland to assess the value of a particular route to hillwalkers. Access to the countryside is a controversial issue in Ireland. Unlike in other European countries there is no right of access and private landowners block many routes. A number of the walkers surveyed were visitors from other European countries. To someone who believes the world works like Marketopia this might seem odd, but many visiting walkers said the maximum price they would be prepared to pay to walk the route was zero. People aren't willing to pay for things they believe they have a right to. You can sell television rights, but you can't put a value on political or human rights. Justice doesn't have a price tag. Whether private landowners have the right to block people from visiting our most beautiful landscapes, or whether walkers have a right of access to such places, is not a matter of price, it is a matter of principle.

In the cases cited above, the contingent valuation method fails even when externalities are simple: more or less pollution, the experience of a single public space or beauty spot. In fact, important externalities can be hugely complex.

One rather subtle externality is diversity. There are many instances where the market may settle on solutions that are very similar in many different places. If there is a pattern to market solutions, which there certainly seems to be, then the casualty is diversity. The result is clone towns containing the same retail outlets, bars and restaurants. People find diversity interesting and a lack of diversity depressing. Places that look just like other places struggle to have a distinct sense of identity.

If you think it is hard to place a value on your local park, try putting a price on diversity. For one thing, we know only the diversity we experience. What would greater diversity than we have now look and feel like? What would it be worth to us? Would more diversity improve our culture, or perhaps enhance our creativity?

Creativity generates all manner of externalities, mostly positive. Music, literature and other art forms don't merely offer the immediate enjoyment of listening to the CD, reading the book or enjoying the experience. They can be the genesis of whole cultural movements that spread through populations. So-called "creative industries" are almost by definition producers of externalities – it is their very aim. The uncertainty that surrounds the benefits of creative activity is so great that markets cannot do it justice. So difficult is valuing creative works that many great authors, from James Joyce to J. K. Rowling, have been rejected by strings of publishers. The singer-songwriter Nick Drake never sold more than five thousand copies of an album during his lifetime, yet 30 years on from his death sales are in the millions and he is cited as a crucial influence by an impressive array of great bands. Who knows how many Joyces and Drakes never broke through at all.

There is a general lesson in these last two examples. Because our economic instincts are to stick with what we know and to seek signals from others regarding what things are worth, markets are particularly poor at valuing things that are original. Marketopian thinking can therefore have a deadening effect on culture, prioritizing what is market tested, obvious and bland over what is creative, groundbreaking and brilliant. Externalities such as diversity and creativity are so uncertain in their impact, especially their future impact, that they cannot be priced. Societies have to find other ways to decide what value they have and to nurture them accordingly.

It may be a matter of regret for economists like me, but not everything can be measured, especially with foresight, in order to slap a price on it. There are times when, to judge what things are worth, we must fall back on principles, traditions and values. Muddleton has plenty of systems, but is bound to have some muddle too.

Theory's not working

Truman Bewley, an economist at Yale, was by his own admission perplexed for years. Why? He couldn't understand what pushed unemployment so high during recessions. In the current recession, as in previous ones, many firms have allowed wages to stay put or even to rise a little, while simultaneously letting people go. This is not easy for standard economics to explain. When firms face falling sales, the only way to survive the loss of revenue is to cut costs. Labour is usually a significant cost and it can be cut either by cutting jobs or wages. Now, if wages were governed by supply and demand, they would fall during a recession. Firms would require less labour – reduced demand. If some firms did let people go, there would be a larger pool of willing labour available to other firms – increased supply. With less demand and more supply, standard theory says wages ought to fall – but they don't. Truman Bewley has probably worked out why, and in a world where unemployment is once again threatening to damage a generation, his explanation deserves to be much better known than it is.

During the recession of the early 1990s, Bewley abandoned the diagrams and equations on the blackboard and, instead, went to talk to managers, recruiters, union leaders and unemployment counsellors, to try to find out why the orthodox economics he knew didn't match the world he watched. What he found, after recording hundreds of interviews across the various industries of Connecticut, provides a neat match with some of the evidence on the instincts of workers and firms.

Bewley's interviews revealed that workers, understandably, did not want their pay cut. But the main reason why wages were not reduced was that managers didn't even try to reduce them. Why? Because they feared what it would do to morale. The bosses told Bewley that they understood that the performance of their firms depended crucially on the voluntary efforts of workers and their loyalty to the firm. Managers believed that the shock of a pay cut and the implied insult to the commitment of workers would damage relations, leading to less willingness to put the good of the company first. Using different language, the bosses were describing the importance of voluntary social exchange in the workplace, underpinned by mutual trust between workers and bosses. Many insisted to Bewley that laying people off was actually less damaging to morale than pay cuts. Only when the workforce could be convinced that moderate pay cuts would save a large number of jobs, or were necessary to ensure the survival of the firm, would management consider the option. Even then, they worried about the impact on trust.

So falling demand for labour didn't push down the wage. What about the extra supply once substantial numbers had been laid off? Bewley wanted to know why firms didn't take on willing workers at lower rates of pay. He found that recently laid-off workers couldn't even get jobs that paid substantially less than their previous wage. Employers didn't want to hire them at lower wages, even though it might in theory be profitable to do so. Managers were concerned that overqualified workers might be discontent with what seemed to be an unfair wage. They also worried that the presence of lower-paid workers might make the company pay structure look unfair, damaging morale. What Bewley found is inconsistent with the traditional view of the labour market, but consistent with behavioural evidence, and the wage differences between industries described earlier. Wages do not simply match supply and demand, but also reflect people's perceptions of fairness.

Bewley's insight has the potential to be hugely important in the current crisis, as all countries struggle to keep unemployment down. But to put the study in context, here is a brief history of the macroeconomics of unemployment. In nasty recessions like the present one, people buy fewer goods and services, and so across the whole economy there is less revenue from sales to go around. In theory, if society could find a way to spread the pain evenly, rather than letting the axe fall on an unlucky fraction, unemployment need not rise. Where economists have long disagreed is on whether an unregulated labour market will do the job for us.

Following the Great Depression, the outstanding economist of his generation, John Maynard Keynes, convinced many that it could not. Keynes argued that markets are not efficient because prices and wages are inherently "sticky", so when there is less demand for goods and services, the result is more unemployed people rather than lower wages for all. The great man would doubtless have found Truman Bewley's study a confirmatory experience. Keynes said that, during bad times, the government should not wait for the market to sort it out, but should stimulate demand in the economy, first by increasing its own spending or perhaps cutting taxes and, second, through monetary policy (to which we will come in the next section). For several decades, governments in the developed world did pretty much what Keynes suggested.

Then came the 1970s, when Keynesianism took a hammering. What is well known is that the trouble followed two big hikes in oil prices, one caused by the Arab oil embargo of 1973–74, the other by the Iranian revolution and the Iran–Iraq war at the end of the decade. What is less well known is that these events coincided with what economists call a "productivity shock". Over time, technology, business organization and industrial techniques improve. The result is that work becomes, on average, more efficient – workers produce more in the same amount of time. For several decades prior to the 1970s, productivity was increasing at about 5% a year. Then, suddenly, it slowed to more like 2%. No one is really sure why, although there is no reason to assume that technology will always improve smoothly rather than in jumps. In many countries, these events occurred at a time of considerable industrial unrest. Firms struggled to keep costs down. They produced less, at higher prices, with fewer workers. Many governments borrowed money to stimulate the economy, but couldn't stop rising unemployment and inflation – or "stagflation", as it became known. In 1976, the UK government almost ran out of money and suffered the indignity of calling on the IMF for assistance. In economics, whatever your perspective, the 1970s were "the bad old days".

Perhaps unsurprisingly, the apparent failure of Keynesian economics produced a backlash in favour of markets. Many economists thought excessive pay claims by unions and workers were to blame for inflation and unemployment. You may recognize something in the logic here. Nobody could argue that the 1970s experience suggested that the economy worked like Marketopia – far from it, given the inability of markets to adjust to the oil price and productivity changes. Instead, many economists argued that while prices and wages might deviate from the law of supply and demand in the short term, in the long term they would eventually have to adjust. Hence, the logic went, we should do whatever possible to speed up the process – let the market rip. In the labour market, this meant tackling whatever was preventing wages from falling, including unions. The logic was that the less the world appeared to be like Marketopia, the more urgent was the need to make it more so. Thus, the economic analysis was again based on assumption not evidence.

From the 1970s onwards, this analysis dominated debate about unemployment. Prior to that decade, unemployment in the EU-15 countries taken as a whole was around 2%. Since the end of the 1970s, it has struggled to fall below 8%. Ask an economist why and almost all of them will tell you it is because of "labour market rigidities" – factors preventing wages from falling to match supply and demand, such that firms can take on more workers. Ask a politician what needs to be done and almost all of them will repeat the argument in different words: we need "more flexible labour markets". When it comes to the cause of inflexibility, the usual suspects are: unions; unemployment benefits so generous that workers won't accept the going wage; the cost of firing people, which makes it too expensive to hire them in the first place; minimum wages; and taxes on labour. Our understanding is so influenced by Marketopian thinking that it never occurs to people to ask whether inflexibility might occur because managers don't want to cut wages, or to ask whether, even in the absence of interference, the labour market is capable of working like Marketopia – Truman Bewley is an exception.

The evidence is at best mixed, even according to those who believe in flexible labour markets. On the one hand, researchers have found that countries with high labour market regulation do tend, on average, to have higher unemployment. But, on the other, there is a lengthy list of inexplicable facts. Why were "inflexible" labour markets not a problem in the 1960s?* Why did Sweden, with a highly regulated labour market, manage to buck the trend and keep unemployment at just over 2% until the end of the 1980s? Why did Spain, with a similar history and labour market laws to Portugal, have unemployment of almost 20% for a decade, while Portuguese unemployment averaged below 6%? How did Austria, Denmark and the Netherlands return to effective full employment without disempowering unions and tearing up regulations?

In order to answer these questions, some economists look for ever more subtle differences between labour laws and welfare benefit systems across nations. But even if there is some truth in the "flexibility" claim, which is highly contestable, it is far from the whole story and, given the patchy evidence, probably not the central one. The French economist Olivier Blanchard, arguably the world's leading expert on European employment, has spent years trying to solve the flexibility riddle. He is beginning to have doubts. In his words: "I'm not sure that our explanations are much more than ex-post rationalizations." Writing in the journal *Economic Policy* in 2006, Blanchard said he had two "reasons to worry" whether more labour market flexibility would solve the unemployment problem. Both reasons take a more Muddletonian view of our economic instincts and may determine which countries suffer less from this latest bout of unemployment.

The relative economic success of the Nordic nations, especially Denmark and Sweden, led Blanchard to the issue of trust. One noticeable difference between the Nordic nations and the Continental and Mediterranean ones is that collective wage bargaining between unions, employers and government happens at a national level. At the end of the 1970s, with firms facing higher costs and decelerating productivity, wage restraint was called for. Blanchard and fellow economist Thomas

---

* A frequent answer to this question is the suggestion that globalization requires greater flexibility. Interestingly, although it is widely believed, there is very little evidence for this. The rate of job creation and destruction has not changed over the period in question.

Phillipon wondered whether the coordination of pay bargaining at a national level made it easier for unions to believe that calls for wage moderation were not merely pressure from employers trying to lower wage bills to increase profit, but a genuine attempt to produce a fair response to an economic predicament. To test the theory, Blanchard and Phillipon looked for ways to measure trust between unions and employers across countries. They obtained data from the 1960s on the number of workers involved in strikes, the number of days lost to strikes and the quality of management–worker relationships. They also quantified the degree to which pay agreements were nationally coordinated. What they discovered was that these measures of pre-existing trust were strongly related to happenings in the turbulent decade that followed – higher trust meant less unemployment.

Blanchard does not explicitly relate these findings to behavioural economics, but the link is clear. Take the Ultimatum Game, where unfair splits by the proposer induce the *yucki* instinct from the responder. Researchers have tried the game when the responder is uncertain about the size of the sum the proposer has to split. For instance, the responder may receive an offer of £2.50 but not know whether the proposer is offering just a quarter of £10, which is a proportion most people instinctively reject, or a fair split of £5, which overwhelmingly people accept. In these circumstances, some more selfish proposers take advantage, offering splits just like £2.50, which imply that the overall sum is smaller than it actually is. Because of this, responders can't entirely trust offers, and some are rejected even though they are in fact a fair split.

There is a simple analogy between the Ultimatum Game and wage negotiation. Following a productivity shock, the amount of revenue firms have to share with workers will fall. But workers may be uncertain about how much margins have truly been eroded. Where there is trust between workers and employers, the information from employers is more likely to be believed. Change may therefore be viewed as a common problem and wage moderation will be more likely. But where trust is absent, where firms or unions have fought or sought unfair shares in the past, moderation may be less likely. Furthermore, we know that if the *endian* instinct comes into play, because those in negotiations share a common identity, agreement over fair shares is a more likely outcome. Thus, where workers and employers feel part of a nationally coordinated response, wage moderation might be easier to agree. In this respect, it may be no coincidence that the nations that suffered least unemployment in the 1980s and beyond were small and arguably more cohesive, socially and ethnically.

There is a neat match between Bewley's observations of real companies, Blanchard's study of trust, and behavioural evidence on the importance of fairness and common identity in bargaining. It represents an alternative to the traditional supply and demand approach, which cannot explain the level of unemployment during and after recessions. If this alternative is more realistic, then the doctrine of flexibility might actually cause more unemployment, by undermining fairness, trust and coordination in wage negotiations. As mass unemployment again darkens our door, such arguments need to be heard.

The role of trusting, coordinated and fair wage negotiations during periods when employers are under pressure is one of Olivier Blanchard's "reasons to worry" about the flexibility mantra. There is a second, which arises from a long-standing debate in macroeconomics and requires a section of its own.

Prices set in stone

I doubt that the island of Yap has ever witnessed a heist. It is also unlikely that the Yapese have suffered at the hands of pickpockets. Until very recently, the official currency of this tiny Micronesian island, the *rai*, was made from shimmering limestone carved into huge ornate discs with holes in the middle.* They look like large

---

* *Rai* are rumoured still to be used in transactions, although in 1986 Yap officially adopted the US dollar.

Stone Age wheels, ranging in size from about a foot in diameter up to an impressive 12 feet. As the anthropologist William Henry Furness put it in *The Island of Stone Money* in 1910: "when it takes four strong men to steal the price of a pig, burglary cannot but prove a somewhat disheartening occupation". In fact, for the same reason, most *rai* are not physically exchanged at all but stay put, leaning against walls and houses. Ownership of them is simply acknowledged, wherever they happen to lie. Like most other forms of money, including notes and coins, the *rai* is basically useless but for the promise that it may be exchanged for something useful in the future. On an island of just a few thousand inhabitants, keeping track of individual wealth does not require physical possession of or proximity to one's *rai*.

One crucial property of a unit of currency is that the total amount of it in circulation can be controlled. This is one reason why precious metals make for good currencies; another being that, unlike the *rai*, they have the portability necessary for use by larger populations. Yap probably adopted the *rai* because there was no metal on the island. In fact, there was no limestone either. The stones originated in the islands of Palau, more than two hundred miles of Pacific Ocean away. This is what gave the Yapese the necessary control over their money supply. Historically, the Yap chief commandeered a proportion of the stones that made it to the island. He pronounced on the value of individual stones, which depended only partly on their size. Peril endured by sailors and lives lost on the voyage also had a bearing on valuations. Thus, in economic terms, the chief of Yap issued currency, decided denominations and controlled the money supply. In short, the chief was a central banker – Yap's Ben Bernanke, Jean-Claude Trichet or Mervyn King.

Curious though they are, you might wonder about the relevance of Yap's stones to modern macroeconomics. In fact, they provide a nice example to help people see the importance of behavioural economics to the way modern central bankers set interest rates, which are crucial to economic growth, inflation and unemployment.

When the Fed, the Bank of England or the European Central Bank lower interest rates, it is just like the chief increasing the money supply on Yap by releasing more stones. When interest rates are raised, it is like the chief refusing to supply more stones. There is a strong link between the money supply and interest rates, because central banks control the supply of money over time to match the interest rate they announce. When there is more money in circulation it is cheaper to borrow – lower interest rates. When there is less money to go around, it is more expensive to borrow – higher interest rates.* For many decades now, one of the key issues of macroeconomics has been what impact these changes have on people's behaviour.

Back to Yap, which is one of the Caroline Islands. Germany bought the Carolines from Spain in 1898 for just over $3 million, back in the days when colonial powers could, with impunity, buy and sell far-off islands and power over the islanders. The Germans, fond of efficient roads, declared themselves unhappy with the quality of the island's highways, and ordered the inhabitants to repair them – with little effect. After repeated instructions were ignored, Germany decided to impose a fine. But how? The debt collector's job on Yap would be as disheartening as that of the burglar. Eventually, the Germans dispatched a man to the island who simply marked a number of the larger stones with a black cross, to indicate that they now belonged to the German government.

Now, here is the key logical leap. The "fine" need not actually have made the Yapese any poorer, in terms of their real living standards. After it was imposed, the island had the same physical resources, and the islanders could generate the same amount of food, clothing and houses, and do the same amount of fishing, tool-making, cooking, whatever. In short, Yap could produce the same goods and services

---

* You might wonder who the central bank gives the extra money to or takes it from. In fact, the way it works is that central banks trade government bonds with the large commercial banks. So, to reduce the money supply they sell them bonds, while to increase it they buy some back. Also, central banks often lend major banks money for reserves, which they can do at the target interest rate.

as before. In real terms, nothing had changed. What had really happened, technically speaking, was a dramatic cut in the money supply – there were suddenly fewer *rai* in circulation.

Suppose that the Germans put black crosses on stones equivalent to 25% of the total value of *rai*. The Yapese could simply drop the price of everything on the island by 25% too. Then, absolutely nothing would change. Everyone would be able to buy and sell exactly as much as before. The islanders could leave the roads alone and continue to give their colonial "masters" the Yapese equivalent of the two-fingered salute.*

This is not what happened, however. In fact, the Yapese felt poorer and did their colonial master's bidding. History does not relate what happened to the amount of economic activity on the island when the black crosses appeared, whether people actually traded less with each other, but the islanders must have at least believed their capacity to buy and sell had fallen. In other words, even though Yap was really no poorer than before, the cut in the money supply meant the islanders felt they could afford less. The Germans had induced a recession. It was severe enough that the islanders finally succumbed to colonial power and improved the roads.

The Germans were not actually the first outsiders to cause problems with Yap's money supply. In 1874, an Irish-American named David O'Keefe was shipwrecked on the island. O'Keefe realized an opportunity when he saw one and returned some years later with a suitably sized ship, capable of transporting large amounts of *rai* from Palau. He used them to buy coconut meat to sell on elsewhere. The *rai* that O'Keefe shipped in were not valued as highly as pre-existing stones, given that he had obtained them more easily than the

---

* I have simplified the story a little for the purpose of explanation. For one thing, where some Yapese had more of their stones requisitioned than others, the distribution of wealth would have changed too. Thus, to restore people's relative riches to their original state, there would also have to be a compensation scheme for those unlucky enough to have lots of their *rai* marked with black crosses. Also, the stones were not in fact used for all transactions, as smaller trades relied on simple exchange.

canoeists and rafters who had previously risked their lives to obtain their quarry. Nevertheless, the result was more *rai* in circulation on the island – a significant increase in the money supply. It seems that, initially, O'Keefe's actions increased the economic activity on the island too, as islanders sold him coconut meat and sought to spend the proceeds. Although we don't know the extent of it, O'Keefe seems to have caused a mini-boom. But, over time, with so many more *rai* about the place, people had to offer more *rai* to buy things – prices went up. O'Keefe had eventually caused a bout of inflation. At higher prices, trade fell away again.

For decades, macroeconomists have argued over whether changes in the money supply cause changes in the amount of real economic activity. Keynesian macroeconomists believe they do, while monetarist macroeconomists believe changes in money supply lead merely to changes in prices and wages.

The reason why this rather theoretical-sounding debate matters is that when the amount of economic activity changes, so does the level of employment. Suppose a Yapese craftsman runs a little firm involving just himself and an apprentice. After more money appears on the island, he may find more people offering him *rai* for his goods. He might decide to hire an extra apprentice to meet this increased demand. Alternatively, he may decide that the increase in demand is temporary because prices are about to rise and make it disappear. If so, he may ignore the temptation to expand the business, for fear that he will just have to let the new apprentice go again. Now imagine what happens after the Germans reduce the amount of money by requisitioning some *rai*. There might be an immediate fall in demand for his goods. The craftsman may decide he has no alternative but to make his existing apprentice redundant. Or he may reason that prices are about to fall and so, provided his apprentice agrees, he can reduce the wages he pays. Thus if the Keynesians are right, the changes to the money supply alter the employment prospects of the apprentices. If the monetarists are right, everyone carries on as before but prices and wages change.

The modern consensus of the last few decades is that Keynesians were right in the short term, but that monetarists were right in the long term: employment may initially change in response to the money supply, but eventually prices and wages adjust. Thus, increases or decreases in employment should be merely temporary. If this consensus view is correct, then it has strong implications.

For a start, we all need to hope that Keynes was at least right in the short term. The speed of the economic downturn since late 2007 does indeed parallel that of the 1930s. Two economic historians, American Barry Eichengreen and Irishman Kevin O'Rourke, are making an explicit and ongoing comparison between now and then. Having matched the peaks in world production of June 1929 and April 2008, they are tracking world industrial output, world stock markets and the volume of world trade, comparing each with its path in the early 1930s. The parallel is both striking and unnerving. It shows that, if anything, the initial downturn we have just gone through is marginally *faster*. What is different this time, however, is the response of governments and central banks, which have massively expanded the money supply (those exceptionally low interest rates) and greatly increased government spending (those stimulus packages). In other words, they have done exactly what Keynes said should have been done in the 1930s. So if the greatest economist of the twentieth century was right, it may be of great benefit to the twenty-first.

In the longer term, the modern consensus underpins central bank policy, which is to commit to changing interest rates only in order to hit a constant inflation target, in most cases of around 2%. As the world economy recovers, hopefully sooner rather than later, this will be the guiding principle for when to raise interest rates again. It is based on the idea that such low and stable inflation has no long-term impact on the level of unemployment, while its very stability makes life less uncertain for firms and so reduces fluctuations in employment. But is the consensus of recent decades right?

Try this example, adapted from Kahneman's study of fairness

which we encountered before. Suppose there is a company making a small profit at a time when the economy is in recession. There is substantial unemployment but no inflation. The company decides to decrease salaries by 7%. Is the company's behaviour fair? Now suppose that there is another company that is in very similar circumstances in a different economy. This time the inflation rate is 12%. The company decides to increase salaries by 5%. Is the company's behaviour fair?

In the first example, over 60% of people think the company's behaviour is unfair. In the second example, 78% of people think the company's behaviour is fair. Now, one interpretation of this result is that we suffer from what economists call "money illusion", whereby a substantial number of us behave "irrationally" and do not take inflation into account. But I'm not so sure this response is irrational.

Try another example, a version of an experiment devised by American psychologist Eldar Shafir and some colleagues. Compare two workers, Ann and Barbara, living in two separate countries. Ann lives in an economy with no inflation. She receives a 2% pay increase. Barbara lives in an economy with 4% inflation. She receives a 5% pay increase. Who will be happier?

The results show that about two-thirds of us say that Barbara will be happier than Ann. Similarly, two-thirds of us believe that Ann is more likely to leave her current employer. This again looks like money illusion. But here is an interesting thing. When Shafir's team asked which of the two workers was "doing better in economic terms", the result was reversed, with 71% picking Ann. This suggests that most people did understand the effect of inflation, in the sense that Ann got a larger increase in her spending power. But we think the increase in pounds, dollars or euros matters too, perhaps because it can be an indication of how much the firm values the employee, irrespective of the rate of inflation.

These results have an interesting implication. If people find pay cuts less objectionable when they consist of pay increases below the rate of inflation than when they are actual reductions in terms of pounds, dollars or euros, then it may be much harder for firms to reduce wages in times of very low inflation. A moderate level of inflation allows firms some scope to give pay increases in pounds, dollars and euros, but cut their wage bills in real terms. There is, in fact, a considerable amount of data supporting this hypothesis. Although it varies by country and by year, on average workers get pay increases at or just above inflation.* There is much variation, fairly evenly distributed either side of the average increase. But there is usually a big cluster of pay deals at exactly zero: pay freezes. Very few firms will go beyond zero and actually cut the wage in pounds, dollars or euros.

This adds an interesting wrinkle to the debate about what causes unemployment. Truman Bewley found that managers in struggling firms were more willing to lay people off than to cut wages. The data shows that firms are particularly unwilling to cut wages in pounds, dollars or euros. This matches experiments that show we find a below-inflation rise more acceptable. Thus, struggling firms are more likely to lay people off at times of very low inflation. When there is moderate inflation, it gives them more flexibility to keep their wage bills down.

If this is right, then the modern consensus that in the long term there is no relationship between the rate of inflation and unemployment may be wrong. Years of very low inflation may lead to struggling firms shedding more workers. A team headed by George Akerlof has recently tried to use this theory to explain why unemployment continued to be so high during a period of consistent low inflation after the Great Depression. The theory may also explain why European unemployment has remained so stubbornly high in the low-inflation climate that surrounded the introduction of the euro, especially in countries where less trust surrounds pay negotiations between workers and employers.

---

* The big exception to this is the USA, where, especially among the lower paid, wages have struggled to keep up with inflation in recent decades.

This is Olivier Blanchard's second "worry" about the doctrine of labour market flexibility. For years, economists and politicians have blamed high unemployment on workers' wage demands, unions and the protections offered to workers by governments. This view is in line with the orthodox assumptions about our economic instincts. A more accurate assessment of our economic instincts suggests, first, that trust established through a process of national pay negotiations may keep unemployment down in tough times and, second, that the oft-repeated economic principle of low inflation might actually increase unemployment. As we once again enter an era of high unemployment, these issues are vital.

The power of ideas, good and bad

The evidence that has emerged regarding our true economic instincts leads to much greater emphasis on the roles of risk and uncertainty, relationships of trust and social exchange, and the seeking of best common solutions. It has begun to change how the major issues of national economic policy are understood. It is starting to give insight into the economic differences between nations, the reasons behind the success or failure of macroeconomic reforms, and the relationship between unemployment and inflation.

The argument about unemployment since the 1970s exemplifies the degree to which traditional theory has until recently maintained a stranglehold. For instance, at successive EU summits over many years, Europe's political leaders agreed with each other that they must make their respective labour markets more flexible. This agenda was not based on evidence, but on theories derived from the traditional assumptions about our economic instincts.

There is now evidence. It shows that those instincts are not as economists had thought, which may help to explain why there are European governments, especially the Nordic nations, that manage to provide security of income for workers made redundant, to maintain workers' rights to organize, and to fund their generosity through progressive taxation, without experiencing higher unemployment or lower economic growth. They also have a narrower gap between rich and poor, largely because their labour market policies narrow the gap between the higher and lower paid. From a political point of view, it is a matter of choice whether you prefer to live in such a place, or whether you prefer a less equal society with lower taxes. But that is politics. As for the economics, it can now be based on evidence, not assumption.

These issues are truly pressing. Following the 1970s, the result of continuing high unemployment in many countries was social unrest, crime and urban decay; or more simply, many people who experienced ongoing deprivation and unhappiness. As of 2009, we don't yet know how bad unemployment will get over the next few years. But if we can improve our theories as to what causes it and what might reduce it, then perhaps we can avoid the worst consequences this time around.

The crisis is speeding up an ongoing revolution in economic thought, but the improvements on traditional theories remain at an early stage. We have a better yet still incomplete understanding of people's real economic instincts, let alone the outcomes when people interact, in markets, workplaces and governments. There are many economists, probably a majority, who still cling to traditional theory, although more and more are beginning to question its assumptions and engage with alternatives. Our final task is to establish what might be done to open minds and hasten change.

10

Corners and turning points

INSIGHTS INTO PEOPLE'S real economic instincts help us to understand what we see when we walk to the end of the street to take part in and watch economic life. It is now some time since I wandered into town to buy new work clothes and to pick up turmeric and razor blades at Leonard's Corner on the way home. A number of local businesses have closed. There are more people of working age hanging around during the day. The late-night pharmacy, I'm glad to say, appears to be thriving and has even had a facelift. Spices are still sold with a 150% price difference, in shops just yards apart.

People's instinct to stick with what's familiar explains why the price of spices defies supply and demand, although the *endian* instinct might play a role in this too, since the shops are run by people of different ethnic backgrounds. The ones with cheaper spices are laid out and marketed with their own ethnic community in mind, as this provides the bulk of their customers. They don't look like traditional Irish shops, so the shopping experience and the brands are unfamiliar to many locals. You sometimes see people hovering around the thresholds, trying to summon the confidence to take the plunge and do business inside. For new Asian immigrants, the shops are doubtless reassuringly familiar. Where customers and shopkeepers share a common ethnic identity, trust is easier to come by. Overcoming uncertainty and establishing mutual trust in exchanges determines who is trading with whom more than relative prices.

Relationships and perceptions determine the buoyant trade at the pharmacy too. Customers are not so sensitive to price differences when they can see the extra effort that goes into running the shop, compared with the larger chain stores. The price seems fair, so we pay it. The *witt* instinct is important too. Provided enough locals make the effort to support the local shop we all get to keep our late-night pharmacy – the best common solution.

The majority of the razor blades stacked on the shelves are, as ever, made by Gillette. Why, in this supposed era of fierce global competition, has Gillette still got a virtual monopoly over a cheap manufactured product? Because it constantly innovates, producing a new type of razor every few years, backed by massive and persuasive marketing. All the razors, meanwhile, seem oddly cheap compared to the packets of blades. Consumers are buying the razor now and the packets of blades in the future, but their impulse is to ignore the future expense and to go for the latest new razor. Because Gillette is so much larger than its competitors, larger still now the brand is owned by Procter & Gamble, it can afford to invest time and money in product and marketing development, always keeping itself one step ahead of the competition. Three things usually apply to the latest design of wet-shave razor to appear on the shelves: it is made by Gillette, the razor blades are more expensive, and people buy it.

Further on in town are the clothes shops where I kitted myself out for what was then my new job. In the new workplace, I have met many people who could earn more elsewhere, but believe in what they do, feel valued in return and, in a national research institute, identify with their organization's aim. The organization is not-for-profit, but people work just as hard as in the private company I worked in before. Most colleagues are very cooperative, trading favours and ideas willingly. A few are not, but are held in check by the majority.

Back in the menswear departments, clothes were not made to

match my tastes, or indeed anybody else's, because the fashion industry capitalizes on the uncertain value of fashion by continually altering the latest styles to increase the perceived value of new clothes and decrease the perceived value of old ones. How other people view what we wear matters to us, so no individual can ignore fashion without paying a price, and the industry's method of keeping the target moving works.

During my shopping trip, I became more confident and willing to buy clothes the longer I shopped, because my uncertainty about what was available and what it was worth diminished. My brand preferences suggested I was susceptible to marketing, because we all are. Each of the clothing companies has a clever brand manager who researches the images and values associated with their target demographic group, and it works. Although I would like to, I will never know what the person who made the clothes was paid, but I'm confident that if they only knew the price I paid for them they would be holding out for more of it.

Like all trained economists, I was taught the model of competitive equilibrium, the model behind Marketopia, as the centrepiece of economic understanding. The gap between this standard economics and the economic life around me has always appeared wide to me. People never seemed to behave like Marketopians, but casual observation is not scientific evidence. In recent years, experiments, surveys and data have started to provide abundant evidence about our true economic instincts. Whether it is down to the accumulation of such evidence, or a crisis that has placed a premium on new thinking, economics is at last beginning to take this evidence seriously. Good science involves constant interplay between theory and evidence. It is this interplay which causes scientific revolutions – great leaps in our understanding of the world. Is economics about to be revolutionized? If so, what impact might the revolution have?

Blinded by science

It was Prague, 1601, and Tycho Brahe was on his deathbed. The Dane, known simply as Tycho, had proved himself the greatest astronomer with the naked eye. He had recorded the positions of planets and stars more accurately than anyone prior to the invention of the telescope. Yet, as he lay dying, Tycho's legacy was on his mind. Beside him was his assistant, a brilliant young German, Johannes Kepler. The two men had never agreed.

Tycho believed the Earth was the centre of the universe, while Kepler thought the planets, including Earth, circled the sun. As the better mathematician, Kepler reasoned that the heliocentric (sun-centred) model of the Polish astronomer Copernicus provided a superior fit with the periodic motion of the planets. But Tycho could not be convinced. He was not naturally conservative, as a man or as a scientist. He had scandalized the Danish court by marrying a peasant girl. He had disproved Aristotle's theory of the unchanging heavens by observing an exploding star. But Tycho could not bring himself to believe that Earth moved through space. The great astronomer's final words to his assistant were: "Let me not have lived in vain." To the last, Tycho was apparently desperate to be right.

Alas, within a few years, Kepler had used his former master's observations to improve Copernican theory, showing that planets orbited the sun in ellipses, not circles. Tycho's major contribution to astronomy was to provide data excellent enough to undermine his own theories. That's science for you.

How and why do highly intelligent and talented scientists like Tycho stubbornly cling to theories? Perhaps the best answer was provided by the philosopher of science Imre Lakatos. After fleeing cold-war Hungary, Lakatos worked at the London School of Economics in the 1960s and early 1970s, where he revolutionized his own subject. Lakatos argued that scientific progress was made by competing schools of thought, or "research programmes". Examples are geocentric (Earth-centred) astronomy, Newtonian physics, Freudian psychology, evolutionary theory or, indeed, neoclassical (standard) economics. Each research programme has a "hard core": one or more central claims that adherents strive to uphold. The hard core of geocentric astronomy is simple: "Earth is the centre of the universe." For Newtonian physics it is Newton's three laws of motion, plus his theory of gravity. For evolutionary theory it is a chain of reasoning: organisms inherit variable traits, natural selection favours particular traits, successful traits lead to the evolution of new species. Around these hard-core propositions, scientists create a "protective belt" of auxiliary hypotheses – add-on theories that account for troublesome observations or highlight findings that only the specific research programme can explain.

Tycho provides a classic example. Rather than abandon his central belief, he added extra theories to defend it. Planetary motions were troublesome for this theory, so he tried to account for them by arguing that while the other planets orbited the sun, the sun nevertheless went round the Earth, which remained the centre of the system. He also constantly challenged the heliocentric school to explain how, if the Earth was moving, the positions of the stars in the sky remained fixed. This was indeed a puzzle for a heliocentrist like Kepler, because if the Earth was in motion then the relative positions of stars ought to move in the sky, which they appeared not to. In fact, we now know that the positions of stars do change, but they were too far away even for Tycho's eyes to detect such small movements without a telescope.

Lakatos argued that all scientists faced with troublesome evidence defend their hard-core propositions with add-on theories, just as Tycho did. Scientists deal with unsolved problems and anomalies all the time, so their most powerful ideas should not be abandoned at the first sign of trouble. But Lakatos also provided wisdom about what separates good science from not-so-good science. A good research programme combines the capacity to find explanations for troublesome observations with the ability to predict new, surprising ones.

For example, Newton's laws had to be protected by add-on theories of air resistance and friction, but their power to predict the motion of heavy objects was impressive, and their use to predict the return of Halley's comet in 1759 stunned the scientific world. Evolutionary theory had to be protected by additional and rather arbitrary theories of mutation to explain big differences between species, until its explanations were supported by better biological data, and the power of its predictions truly unleashed through modern genetics. These are successful scientific research programmes, where some defence is required but the core theories have predictive power. Unsuccessful ones are characterized by constant tinkering with add-on theories and poor predictive power. Alchemists ran out of excuses for failing to make gold. The few remaining Marxists still play with add-on theories to explain why the inevitable collapse of capitalism is, to say the least, delayed. A degree of defence is inevitable, but when intellectual effort is primarily spent defending core propositions rather than finding new phenomena, then, as Lakatos put it: "blind commitment to a theory is not an intellectual virtue, it is an intellectual crime".

The hard core of standard economics, the set of central claims behind Marketopia, comprises the assumptions of the model of competitive equilibrium: the economy consists of selfish, independent, rational individuals; together with firms that aim for maximum profits in markets where prices and wages match supply and demand. Lakatos provides two key insights to help us assess the state of play. First, although highly intelligent professional economists believe and skilfully defend the hard-core propositions of standard economics, that is no test of good science. Second, if talents are used more to protect these hard-core propositions from troublesome observations than to predict interesting new findings, then the hard-core propositions need to be changed.

Lakatos, whose insights into the nature of scientific progress dominate modern philosophy of science, provides us with a scientific benchmark against which to judge the science of economics. A healthy, progressive science involves constant comparison of theory and evidence. Where its central theories are found wanting, it avoids blind commitment and looks for alternative propositions around which to build new theories.

Doing it by the book

The shelf next to the desk where this is being typed holds ten modern economics textbooks, each of which was published or updated in the last ten years. There is an even split between microeconomics and macroeconomics, and the books are a mix of undergraduate, postgraduate and professional texts. The index of all ten contains an entry for "competitive equilibrium". Not one of them has an entry for "Ultimatum Game", even though the results of Ultimatum Game experiments challenge the very theory of everyday transactions; the equivalent of the atom in economic analysis. Every textbook does have an entry for "Prisoner's Dilemma". Turning to the appropriate sections reveals that this key concept, the possibility of situations in which individual incentives are at odds with the best common solution, is routinely introduced in the context of two companies competing for market share, where the best common solution (for them, anyway) is to engage in price collusion instead of competing with each other. Not one of my textbooks reports the result of experiments in which people, or firms, actually confront a Prisoner's Dilemma situation for real. Instead it is simply assumed, wrongly, that the best collective outcome is unlikely to occur, because people are too selfish. No index contains an entry for "trust" (although a number contain "anti-trust", meaning regulation of monopolies), even though evidence suggests that trust and how it is established are vital ingredients of a successful market economy. The occasional entry for "uncertainty" turns out not to be about uncertainty, which cannot be accurately quantified, but about risk and probability, which can.

Although it is fair to say that there has been an explosion in behavioural research in the past decade, and there is bound to be a time lag in the production of textbooks, there is little excuse for these oversights. It is over 25 years since the first Ultimatum Game results were published. People's ability to cooperate at Prisoner's Dilemma was first recorded over forty years ago. One of the most interesting observations, flicking through the texts, is that there are virtually no references *at all* to observations that are troublesome for conventional theory.

What, you might wonder, do all the hundreds of pages contain? The answer is a very large number of equations and diagrams that budding economists have to be able to replicate to pass exams, or adapt in some new way to produce research papers. Every one of them assumes that people are independent, selfish and rational, and that firms maximize profit. Evidence to the contrary is not even considered. Where these mainstream texts do refer to evidence, it is anecdotal and supportive of standard theory.

The conclusion is inescapable. Comparison of theory and evidence is almost absent in the teaching of economics, where the primary skill required to obtain qualifications is the recital of algebra; the ability not to question but to copy. Where is the interplay between theory and evidence? Where are the groundbreaking theoretical predictions that predict real-world findings? To put it bluntly, where is the science?

One could argue that before getting to the cutting edge of research, it is essential to have a grounding in basic theory. But even school textbooks in physics and chemistry talk children through some simple experiments to test the fundamental claims. The interplay between theory and observation is the essence of good science; it is what links scientific understanding to truth.

The way economics is taught means that a large number of professionally qualified economists, especially those working outside academia, in private business, in journalism or in government, have at no stage been exposed to any evidence concerning the theories that underpin their professional status. To a scientist, this should be alarming. It is worrying too how many academic economists, including very good ones, have had no exposure to contrary evidence. There are of course notable exceptions and many excellent scientists doing research in economics. But, as an economist, I am in general ashamed to admit that rather than training sceptical, creative minds, the profession has for years been teaching students and practitioners to recite doctrine.

Economics has been similarly criticized on previous occasions. Many writers, social scientists from other disciplines, journalists and more radical economists have objected to the subject's assumptions, seeing them as political statements, not scientific propositions. Others have expressed dislike for the way economic reasoning has invaded seemingly non-economic issues. There is substance to both criticisms. Willingness or unwillingness to accept the proposition that our fundamental economic instinct is to be selfish is partly a political judgement. And for some time now, if you want to change, or preserve, anything about society, you have to make a persuasive *economic* case. This applies to seemingly non-economic issues such as what schools are available to which children; who locks up prisoners; the selection of movies offered by the local cinema; the workplace rights of women; or what time a sports event kicks off. Economists have invaded territory and incurred the wrath that occupying forces face. If the critics knew what flimsy evidence backed up some of the economic theory, they might fight back more strongly.

But things are truly changing. Research teams in behavioural economics are expanding. Top journals are publishing more behavioural work. The number of behavioural presentations at major conferences has grown. The approach is proving to be particularly popular with younger economists and students.

When, in 1998, Matthew Rabin described the attitude of fellow economists towards behavioural economics as one of "aggressive uncuriosity", the quote succinctly captured the attitude of many at the time, who dismissed it as wacky, fringe or just not "proper economics". Lakatos would have recognized this defensive pattern of behaviour as symptomatic of a failing research programme. Ten years on, in late 2008, I met Rabin at a European Commission conference. The event was designed to spread the word about the importance of behavioural economics for consumer policy and was itself a sign of the area's growing impact. I asked Rabin if the phrase still applied. His answer? "Not any more."

Economics has many important things going for it. Among the social sciences it is the most numerate. It prides itself on analytical rigour and refuses to tolerate the imprecise definitions and rambling arguments that characterize so much social science. If it can combine these attributes with greater respect for evidence and an open-mindedness towards fresh ideas, then genuine leaps in our understanding may well be within our grasp. We don't need less economics; we need better economics.

Evidently in need of change

Each of the hard-core theoretical propositions of economic orthodoxy fails when forced to collide with evidence.

People are not "rational", in the sense that economists use the word. We value something we own more than something we do not, even when it is the same object. We try to avoid risk and uncertainty, even at a cost to ourselves. More generally, we instinctively value what is familiar more highly than what is not when there is no objective reason to do so, whether it be with reference to products, people or firms. We make systematic errors in relatively simple probability judgements. We take different options when faced with the same economic decision presented in a different social context, or described a different way. Our judgements about what things are worth are not consistent over time. We fall for marketing tricks and are persuaded by adverts.

We are not "independent", in the sense that economists use the word. We seek opportunities to learn whatever we can about how other people value products, instinctively picking up small and subtle social signals. We form alliances of mutual trust, even with strangers. Our happiness depends as much on our economic circumstances relative to those around us as it does on our ability to buy goods and services.

We are not "selfish", in the sense that economists use the word. We do aim to improve our lot and at times we can be selfish. Some people are more selfish than others. But we make sacrifices to punish unfairness, to seek the best common solutions and, in many cases, just to be generous to complete strangers. We trust people to behave unselfishly towards us and most of the time they repay that trust. We constantly engage in unselfish cooperation with colleagues – organizations could not function as effectively as they do if we didn't.

The evidence suggests that the central assumptions of conventional economics with respect to individuals are not true. Sure, there is some truth in them. Sometimes our behaviour is independent, rational and selfish. Standard economic models will therefore be accurate some of the time. The models are very much better than having no models. They offer a limited understanding of how the economy works. But the evidence shows that departures from orthodox theory are not the result of random errors, but of consistent behaviours. Thus, the evidence does not suggest that orthodox theory is approximately true, in the sense that it is accurate on average but not in individual cases. It suggests that it is inaccurate on average; arguably very inaccurate.

The evidence shows that our true economic instincts when conducting transactions are deep and systematic, because they have evolved and developed as a response to our uncertain economic environment. Traditional economics has these instincts wrong because it assumes that transactions are straightforward, which they are not. In any transaction we can make mistakes, lack information, be surprised, suffer bad luck, change our mind in the light of future events, or be a victim of dishonesty – we can be MISLED. The economic environment is uncertain – we inhabit Muddleton not Marketopia.

In our uncertain economic environment we try to stick with what is most familiar and seek the assistance and cooperation of others. We try to form mutual alliances based on fairness. We punish people who do not treat us fairly. The *yucki* instinct means we would rather have no share than an unfair share. The *witt* instinct shows that we will often be selfless and trusting in search of common goals, even with total strangers. The *endian* instinct shows how we exploit anything we have in common with others to strengthen mutual alliances. Again, these are not random deviations from the orthodox model, they are human instincts that have adapted to deal with our uncertain environment. We are instinctive Muddletonians because we inhabit Muddleton, not Marketopia.

The alternative perspective on the economic instincts of individuals, implied by evidence from experiments and surveys, predicts new findings in economic data and offers new explanations for longstanding economic puzzles. Our aversions to risk and uncertainty may explain why more able children from poorer backgrounds decide not to go to college, even though it appears to be in their economic interest to go. The *yucki* instinct may well be behind the large differences in wages paid for the same work in different industries, the failure of prices to rise on products in very short supply, and more generally why prices and wages frequently do not match supply and demand. It may explain the persistence of high unemployment in times of stable, low inflation. The *witt* instinct explains why people comply with honesty boxes, tip waiters and contribute to good causes; why people will do jobs for less money than they could earn elsewhere. In combination with the *endian* instinct, it may also explain why communication, trust and loyalty are hallmarks of successful organizations, and why companies that discriminate do not seem to suffer lower productivity.

Executives running firms do not behave as standard theory says they should either. Again, uncertainty in the commercial environment is the reason. In a changing and uncertain market environment, maximizing profit may not be the best survival instinct. Many firms do not appear to maximize profits. Managers believe instead that their survival can be threatened by the overambitious pursuit of profit. Instead, the instinct of many successful executives is to prioritize market share, innovation or the long-term relationship with customers. Thus, they do not aim to deliver products at market prices as efficiently as possible. Firms mostly aim for distinctive products, fairly priced, with sufficient margin to invest in innovation. Perhaps there are firms that match standard theory, but there are clearly very many that systematically depart from it.

The alternative perspective on the instincts of firms, implied by evidence from experiments, surveys and data, offers a different view of the driving force of capitalism. Firms actively aim to be distinctive. The different individuals, skills and trial-and-error processes within each firm mean that industries have firms of a variety of shapes and sizes, each with its own changing solution to the challenge its market presents. Successful firms innovate throughout the product life cycle, first with respect to products and marketing, later with respect to production processes. This perspective on successful companies explains why firms of different sizes compete in the same market, why some markets are dominated by a few firms, and why the pattern tends to be replicated across countries.

As many, including some of its long-time proponents, have recognized, traditional economics cannot account for what has occurred since 2007 in the world economy. Many individual families took on loans they could not really afford or made purchases they would come to regret. Major financial institutions traded assets worth a fraction of what they paid for them, incurring massive losses and in some cases destroying the company. Financial markets across the world froze. Mistakes were compounded and copied.

These happenings can be largely explained by a deeper understanding of our real economic instincts. Consumers are sensitive to recent trends, value the immediate more highly than the future and copy the behaviour of others, leading to repeated bubbles in property and stock markets throughout history. People, including financial traders, react differently to what they perceive as quantifiable risk and unquantifiable uncertainty. Traders, consumers and even regulators herd, leading erroneous valuations to multiply. These insights, and perhaps others like them, are essential for understanding how we got into the mess we are in.

Go wild

Believers in traditional economics can, and do, try to account for many of the troublesome observations by producing add-on theories that protect their core theoretical propositions, as Lakatos' theory of scientific progress correctly predicts. They insist that people behave differently in experiments. They argue that market selection will force people to be rational and selfish, or will force firms to maximize profits. They say that survey answers don't match real behaviour. Finally, when all else fails, they sometimes resort to an argument that a physical scientist like Tycho could only dream of. Economics is a social science, so if people don't behave selfishly, rationally and consistently, economists can always argue that the economy would actually work better if they did. It is as if Tycho turned to God and said, "OK, I give in, Earth goes round the sun, but your system would work better if you made it the other way round."

If we take Lakatos' view of science seriously, then the key issue is this: will a new set of hard-core theoretical propositions emerge in economics to replace the old ones? Some economists who admit the weakness of the traditional assumptions argue that instead of abandoning them altogether, we should relax them one by one. There are many economic research papers that do this. The conventional model is maintained, but one of the assumptions is abandoned or changed, perhaps by introducing imperfect information or allowing one individual to care about the outcomes of another. The problem with this methodology is that the evidence against each of the assumptions is too strong. There are fundamental aspects of our natures missing from the hard-core theoretical propositions, instincts more powerful than those that are included.

A scientific revolution is occurring. A new hard core of theoretical propositions in economics will emerge, to replace the old ones. It is not yet clear exactly what they will be, but the influences upon them are probably clear. Our economic instincts have evolved and developed to cope with the uncertainty of our economic lives. The scientific task ahead is to find a concise description of our most powerful instincts, which can be combined to predict our behaviour in individual transactions, in individual markets or organizations, and finally can be built up into bigger models of the economy – a more behaviourally accurate equivalent of competitive equilibrium.

Evolutionary influences almost certainly contribute to our deepest and most powerful economic instincts. We are only partly domesticated; still partly wild. One of the most compelling aspects of behavioural economics is the degree to which people refuse to accept that their instinctive reactions to many different scenarios are somehow irrational, when viewed as mathematical problems. Our most powerful instincts are there for a reason, and to understand how they have come to be is part of the job of piecing together new, better economic theories.

In such times of revolution, intriguing things happen. To a trained economist, it can feel very odd to be confronted with a paper suggesting it is time to pay attention to what is happening in the lateral prefrontal cortex – a part of the brain associated with rational thought processes. The arrival of "neuroeconomics", the application of the techniques of neuroscience to economic problems, is perhaps the ultimate indication that economists are going to have to deal with the fact that humans are flesh and blood. "Magnetic resonance imaging" (MRI) is a technique for measuring blood flow in the brain and can be performed on people while they are fully conscious and engaged in any kind of mental task. Papers are now being published that record which brain areas are most stimulated when individuals make different kinds of economic decisions. Studies have shown that the insula cortex, a brain area associated with reactions to pain and disgusting smells, becomes active when people receive low offers in the Ultimatum Game. Neuroscientists have also shown that there is an anatomically distinct sequence involved when people try to solve probability problems, which may be linked to our inconsistent responses. It has also been shown that when people reason about risk it involves different brain areas from when they reason about uncertainty.

Neuroeconomics has inevitably produced a backlash. Princeton economists Faruk Gul and Wolfgang Pesendorfer recently penned a paper entitled "The case for mindless economics". They argue that neuroscientific evidence consisting of patterns of brain activity cannot be used to assess economic theories because economics makes no predictions about the physiology of the brain.

When revolutions happen, people in the old and new regimes frequently fail to understand each other. The problem with Gul and Pesendorfer's argument is that while it is true that standard economics makes no predictions about the physiology of the brain, it is not true that it makes no predictions about the human mind. It very precisely predicts that when we face a scenario in which we must choose between a selfless but fair share and a selfish but unfair one, we will prefer the latter. When it becomes clear that people frequently choose fairness over selfishness, some economists try to adapt their theory to suggest that we value feelings of generosity in the same way that we value cars, haircuts and tins of beans. But once the theory becomes one in which people selfishly choose to be selfless, it becomes circular. Whatever behaviour we observe is designated as selfish after the fact, and so the theory can no longer be used to predict what will occur in the original scenario. Economists have to base theories on a simplification of our economic instincts and, in doing so, they employ theories of the human mind that may be true or false. Had their paper been called "The case for brainless economics" then the argument would have been stronger.

Nevertheless, there is a strong link between mind and brain. Thus, it is quite possible that a neuroeconomist could observe that in a particular kind of economic scenario, such as a Prisoner's Dilemma game, playing with our offspring engages a different brain area than when playing with non-relatives, perhaps an area usually associated with unconscious or emotional processes. Based on such a result, it would be possible to construct an economic hypothesis about how family income is shared in different types of families, then test it with household budget data. Like it or not, there is, in theory, a link between brains and economics.

Nevertheless, having originally trained as a neuroscientist, I am sceptical about whether brain research will have an important impact on economics any time in the near future. The problem is that we just don't understand the relationship between the brain and the mind well enough that many useful hypotheses are likely to emerge. Knowing that different brain areas are involved in different types of decisions tells us the physical location associated with decisions, and perhaps which other mental tasks employ the same areas, as with the Ultimatum Game and disgusting smells. It doesn't tell us how the brain makes decisions, which is what we need to know to be able to predict people's behaviour. How the brain works, and, in particular, how it manages to produce consciousness, is probably the greatest unknown of modern science.

For the revolution in progress, neuroeconomics is probably no more than an entertaining sideshow. But it is symptomatic of changing and refreshing times in economics. A new economics, based on a more accurate theory of our economic instincts, and a more accurate idea of the economic environment in which they prevail, is emerging. Our inability to see where it will take us is part of the fun of the ride.

Political instincts

Economics is political. It indicates what the likely outcomes of some policy changes will be. It provides theories of why some people benefit more from our available resources than others, on the basis of which people make judgements about whether such disparities are fair. It suggests ways in which the total resources at our disposal might be increased, used more efficiently or more sustainably. Because economics is political, a revolution in the subject could have profound political implications, as previous revolutions in economics have done. Understanding our real economic instincts will change political instincts. To make many political decisions, people have to have some idea in mind of how the economy works. Nobody put it better than Keynes, who pointed out that even practical, objective people are "usually the slaves of some defunct economist".

Scattered throughout this book are ideas regarding some of the potential implications of the changing economics for the political arena. A better understanding of our aversion to risk and uncertainty, and our liking for the familiar, is likely to change how we view economic decisions that appear to go against people's best interests, such as decisions not to go to college or not to save adequately for retirement. Because uncertainty is greatest over the biggest financial decisions in life, there may be a major reappraisal of some of the causes of poverty and inequality, and how to design potential solutions. The role of fair shares in transactions, and how markets can be designed or regulated to promote fair shares, are likely to feature strongly in arguments about free trade and development. People in less developed nations, from sweatshop workers unaware of the revenue they create to small businesses trying to trade with multinational corporations, could potentially be the beneficiaries. Recognition of the factors that support selfless collective action in pursuit of common goals has huge untapped potential for all kinds of political action. It applies to systems of environmental protection, efforts to increase productivity, policies to combat discrimination, and more.

The arbitrary power of marketing may come into greater political focus – consumers deserve something in return. Ways to promote voluntary social exchange promise to improve workplace practices, making organizations more efficient and more enjoyable to work for, in public and private sector alike. Evidence for the importance of plurality and innovation to the success of capitalism may lead to better understanding and promotion of competition, and less short-term pressure for profit. Central banks may be permitted to allow a bit of inflation (just a bit, mind), which may not be such a bad thing after all. Financial regulators may find methods for curbing excessive lending or assisting consumers to take better financial decisions, or at least helping them to avoid ruinous ones.

Perhaps above all else, appreciation of the uncertainty inherent in transactions and the mutual trust necessary to overcome it might result in a more judicious and sceptical approach to what markets can and cannot do. Markets are not deterministic and efficient allocation machines. They behave differently according to levels of trust, common identity, the availability of information, perceptions of fair prices, and uncertainty about value and about the future. Given events since summer 2007 it hardly needs to be said, but some markets have the capacity to cause havoc and misery.

Ultimately, what political conclusions we draw from an improved understanding of our economic instincts doubtless depends on our individual political perspective. Knowing how things work does not tell us how they should work. But a revolution in our knowledge of how the economy works is very unlikely to leave opinions unchanged. For those of us interested in such things, these are exciting times.

Further reading

THE AIM HERE is not to provide a full set of academic references to justify each and every claim in the book. To do so would have demanded that the main text be written in a more formal and less readable fashion, as the list of relevant research that informs the book runs to several hundred papers. For those studies described in more depth, however, the original reference is given below. Beyond that, I have supplied a range of papers relevant to the material in each chapter, such that the interested reader should be able to follow up any area of particular interest.

Unfortunately, there is a lack of good material on behavioural economics for the general reader, a fact that formed part of the motivation to write this book in the first place. Most, but not all, of the papers listed below require a knowledge of economics, and I have indicated those that are more accessible. It is a pity that so many good ideas lie hidden behind so much jargon and opaque language.

One of the best popular articles I have encountered is "The marketplace of perceptions", by Craig Lambert, which appeared in the *Harvard Review*. Another useful source for non-economists is *Behavioural Economics: Seven principles for policy-makers*, published by the New Economics Foundation, which does what it says by interpreting some of the classic findings of behavioural economics in the context of arguments about policy. A specific and highly accessible take on how behavioural economics can be useful for making policy is provided by *Nudge* (Yale University Press, 2008), by Richard Thaler and Cass Sunstein.

Moving to less popular writing, the entry on behavioural economics in the *International Encyclopaedia of the Social and Behavioural Sciences*, by Mullainathan and Thaler, is a good introduction. The subject now has an introductory textbook, *An Introduction to Behavioral Economics* (Palgrave, 2007), by Nick Wilkinson. Richard Thaler's *Winner's Curse* (Princeton University Press, 1994) is getting a bit old and requires some knowledge of economics, but covers the classic results and is a refreshingly entertaining read for an economics book. For anyone looking for a general introduction to economics with which to contrast the behavioural approach, there are many introductory texts, but I recommend *Economics* (McGraw-Hill) by Begg, Fischer and Dornbusch, which is thoroughly orthodox but more worldly and open-minded than most. For anyone interested in the evolutionary approach, not only to economics but to other social sciences, there is an excellent introduction written by Cosmides and Tooby, *Evolutionary Psychology: A primer*, which at the time of writing is online at www.psych.ucsb.edu/research/cep/primer.html.

For those more familiar with economics, *Advances in Behavioural Economics* (Sage, 2004), edited by Camerer, Loewenstein and Rabin, is the place to start. A bit older but with excellent coverage of experimental work is *The Handbook of Experimental Economics* (Princeton University Press, 1995), edited by Kagel and Roth. On the influence of evolutionary thinking, "Better than rational: evolutionary psychology and the invisible hand", by Cosmides and Tooby (*American Economic Review*, 84, 1994), outlines the main argument for individuals, while Nelson and Winter's "Evolutionary theorising in economics" (*Journal of Economic Perspectives*, 16, 2002) does so for firms.

Lastly on general work, with a preference for macroeconomics, George Akerlof and Robert Shiller's *Animal Spirits* (Princeton University Press, 2009) is a provocative and relatively jargon-free account of recent events, from a more behavioural perspective. That said, I advise my economist friends and colleagues to read Akerlof's "Behavioral macroeconomics and macroeconomic behavior" (*American Economic Review*, 92, 2002), which is a great place to begin grappling with the work of one of the most creative thinkers in economics.

On competitive equilibrium (Chapter 2), the original reference for the proof that a competitive equilibrium economy can be perfectly efficient is: "Existence of an equilibrium for a competitive economy", Arrow and Debreu (*Econometrica*, 22, 1954). Unless you have a taste for tricky mathematics, this is useful only as an indication of the intentions of the authors, who clearly believed they were engaged more in an abstract technical exercise than the production of a theory of how the world works. For the argument that it does actually describe how the world works, see *The Armchair Economist: economics & everyday life* by Steven E. Landsburg (Free Press, 1994). The attack on the "perfect information" assumption of neoclassical economics is still nicely and simply articulated nearly forty years on by Akerlof in "The market for lemons" (*Quarterly Journal of Economics*, 84, 1970), while a more up-to-date account is given in Stiglitz's "Information and the change in the paradigm in economics" (*American Economist*, 2003). For a non-technical argument describing the importance of information economics (and more) to the globalization debate, *Globalisation and Its Discontents* (Penguin, 2002) by the same author is the place to go. Two articles that nicely summarize the undermining of the standard assumptions by experimental psychology are Kahneman, "A psychological perspective on economics" (*American Economic Review*, 93, 2003) and Rabin, "Psychology and economics" (*Journal of Economic Literature*, 36, 1998).

Turning to risk (Chapter 3), there is very little in the way of work accessible to the general reader. The outstanding exception is Dan Ariely's *Predictably Irrational* (HarperCollins, 2008), which describes many ways in which our economic behaviour falls short of the ideals set by standard economics. The mug experiment can be found in Kahneman, Knetsch and Thaler's "Experimental tests of the endowment effect and the Coase Theorem" (*Journal of Political Economy*, 98, 1990). The classic reference on people's willingness to take gambles is Kahneman and Tversky, "Prospect Theory: an analysis of decision under risk" (*Econometrica*, 47, 1979). A summary of work since is *Choices, Values and Frames*, edited by Kahneman and Tversky (Cambridge University Press, 2000), which includes an accessible chapter on real-world applications by Colin Camerer, called "Prospect Theory in the wild: evidence from the field". The study of the endowment effect among collectors is by John List, "Neoclassical theory versus prospect theory: evidence from the marketplace (*Econometrica*, 72, 2004). A non-technical early introduction to framing effects is Tversky and Kahneman, "The framing of decisions and the psychology of choice" (*Science*, 211, 1981). The mere exposure effect appeared in Robert Zajonc's "Attitudinal effects of mere exposure" (*Journal of Personality and Social Psychology*, 9, 1968), while an entry to modern research on the phenomenon can be had via Fang, Singh and Ahluwalia, "An examination of different explanations for the mere exposure effect" (*Journal of Consumer Research*, 34, 2007). Summaries of the work on status quo bias, belief perseverance and other apparent irrationalities are in Camerer's chapter in *The Handbook of Experimental Economics* (Princeton University Press, 1995; as before). A technical theory of the evolutionary benefits of the endowment effect is in Huck, Kirchsteiger and Oechssler, "Learning to like what you have – explaining the endowment effect" (*Economic Journal*, 115, 2005). Finally, evidence regarding the educational decisions of people from less well-off backgrounds can be found in Callender and Jackson, "Does the fear of debt deter students from higher education?" (*Journal of Social Policy*, 34, 2005).

Less has been written about true uncertainty (Chapter 4), as opposed to risk. Hogarth and Einhorn's "Venture Theory: a model of decision weights" (*Management Science*, 36, 1990) shows how we distinguish risk and uncertainty. For how consumers change preferences given different options, see Simonson and Tversky, "Choice in context: trade-off contrast and extremeness aversion" (*Journal of Marketing Research*, 29, 1992). For the behaviour of stock markets, a good place to start is Shiller, "From efficient markets theory to behaviour finance"

(*Journal of Economic Perspectives*, 17, 2003). Evidence on the relevance of winner's curse can be had from Hong and Shum, "Increasing competition and the winner's curse: evidence from procurement" (*Review of Economic Studies*, 69, 2002), which refers to previous work also. A good review of how preferences change over time is Frederick, Loewenstein and O'Donoghue, "Time discounting and time preference: a critical review" (*Journal of Economic Literature*, 40, 2002), while the application of behavioural economics to savings behaviour is taken from Thaler and Benartzi, "Using behavioral economics to increase employee saving" (*Journal of Political Economy*, 112, 2004).

With respect to our motives (Chapter 5), two useful reviews of behaviour in experimental games are the chapters by Crawford and by Camerer in *Advances in Behavioural Economics* (Sage, 2004; as before). The original reference for the Ultimatum Game is Güth, Schmittberger and Schwarze, "An experimental analysis of ultimatum bargaining" (*Journal of Economic Behavior and Organisation*, 3, 1982). There is a review of follow-up experiments by Roth (*The Handbook of Experimental Economics*, Princeton University Press, 1995; as before). The experiment in Indonesia is from Cameron, "Raising the stakes in the Ultimatum Game: experimental evidence from Indonesia" (*Economic Inquiry*, 37, 1999). The primary reference for inter-industry wage differentials is Krueger and Summers, "Efficiency wages and the inter-industry wage structure" (*Econometrica*, 56, 1988), while Thaler's *Winner's Curse* (Princeton University Press, 1994; as before) contains an account of the behavioural explanation for them. The classic reference for the minimum group experiments is Tajfel et al., "Social categorisation and intergroup behaviour" (*European Journal of Social Psychology*, 1, 1971). A more up-to-date review is Hewstone, Rubin and Willis, "Intergroup bias" (*Annual Review of Psychology*, 53, 2002). The effects of introducing punishment to games are described in Fehr and Gächter, "Cooperation and punishment in public goods experiments" (*American Economic Review*, 90, 2002) and more accessibly by the same authors in "Altruistic punishment in humans" (*Nature*, 415, 2004).

On marketing (Chapter 6), arguably the leading textbook is Armstrong and Kotler's *Marketing: An Introduction* (Prentice Hall, 2006). A nice historical paper that references others is Church, "Advertising consumer goods in nineteenth-century Britain: reinterpretations" (*Economic History Review*, 53, 2000). Theodore Levitt's groundbreaking article "Marketing myopia" appeared in the 1960 *Harvard Business Review*. Becker and Murphy's "A simple theory of advertising as a good or bad" (*Quarterly Journal of Economics*, 108, 1993) outlines their explanation for the influence of marketing, while the other standard economic theory is described very accessibly in Davis, Kay and Star's "Is advertising rational?" (*Business Strategy Review*, 1991). A good overview of research into the effectiveness of advertising is Vakratsas and Ambler, "How advertising works: what do we really know?" (*Journal of Marketing*, 63, 1999). The South African loan experiment is from Bertrand et al., "What is psychology worth? A field experiment in the consumer credit market" (NBER Working Paper no. 11892, 2005). Lastly, a good review of work on happiness is Frey and Stutzer, "What can economists learn from happiness research?" (*Journal of Economic Literature*, 40, 2002).

A comprehensive account of the orthodox economic approach to the motivations of workers (Chapter 7) is Prendergast, "The provision of incentives in firms" (*Journal of Economic Literature*, 37, 1999). Worlds away academically, if not in reality, a readable overview of Cosmides and Tooby's work on social exchange is their chapter "Cognitive adaptations for social exchange" (in *The Adapted Mind: Evolutionary Psychology and the Generation of Culture*, ed. Barkow, Cosmides and Tooby, Oxford University Press, 1995). The Work Foundation in the UK has compiled a number of accessible reports on what makes a successful organization, including "Cracking the performance code", which contains many further references. The Trust Game was developed by Fehr, Kirchsteiger and Riedl in "Does fairness prevent market clearing? An experimental investigation" (*Quarterly Journal of Economics*, 108, 1993). A not-too-technical account of introducing punishment to such games is to be found in Fehr and Fischbacher,

"Social norms and human cooperation" (*Trends in Cognitive Sciences*, 8, 2004), while the implications of laboratory games for labour economics are described in Gächter and Fehr, "Fairness in the labour market" (IEW Working Papers no. 114, 2002). A good overview of economists' puzzlement at continuing discrimination is Darity and Mason, "Evidence on discrimination in employment: codes of color, codes of gender" (*Journal of Economic Perspectives*, 12, 1998). The reference for the study of discrimination in orchestras is Goldin and Rouse, "Orchestrating impartiality: the impact of 'blind' auditions on female musicians" (*American Economic Review*, 90, 2000). Lastly, the description of how group identity changed cooperation and punishment in the Swiss army is derived from Goette, Huffman and Meier, "The impact of group membership on cooperation and norm enforcement: evidence using random assignment to real social groups" (*American Economic Review*, 96, 2006).

As regards the behaviour of businesses (Chapter 8), technical evidence on how prices are set is provided by Lee, *Post-Keynesian Price Theory* (Cambridge University Press, 1998) and Carlton, "The theory and facts of how markets clear" (in *Handbook of Industrial Organisation*, vol. 1, ed. Schmalensee and Willig, 1989). An overview of how prices behave in artificial markets is provided by Holt (in *The Handbook of Experimental Economics*, Princeton University Press, 1995; as before). Chandler still provides one of the most accessible and important accounts of successful business behaviour, charting the rise of corporate giants at the turn of the twentieth century, in *Scale and Scope: The dynamics of industrial capitalism* (Harvard University Press, 1990), while a cut-down version of the implications for economics is available in the 1992 *Journal of Economic Perspectives* (vol. 6). Kahneman, Knetsch and Thaler's "Fairness as a constraint on profit-seeking: entitlements in the market" (in *Advances in Behavioural Economics*, Sage, 2004; as before) describes experiments showing how consumers view prices. Decades of the empirical exploits of conventional industrial economists are to be found in Scherer and Ross, *Industrial Market Structure and Economic Performance*

(Houghton and Mifflin, 1990), while a more behavioural and accessible take is provided by Simon, "Organisations and markets" (*Journal of Economic Perspectives*, 5, 1991). The product life cycle is described by Klepper in "Entry, exit, growth, and innovation over the product life cycle" (*American Economic Review*, 86, 1996), and the importance of innovation is described readably by Nelson, "Why do firms differ, and how does it matter?" (*Strategic Management Journal*, 12, 1991).

On macroeconomics (Chapter 9) the Akerlof paper on behavioural macroeconomics (in *American Economic Review*, 92, 2002; as before) is essential reading. Henrich et al., "In search of Homo Economicus: behavioral experiments in 15 small-scale societies" (*American Economic Review*, 91, 2001), reports cross-cultural behavioural experiments, while the comparison of results from developing and developed countries is due to Cardenas and Carpenter, "Behavioural development economics: lessons from field labs in the developing world" (forthcoming in the *Journal of Development Studies*; also available as a 2006 Middlebury College Working Paper). A non-technical comparison of different European social models is provided in Sapir, "Globalisation and the reform of European social models" (*Journal of Common Market Studies*, 44, 2006). A good reference on the plight of New Zealand is Dalziel, "New Zealand's economic reforms: an assessment" (*Review of Political Economy*, 14, 2002). Original experiments on the valuation of environmental resources were devised by Tversky, Sattath and Slovic, "Contingent weighting in judgment and choice" (*Psychological Review*, 95, 1988), although many others have followed and a review is provided in Carson and Hanneman, "Contingent valuation" (*Handbook of Environmental Economics*, ed. Mäler and Vincent, vol. 2, 2006). Truman Bewley's account of unemployment during the early 1990s can be read in "A depressed labour market as explained by participants" (*American Economic Review*, 85, 1995). A nice narrative of the thinking on European unemployment is Blanchard's "European unemployment" (*Economic Policy*, 21, 2006). Experiments revealing people's attitudes to inflation are provided by

Shafir, Diamond and Tversky, "Money illusion" (in *Advances in Behavioural Economics*, Sage, 2004; as before). Eichengreen and O'Rourke's excellent comparison of the present economic crisis with that of the 1930s can be accessed at www.voxeu.org, where you should search for *A Tale of Two Depressions*.

Finally, to assess the state of economics as a science (Chapter 10), the analysis of Imre Lakatos regarding what characterizes good science is best read in his own words (*The Methodology of Scientific Research Programmes: Philosophical Papers*, vol. 1, Cambridge University Press, 1978) or can even be heard in his own words via a posthumous podcast, which has been made available in an impressive innovation from the London School of Economics (*Science and Pseudoscience*, www.lse.ac.uk/collections/lakatos/, recorded in 1973). Camerer, Loewenstein and Prelec, "Neuroeconomics: how neuroscience can inform economics" (*Journal of Economic Literature*, 43, 2005), provides reasons to think that economics will be changed by neuroscientific discoveries, while Gul and Pesendorfer, "The case for mindless economics" (UCLA Working Paper, 2005), argues that neuroscientific discoveries will do no such thing.

Many, many more papers and volumes contributed to this book than I have listed here, but the suggestions offered should provide access to the relevant literature from which I have drawn. Should it prove difficult to find sources for any of the results quoted or claims made, I am happy to respond, within reason, to requests for more references.

Index

An economist and former BBC journalist, Pete Lunn now works for the Economic and Social Research Institute (ESRI) in Dublin.

Pete has an unusual background for an economist, having originally trained as a neuroscientist. He received a PhD in human perception from the University of London at just 24 years of age. He then spent over a decade in journalism, mostly with the BBC's *Newsnight* in London, but also in Ireland, where he was founding editor of the country's first specialist talk radio station, NewsTalk.

A former English Speaking Union scholar, Pete specializes in bringing original or complex ideas to wider audiences. His work in television and radio has won several national awards. After re-qualifying as an economist, he now devotes his energies to policy research and to spreading new economic thinking.

Pete lives in Dublin with his partner and three children.